T0051479

PRISON JOURNAL

GEORGE CARDINAL PELL

PRISON JOURNAL

Volume 3

The High Court Frees an Innocent Man

1 December 2019–8 April 2020

With an afterword by George Weigel

IGNATIUS PRESS   SAN FRANCISCO

Quotations from George Cardinal Pell's breviary are from *The Divine Office*, 3 volumes (Sydney: E J Dwyer, 1974).

Cover photograph courtesy of George Cardinal Pell

Cover design by Roxanne Mei Lum

Afterword © 2021 by George Weigel

© 2021 by Ignatius Press, San Francisco
All rights reserved
ISBN 978-1-62164-451-4 (PB)
ISBN 978-1-64229-144-5 (eBook)
Library of Congress Control Number 2020945860
Printed in the United States of America ∞

CONTENTS

CHRONOLOGY

16 July 1996	Pope John Paul II names Auxiliary Bishop George Pell the archbishop of Melbourne, Australia.
26 March 2001	George Pell becomes the archbishop of Sydney, Australia.
21 October 2003	Pope John Paul II makes Archbishop Pell a cardinal.
25 February 2014	Pope Francis appoints Cardinal Pell to the newly created position of prefect of the Secretariat for the Economy, which manages the finances of the Holy See and the Vatican.
29 June 2017	Australian police charge Cardinal Pell with multiple historical sexual assault offences.
5 March 2018	Having denied the charges and voluntarily returned to Australia, Cardinal Pell appears in Melbourne Magistrates' Court for the filing of the charges against him.
1 May 2018	After dismissing several of the charges, a Melbourne magistrate rules that the cardinal will stand trial for the others.
2 May 2018	Cases are divided into two trials: the first will concern charges dating to when Pell was the archbishop of Melbourne in the 1990s; the second will deal with charges dating to when he was a young priest in the 1970s.
20 September 2018	First trial, which began 15 August 2018, ends in a hung jury.
11 December 2018	Retrial, which began 7 November 2018, ends in a guilty verdict.

26 February 2019	Prosecutors drop the second set of charges dating to the 1970s.
27 February 2019	Cardinal Pell is remanded in custody and taken to prison.
13 March 2019	Cardinal Pell is sentenced to six years in prison.
5–6 June 2019	Appeal is made to the Supreme Court of Victoria.
21 August 2019	Appeal is rejected 2–1.
10–11 March 2020	Appeal is made to the High Court of Australia.
7 April 2020	High Court overturns all convictions by 7–0 decision, and Cardinal Pell is released from prison.

WEEK 41

Advent Begins

1 December–7 December 2019

First Sunday of Advent, 1 December 2019

The liturgical year is a wonderful invention which the Catholic Church took over from the Jews and adapted to Christian teaching. Like other Australians, I grew up with the secular holidays of Christmas and Easter and always participated in their religious celebration. I took the yearly cycle somewhat for granted, although increasingly I understood and loved it better.

However, I have a new and deeper appreciation for Lent and Easter, Pentecost, Advent and Christmas, and even Ordinary Time, as they give structure and purpose to my quiet life in jail.

Jewish and Christian history is going somewhere and has a beginning with creation and then Adam and Eve. The Jews are still waiting for the promised Messiah, whom we recognize in Christ, who will come again as judge in the end times. Christians don't believe in an everlasting cycle of return, in an afterlife of reincarnations on earth. One can see here another foundation, other than a rational God, for the theories of the Big Bang, evolution, and even the mythology of progress, a mirage of inevitable and universal progress, which was exploded again in the crimes of the twentieth century. But the world has seen spectacular advances, not universal, in longevity and health, literacy, less hunger, and fewer famines on every continent.

Christians have escaped from the Wisdom literature's pessimism that there is nothing new under the sun (Eccles 1:9) as we move toward the final judgement (Mt 25) and the new heaven and the new earth (Rev 21:1). In the yearly cycle of feasts, we celebrate what has been achieved by God's people and look forward in hope.

My reflection on these blessed understandings was prompted by
the fact that the two North American Protestants, both excellent
preachers with huge congregations, whom I watch every Sunday,
don't follow any discernible liturgical calendar. I shall be interested to
see what they do with Christmas, because the celebration was banned
by Thomas Cromwell in the 1600s in England, with December 25th
declared a fast day and the eating of plum pudding forbidden. The
feast was even outlawed in the early days in the United States.

Fr Martin Dixon celebrated the First Sunday of Advent Mass in
blue vestments, which, he explained, the Church allows as an alternative to the harsher purple of Lent. I have learnt something.

Joseph Prince[1] urged us to "find answers in your darkest dreams",
dressed in a dark jacket and jeans, three rings, and darker subdued
bracelets. He preached on chapter 20 of Acts, reminding his congregation that they are the light of the world and will shine more brightly
by coming together. He recounted the story of Eutychus, who was
cured by Paul after falling asleep and then falling out the window
while Paul was preaching. It gives context to Paul's diffidence about
his worldly wisdom and eloquence; but he was a religious genius. The
Anglican bishop and exegete N. T. Wright compared Paul's intellectual contribution to that of Aristotle, which came to me as a great
surprise when I first read it. But Wright knows much more about
St Paul, and possibly Aristotle, than I do. Prince was quite explicit
about sin and told his congregation, "You too are saved to enjoy the
world completely." Adult believers understand this.

Joel Osteen[2] urged us, not for the first time, to "erupt out of the
negative". As I listened, Joel had competition from an angry banger
and shouter at the other noisy, and often smelly, end of the unit. He
explained that the hidden roots of bitterness grow, that God gives us
grace for every season so that we can take our minds off ourselves.
He concluded by talking about the older brother in the story of the
Prodigal Son, who refused to go to the party, which, Joel reminded
us, went on without him.

Songs of Praise was in Chester [England], where Christingles were
invented. The Christmas decoration is a lighted candle inside an

---

[1] The evangelist Joseph Prince leads a televised worship service called *New Creation Church
TV*.

[2] Joel Osteen is a televangelist and an author. He is the pastor of Lakewood Church in
Houston, Texas.

orange surrounded by four inserted toothpicks with threaded sweets. Good traditional Anglican hymns and "Christ Be Our Light".

The Church's prayer for today's feast of the First Sunday of Advent sums things up.

Grant, almighty Father, that when Christ comes again, we may go out to meet him, bearing the harvest of good works achieved by your grace. We pray that he will receive us into the company of the saints and call us into the kingdom of heaven. Through Christ Our Lord.

Monday, 2 December 2019

After living for eighteen years mostly in Sydney and then in Rome, I have grown used to summer coming and staying. The changes in the Melbourne weather are a novelty for me again after my absence, and I was seriously cold during my two hours in the garden. So much so, I placed an open copy of the *Spectator* across my tummy and under my prison top.

My recollection of a variety of flowers from my visit to the garden was proved correct as many small-petal native flowers are in bloom, very attractive. No one is snipping the dead roses, or the good number which are wilting, well past their prime, although many beautiful new blooms have opened. It is as though the roses have no homes for elderly people, so that those in serious decline can be hidden from public view.

An Islamic terrorist in London has stabbed a couple of people to death at a rehabilitation course. He was shot dead on London Bridge near the scene of the earlier terrorist murders, and the father of the man who was stabbed, a Cambridge graduate organizing the weekend, has spoken against using the atrocity to impose much harsher retribution. We have more than a whiff of Satan here, pure evil.

Tony Abbott's[3] visit to me caused a bit of excitement in the jail. As anticipated, the press was quickly informed and was waiting when he left. He said simply that he was pleased to be in Melbourne and was

[3] Anthony John Abbott (b. 1957), a member of the Liberal Party, was prime minister of Australia from 2013 to 2015. Afterward he remained in Parliament. He lost his seat to a Labor candidate in the federal election on 18 May 2019.

visiting a friend. Some media were wanting a comment from us, but we are not making any statement.

Tony is a genuine and loyal friend, who was the most successful opposition leader in Australian history, but much less effective as prime minister. He suffered from the anti-Catholicism which has strengthened once again in Australia, and I believe the paedophilia crisis engulfing the Church spilled over onto him as a prominent Catholic. His friendship with me was another handicap.

Although he is no longer a candidate for office, his visit here still took courage. He mentioned that no one had asked him to provide a reference for me, and I explained that I strongly supported this. He quickly interrupted, "Not to disadvantage me in the election?", and I agreed.

We spoke of the importance of the work of the Ramsay Centre for Western Civilisation especially now, given the stranglehold the secular Left has over nearly all Australian tertiary education, especially in the humanities. It looks as though Australian Catholic University will be the third partner with the foundation along with the Universities of Wollongong and Queensland. I was surprised and delighted to hear that Ramsay had made a donation to Campion College.

Like myself, Tony is an admirer of my recently deceased friend Fr Paul Stenhouse, and I recounted how beautifully Paul was looking forward to seeing the face of Christ. This prompted a discussion on the nature of life after death and Paul's argument for the reality of the human soul. An individual retains his identity, the same soul, although physically his components are completely different from when he was a baby. One or two of Tony's medical friends claimed some physical continuity, i.e., of some components, in (I think) the brain.

Tony was also interested in the recent financial news from Rome. Kartya[4] had me sent the Vatican press office overview of 28 November. Two pieces of information were new to me. A second member of the AIF[5] board had resigned, Juan Zarate, previously an assistant treasury secretary against financial crimes in the United States. More ominously *Il Fatto Quotidiano* of 28 November 2019 cast serious

---

[4] Kartya Gracer is a senior associate and solicitor assisting Paul Galbally, a partner in the law firm of Galbally and O'Bryan and the principal solicitor for Cardinal Pell.

[5] Vatican Financial Intelligence Authority (AIF).

aspersions on the work of the new president of AIF, Carmelo Barbagallo, when he was at the Bank of Italy from 2011 to 2019, during one of the worst periods for banking scandals. The author claims that Barbagallo was invited to resign after suggestions he was slow to provide information and impeded some operations. Such accusations are easily made, often by opponents, but it would be another kiss of death to have someone at the apex of AIF who was not a capable, determined, and courageous opponent of corruption.

My surviving natural right hip is playing up a bit, causing mild discomfort sometimes when I am walking, but I have no pain when sitting, standing, or lying.

These final words of Prospero to the audience at the end of Shakespeare's *The Tempest* are not a perfect fit for the end of this day, but the language is magnificent and the thought deeply Christian.

> *And my ending is despair,*
> *Unless I be relieved by prayer,*
> *Which pierces so that it assaults*
> *Mercy itself and frees all faults.*
> *As you from crimes would pardon'd be,*
> *Let your indulgence set me free.*

Tuesday, 3 December 2019

After turning on the television, I sat down to a breakfast of toast, butter, and jam with a half-litre of milk to find that Tony Abbott's visit to Cardinal Pell was headline news. Channel 7 continues to use my title, unlike the ABC,[6] which prefers the terms "disgraced" and "convicted paedophile". The world of today's media is always on the move with an astounding and almost instantaneous outreach. One of my US correspondents told me how she had heard of my work in the jail garden!

Spoke to Terry Tobin[7] this morning, who is about to leave for Order of Malta work in East Timor; he felt that a public gesture

---

[6] The Australian Broadcasting Company (ABC) is the national, government-funded television and radio network.

[7] Terry Tobin, a Queen's Counsel, is a friend of Cardinal Pell.

like Tony's was worth much more with the general population than learned articles.

Drawing on my nine years' work as chairman of Caritas Australia in the poorer parts of Asia, I gave Terry Fr Sam Dimattina's solemn warning (which I had followed) to drink only beer, avoiding the water, and to eat plenty of boiled rice. I also passed on the fabulous advice that the seriously careful traveller, determined to avoid stomach trouble, would use whisky with his toothpaste to clean his teeth.

An uneventful hour in the gymnasium, although it took me a while to achieve an unbroken series of a hundred shots on my backhand and forehand at the ping-pong. Sped up the treadmill for a bit longer.

Sr Mary[8] brought me Holy Communion and recounted how she had been speaking with Chris Meney,[9] as Archbishop Fisher wished to come to celebrate Mass for me. Unfortunately, this is not possible because personal visitors cannot also come in on official chaplaincy business, and the authorities are fearful of publicity, more so since yesterday. I think we should ask Fr Jerome to celebrate Mass once again.

About a dozen letters arrived today, which is manageable, because I have about twenty to thirty letters that I have read but have not sorted or used in my journal—quite a backlog, without mentioning a number of letters which should be written.

A couple of letters mention dreams about me. One is from a Queensland lady who "had a dream you were in your red and white robes with the sun shining on you through stained glass windows, hope the dream will come true".

She made another point, which I much appreciated, because it has been made rarely, if at all, among my approximately 2,700 sympathetic letters. She wrote, "What man becomes a priest and a cardinal, then spends years of his time dealing with these problems of abuse in the Church; this is a different and difficult level of service; you must have extremely broad shoulders." Whatever about my shoulders, literally (not broad) or metaphorically, my contribution was simply my duty, but it is encouraging to have it acknowledged. She also mentioned my Facebook supporters' prayer group called St Peter in Chains. And in five years in Melbourne, we helped three hundred complainants.

---

[8] Sr Mary O'Shannassy, a Good Samaritan Sister, is a chaplain at Melbourne Assessment Prison.

[9] Chris Meney, chancellor for Archbishop Anthony Fisher of Sydney, is Cardinal Pell's cousin and friend.

Another dreamer, this time from Dundas in New South Wales, explained simply that "in the dream you were cheerful", this prompting her to arrange for another Mass to be celebrated for me. I too hope and pray that the High Court does the right and just thing and quashes my convictions for the sake of all my supporters and for the good of the Church. Even the High Court's acceptance of my appeal brought relief and delight to the "true believers", not my only supporters, who deserve a break.

A couple of other letters went in different directions. A Queensland writer pointed out that the Bible requires two or three witnesses for a conviction, although for the Noahide laws one witness sufficed. He wonders whether this will be the way of the future. He went on to compare my conviction to the Communist show trials under Stalin in the 1930s. This is a step too far, even for the Appeals Court, because the Soviets never had a Justice Weinberg.

Fr David Cartwright has been a great supporter and regular writer, and he quoted from John Cardinal O'Connor's long homily at the consecration of the new altar in St Patrick's Cathedral, Melbourne, in 1997. The cardinal, one of my inspirations, said that the greatest tragedy is not suffering; the greatest tragedy is suffering wasted. All suffering, small and great, can be used for much good.

Some lines from Psalm 24 provide a finale.

> *Who shall climb the mountain of the Lord?*
> *Who shall stand in his holy place?*
> *The man with clean hands and pure heart,*
> *who desires not worthless things.*

Wednesday, 4 December 2019

Yesterday evening, SBS[10] ran an hour-long program on Advent and the Christmas celebrations in St Paul's Cathedral, London, which focused heavily on the choir. I am not brimful of enthusiasm for Sir Christopher Wren's masterpiece, rebuilt after the Great Fire of London in 1666, because when empty it resembles a concert hall. Like

---

[10] The Special Broadcasting Service (SBS) is an Australian public radio, online, and television network.

the Melbourne Cricket Ground, which is awful when it is empty
(the Sydney Cricket Ground is always beautiful), St Paul's was transformed by the huge Christmas congregations and provided a splendid
setting for the carol services and the Catholic-style Eucharists.

My determination to quash my convictions is reinforced by my
pride in the liturgy and music at both St Patrick's and St Mary's and
in my contribution to strengthening both traditions.

A Gothic cathedral is more clearly an environment for worship
and an evocation of the Transcendent than St Paul's, but the liturgies
are similar, reverent, and ritualised. Both cathedrals are thronged by
the devout, the doubters, those seeking quiet and peace, and the
inevitable tourists. Both buildings are expensive beasts, sustained by
efficient staffs, volunteers, and a hard core of "parishioners".

In Rome, I missed the carol services which are part of our tradition, and this year in jail I will only be able to participate in one Mass
around the table in the Unit 8 common area, hoping the prisoners
don't play up too noisily. The rest will have to come through the
television and, more importantly, through my prayers.

The weeks are no longer punctuated with visits from the lawyers,
so today my only outing, apart from my periods in the small exercise
yard, was a visit to the medical centre for my monthly blood tests.
The gymnasium was closed for the day, which eliminated my session.

I finally managed to attack the backlogged pile of articles and letters and made some progress, as well as writing a couple of letters,
both overdue. Also took a siesta sitting in the chair after lunch and
have decided to do so each day.

One lady from Doncaster wrote that when I lost my appeal in the
Supreme Court, she was at first too upset to read the three-hundred-
page judgement. It was only after the High Court success that she
read the three hundred pages, then wrote: "All I can say is that Justice Weinberg's treatise will no doubt become legend in Australian
legal history. It is extraordinary." Amen to that. She quoted others
who had written to support me, mentioning Russell Marks' article
in the *Saturday Paper*.[11] I had not realised how left-wing this paper is
and had therefore underestimated the article's importance. She has a

[11] Russel Marks, "George Pell's Appeal to the High Court", *Saturday Paper*, 16 November
2019, https://www.thesaturdaypaper.com.au/contributor/russell-marks.

Facebook page "Cardinal Pell Trial", which has nine hundred followers and, she claims, continues to grow.

One of my regular correspondents is from Dallas in Texas and had been away in Wyoming. She has regularly provided food for meditation and comment in this journal. She hopes I am writing a journal, prays for me regularly, and asks St Thomas More to do so, too. She paid me a surprising compliment. "Even in prison, your life has meaning and purpose. Without your trial, I would surely not have such a vivid, compelling model to sustain me during my period of doubt and temptation to walk away from our church in a disgraceful state of corruption." Please God, we won't have too many more developments provoking good people to think of schism.

I will close with a piece of advice St Pio of Pietrelcina (still Padre Pio to me) wrote to someone who was deeply regretting his situation (which my Dallas friend quoted).

The path you tread is the one that will lead you to heaven. And it is all the safer because Jesus himself takes you by the hand. Do not upset yourself at your spiritual aridity and desolation.... Remember what Our Lord said, "Blessed are the poor in spirit for theirs is the Kingdom of heaven."

Thursday, 5 December 2019

Today turned out differently from what I expected. Mr Harris had mentioned an hour in the gymnasium before my two hours in the garden, but his replacement felt it was a bit much to organize as I would have to come back for a half hour between the happenings. He eventually said it was my right, but I conceded and said I would only go to the garden.

The sky had a few clouds, but the day was pleasant, in the low 20°s [high 60°s F], and I made some good progress through the manifesto of the Catholics for Renewal.[12] It is a radical book, in a literal

---

[12] According to its brochure, Catholics for Renewal is a group of Australian Catholics who "seek renewal of the governance, teachings, and practices of the Catholic Church", https://www.catholicsforrenewal.org/aboutus.htm.

sense. I can understand the Wagga farmer at a meeting to prepare for the Plenary Council,[13] which was led by Renewal enthusiasts from Canberra, who walked out proclaiming, "It's OK if you want a new church. Go off and do it, but don't come down here upsetting our church." This isn't an option for me, even at my age, but the potential for strife and further damage is real with the Plenary Council.

At 2:30, I asked the guard to see where my visitors were, as they were due then and unlikely to be late. He replied that the warders knew where I was and would call when the guests arrived. After ten minutes, I enquired again, politely but insistently, suggesting he go inside and ask what was happening. He entered, then returned, saying they had not arrived.

Eventually, after twenty-five minutes (thirty minutes were allotted for the visit), I was brought inside by the guards who would take me back to my cell. Naturally I was upset. I enquired directly, asking what was going on, and I was ushered back out of the office into the meeting room, the blind was pulled down, and they spoke with a newcomer. I was then allowed to proceed and told I was returning to Unit 8. I waited until the female warder finished speaking on the phone and enquired, "What is going on?" She replied she was following orders as the visitors were not on the list. I asked who gave the orders, but she was evasive in reply. My recollection was quite clear—namely, that I had submitted their names previously and in due time. This was confirmed by my notes in the cell that the names had gone in on December 2nd.

After checking this information, I wrote it on a note and enquired again what was happening. Following the normal protocol, I pushed the message out into the corridor under the door.

The unit commander had been conveniently absent when I returned, and they eventually sent two guards, one after the other, both of whom were friendly toward me, to tell me that central office had taken over the approval process for my visits and I now had to give five days' notice. This was news to me, and obviously no reason had been given for any such measure.

---

[13] In October 2020, the Catholic Church in Australia was to hold her initial assembly as part of her first Plenary Council since Vatican II. Due to the COVID-19 pandemic, Assembly 1 was postponed until October 2021, and Assembly 2 was rescheduled for July 2022.

I thanked them for the information and explained that it would have been useful to know beforehand, so I could have saved my friends the time and frustration, as both had come down from New South Wales. My visitors were Fr Victor Martinez, the Australian superior of Opus Dei, and Prof Gerald Fogarty, the master at Warrane College at the University of New South Wales.

I will discuss the matter with my lawyers, but I am inclined to think that a polite, direct letter of complaint to the top of the jail could be appropriate. The warder outside in the garden had been cool and uncommunicative and, I suspect, had lied in saying the visitors had not arrived. My suspicion is that it is somehow connected with the publicity over Tony Abbott's visit and vindictive, rather than the end result of muddle. While I don't want to make too much of it, I will certainly discuss it with the lawyers.

On occasions like this, my mother used to say, "It is the fun of the Cork to be alive, and the will of God to be flat-footed." I have asked many of the Irish if they knew the saying, but only one claimed to have heard something like it.

A huge envelope full of letters and photocopied articles was waiting in my cell, on my return, with enough work for some days. I spent a couple of hours reading four more excellent detailed articles on my case written by Christopher Friel,[14] showing how the complainant had been forced to change his stories about the site of the "attacks" in the sacristy and corridor.

My siesta yesterday was probably not such a good idea as I didn't sleep as well as usual last night. Took no siesta today.

St Anselm was archbishop of Canterbury (1093–1109), and his works *Proslogion* and *Cur Deus Homo* on Christ and the Godhead are classics which in some senses balance out and develop another episcopal classic, St Athanasius of Alexandria's *On the Incarnation*—nearly seven hundred years earlier. More effectively than anyone else, Athanasius defended the full divinity of Christ, and his humanity, against the attacks of the Alexandrian priest Arius. His followers, denying Christ's divinity, are alive and well today, although not openly in the Catholic Church.

---

[14] Christopher S. Friel is a theologian and philosopher located in Wales, UK, who wrote a series of more than 130 analytical papers on the Pell case, which he made available online at Academia, https://independent.academia.edu/ChrisFriel.

St Anselm wrote:

And you, O Lord, how long? How long, Lord, will you be unmindful of us? How long will you turn your countenance from us? When will you look upon us and hear us? Give yourself to us that it may be well with us, for without you it goes so ill with us. Have pity upon our efforts and our strivings toward you, for we can avail nothing without you.

Friday, 6 December 2019

Although I have not read most of the Vatican financial news which came to me yesterday, the situation is unsettling; not so much because the Holy Father has appointed a new promoter of justice and president of AIF, although this has helped, but because the Vatican authorities have hunkered down waiting for the attacks to pass, as is their usual practice. It seems to have worked for decades, but one wonders how much damage is being done out of view, under the Plimsoll line,[15] in the hearts of the faithful. Our good standing has been badly damaged by the paedophilia scandals, so we need to be serious in combating financial crimes. I was amazed to see recently that a US poll claimed that around 40 percent of American Catholics had considered leaving the Church.

A deeply pious prisoner has been writing to me regularly. He is a devotee of the saintly Padre Pio, married with teenage children, and claims that he was condemned unjustly, through the corrupt activities of some police. He doesn't have the money to mount an appeal, but today he was to meet the Victoria government's attorney general to explain his claims. It would be over by now (about 6:30 pm), and I hope it went well. I offered up all my prayers today for that intention. I don't know how many prisoners are unable to find any money for lawyers, but there would be quite a few. I don't know much about the Victoria attorney general and am sceptical about the anti-Catholic

---

[15] The Plimsoll line on the hull of a ship shows the maximum depth it can be safely immersed when loaded with cargo.

Andrews government,[16] but I admire an attorney general who would meet a prisoner like my friend.

A wide range of prisoners continues to write to me. One fellow from country Victoria is much in the wars as his son has just passed a month in jail, his sister has recently attempted suicide, and his mother has been diagnosed as only having some months to live. He asked me to try to ensure someone from the parish made contact with his dying mother. Sr Mary agreed to contact the parish priest, asking him to visit, although at the moment we don't have an address! We shall see if we can make any progress.

Paul Galbally duly called this afternoon to discuss the visitor fiasco of yesterday. I live at the Toorak[17] end of the unit, quiet and fresh-aired, but the guards insisted we leave by the main entrance, and not past the noisy, often smelly other end of the unit. This was a good decision because the smell was terrible, as some prisoner, probably our shouter, had deliberately fouled his cell. It is not an easy unit for the warders, who laughed and are used to such indignities.

After briefly recounting yesterday's story to Paul, we agreed that he would contact the director of the jail to discuss the situation. Fr Victor had phoned him yesterday after they were expelled, but Paul was tied up in court. He also explained to me that I would not be able to watch the High Court proceedings live, as they will not be streamed, and I could not attend in person, even if I could get to Canberra. We discussed some aspects of Friel's articles on the trials, and I indicated that I would prepare a list of those I would want them to read.

The day was cloudy, but the weather was pleasant for my two spells in the exercise pen. My right hip is less of a bother, helped by the fact I am no longer bending to touch my toes, although I can put each foot in turn onto the bench for stretching exercises without provoking discomfort.

I have yet to read my daily quota of St Thomas More's *The Sadness of Christ*. Obviously, the language is different, the sentences are long,

---

[16] Daniel Andrews (b. 1972), leader of the Labor Party in Victoria, has been premier of the state since 2014.

[17] The upper-class suburb of Melbourne.

but we have the classic Catholic teaching on redemptive suffering. So far it is more predictable, even conventional, than I thought it might be.

A couple of lines from Psalm 19 hit the spot.

> May the Lord answer in time of trial;
> may the name of Jacob's God protect you.

Saturday, 7 December 2019

Another quiet day when a small avalanche of mail arrived while I was still working through the backlog. Unfortunately, my gymnasium time was again eliminated, because the jail was in a state of lockdown due to some trouble, I know not what. However, I had my exercise times in the small yard in both morning and afternoon. The weather was pleasant, and while the phone service was down in the morning, I was able to make three phone calls in the afternoon. Danny Casey[18] reported that there had not been much financial news in the last days from the Vatican, although the forces of righteousness are busy. Mark Withoos[19] sent me a series of older news items from Italy, where the scandals have received a lot of coverage from a variety of sources, ranging from the *Wall Street Journal* to *La Repubblica* and the gossip sheets, a heady mix of financial and sexual impropriety.

My good friend and regular correspondent Eugene Ahearn wrote to enthuse about Tony Abbott's visit and to lament the Victoria premier Daniel Andrews' condemnation of the visit as "shameful, absolutely shameful". Derryn Hinch's[20] comments were predictable, but I was surprised that Andrews would be so injudicious publicly. I could have predicted his private views, but such public comments are revelatory, demonstrating how much the secular revolutionaries have invested, at least emotionally, in obtaining and securing my public disgrace. It reveals also his estimate of where Victoria public opinion

---

[18] Danny Casey is a close friend of Cardinal Pell, former business manager for the Catholic Archdiocese of Sydney, and former director of the Secretariat of the Economy.

[19] Fr Mark Withoos was Cardinal Pell's personal secretary in the Vatican.

[20] Derryn Hinch is an Australian politician, actor, media personality, and author who served as a senator for Victoria from 2016 to 2019.

lies, although he won't be gaining any new votes for such an outburst. Today, Danny Casey recounted how an elderly man in his Sydney parish, during the rosary after Saturday Mass, always asks for prayers for political prisoners, especially Cardinal Pell, in the People's Republic of Victoria. I cannot remember meeting Andrews.

Fr John O'Neill from St John Vianney parish in Doonside in the Parramatta Diocese wrote to me again. Educated at St Mary's in Sydney, where he sang in the cathedral choir, he had, and probably still has, a magnificent tenor voice. He is larger than life, like his achievements, and has led his booming parish, alive with faith and prayer, for many years. In most ways, he represents the best of the old school but knows all the tricks necessary to survive today. On my last visit to his parish, he had more than twenty altar servers in procession and a larger group of veiled young women, members of the Handmaids of the Lord. His parish has produced many vocations, with three in the seminary now and another, Fr Jack Green, in the parish next door. Three younger servers are interested in the priesthood. It is an exotic garden, but it is flourishing, and the fruits are good.

He is also an author with a wry, somewhat uncharitable sense of humour, whose characters are dangerously lifelike. The best comparison I can think of for the piece he sent to me is the stories of Don Camillo in Italy, but the parish priest is not fighting the Communist mayor, but the trendies. The hero is Fr King, who is not to be called Freddie, who suffers from "ospeditis", i.e., he keeps putting his foot in his mouth, and wins most of his verbal encounters with his foes, which include his bishop and the diocesan personnel adviser Edna Bacciatutti. All the parish committees resign, the bishop tries to remove him as parish priest, but he survives, and the parish thrives. I told him it was wicked stuff and sentimental, but I thoroughly enjoyed it. He wrote earlier a more polished short novel on the absurdities of postconciliar seminary life, a comedy of errors. Fr John is full of faith, a man of prayer, can charm a vulture off a corpse (as someone said of Lord Louis Mountbatten, last viceroy of India) when he chooses; but he is also tough and savvy. He needed to be to survive. In the last few weeks, he signed an international letter of protest against the placing of the pagan idol Pachamama in St Peter's Basilica in Rome during the Amazon Synod. I congratulated him.

St Cyprian, bishop of Carthage, was martyred in A.D. 258 under Emperor Valerian and wrote in *On the Advantage of Patience*:

The very fact that we are Christians is the substance of faith and hope. But in order for faith and hope to attain their full fruit, there is need of patience. We are pursuing a future, not a present, glory, in accordance with the admonition of Paul the apostle: "It is in hope that we were saved" (Rom 8:24).

WEEK 42

Breaking News at the Vatican

8 December–14 December 2019

Second Sunday of Advent, 8 December 2019

For the first time during my stay in jail, I felt unwell with a stomach upset. During yesterday, my stomach was disturbed, so I woke up to find I had slightly soiled the bed while I was asleep. The inevitable visits to the toilet followed, and I started the day by taking a shower. The senior warder to whom I reported my problem was helpful, and the nurses from the medical centre came while I was briefly outside for exercise in the morning and gave me a couple of tablets, before I beat a hasty return to my cell.

I had very little for lunch, but started to feel better during the day, which I spent quietly, rather than continuing through the backlog of articles. Later in the afternoon, I watched the finish of the Australian Open golf tournament.

Fr Martin Dixon again celebrated Mass in his blue vestments and preached a good short sermon on John the Baptist's call to repent and believe, which leads us to our personal centres, often a long journey, like travelling from the Australian coast to Uluru, or Ayers Rock, as it used to be known.

Joseph Prince preached on the healing power of Communion, soberly dressed in a dark suit, open-necked white shirt, dark blue sandshoes, and only two rings. He gave an exegesis of the New Testament texts on the Eucharist, explaining that all followers of Christ were priests. We ourselves can make and take Communion, which is not merely a symbolic presence. When his young son was recently in hospital with a head injury, the young lad took Communion three times a day. When we drink from the cup, our sins are taken away as a result of Jesus' death on the Cross, although Joseph nowhere mentioned the need for an explicit repentance of our personal sins. For reasons I did not fully comprehend, the order of things is important, so that we drink from the cup before the covenant is announced. From his own evangelical premises, he is genuinely wrestling with the New Testament evidence. It will be interesting if he ever moves beyond the New Testament to examine the other evidence over the first few Christian centuries. It is this study, of patristics, which has brought many former Protestant pastors, such as Scott Hahn, into the Catholic Church, as it did for St John Henry Newman.

Joel Osteen urged us to "wake up to hope", to fight for our future. We need to step out into our greatness as Moses and David battled on, because the forces against Christians are not random; they sense the Christians' capacity for good and strive to destroy it. Storms cannot stop God; we need to stand still and firm, so that we will see the deliverance of the Lord. Joel does not deliver all the Lord's message, but he is right as far as he goes, and his preaching encourages me to persevere.

Songs of Praise was devoted to carols, a term which derives from the Greek word meaning "to dance" and which were introduced into Britain about seven hundred years ago by the followers of Francis of Assisi. They were banned with the feast of Christmas by the Puritans in the seventeenth century. It was mentioned that the traditional carol service begins with a single young chorister singing "Once in Royal David's City", a hymn dating back to 1848. The three Irish priest tenors The Priests sang, and the show featured the Sheffield tradition of carols in the pubs. Still one of my favourite TV shows of the week.

Spoke to Bernadette Tobin,[1] in Sydney, who relayed Terry's account of the story in the *National Catholic Register*,[2] taken in turn from the Italian *Corriere della Sera*,[3] alleging that Peter's Pence money

---

[1] Bernadette Tobin is the director of the Plunkett Centre for Ethics. She and her husband, Terry, are friends of Cardinal Pell.

[2] Edward Pentin, "Report: Vatican Invested Peter's Pence Funds in Elton John Biopic", *National Catholic Register*, 6 December 2019.

[3] Mario Gerevini and Fabrizio Massaro, "Vatican Invested in Lapo Elkann and Elton John Film", *Corriere della Sera*, 4 December 2019.

had been invested by the Secretariat of State, with the help of a dubious Maltese intermediary, in a biopic of the life of Elton John, complete with homosexual activity. It would be nice if recent experience warranted an immediate denial of such a bizarre possibility, but the probabilities are that the story is true. If further proof is needed, it is another conclusive reason why the work of the external auditors was brought to an end, the auditor general was forced to resign, and the Secretariat for the Economy was impeded when it tried to inspect their accounts.

One Advent intercession prays:

Prince of Peace, turn our grievances into life—teach us to forgive rather than give way to anger.
Come, Lord Jesus.

Monday, 9 December 2019

It was supposed to be 38°C [100°F] today, before a change of weather in the evening. The clouds did come in, and it was warm to hot for my two hours in the garden, but I don't think it was century heat[4] (to slip back to the old imperial measure).

Am feeling better after my tummy upset yesterday, but I am short of energy and careful about what I eat. All of this is a normal progression for me after an upset. Like many of my Aussie friends at Propaganda Fide[5] in Rome in the 1960s, the food there damaged, or at least changed, my stomach, so that it reacted badly to rich foods or changes of food. To my regret, I couldn't then eat fruitcake without an upset. Please God the jail food doesn't curtail my appetite, although I am living mainly on salads. I also suspect I was eating too much chocolate.

I look forward to the final ritual of my day, a cup of hot chamomile tea, with a couple of bars from a block of Cadbury's chocolate, while I pray compline. Tonight, like last night, I won't touch the chocolate.

---

[4] "Century heat" is a term used to describe prolonged temperatures of more than 100°F.
[5] The College for the Propagation of the Faith, the international missionary seminary where Cardinal Pell trained for the priesthood.

It was quiet also today in Unit 8, but not everywhere in the jail, apparently. The unit commander explained that there had been a serious incident and the phones were deactivated to prevent word getting out to the press. As Tony Abbott's visit and my brief gardening career demonstrated, MAP [Melbourne Assessment Prison] leaks like a sieve.

The Greek Orthodox chaplain, a friend of Msgr Charlie Portelli,[6] called with his younger assistant chaplain, both in full-length robes, and with the Muslim (Sunni) chaplain. We sat around the picnic table in the garden for nearly a half hour before the sun drove us indoors. The chaplain is a friend of the brother, who lives in Mentone, of Patriarch Bartholomew of Constantinople. I dined there with the patriarch and his entourage during his 1996 visit, when his niece was singing in the choir at St Patrick's Church in Mentone. I recounted that the patriarch mentioned that I was her *didaskalos*,[7] which I wasn't, although I was pleased to be so commended. The younger Orthodox chaplain offered to buy me a new shirt as my sleeve is torn and a couple of front buttons have disappeared, torn off in the washing machine. I thanked him, explaining that was not necessary, but it was a kind and appreciated gesture.

Fr Bill Miscamble, the Australian historian and friend who is at the University of Notre Dame in Indiana, forwarded a disconcerting quotation from C.S. Lewis, which had been sent to him by a professor of Catholic studies at the University of St Thomas in St Paul, Minnesota. I suspect the words, which I did not know, were written after the death of Lewis' wife.

I will give the quotation in full.

It would be [bad] to think of those who get what they pray for as [some] sort of court favourites, people who have influence with the throne. The refused prayer of Christ in Gethsemane is answer enough to that. And I dare not leave out the hard saying which I once heard from an experienced Christian: "I have seen many striking answers to prayer and more than one that I thought miraculous. But they usually come at the beginning: before conversion, or soon after it. As the Christian

---

[6] Msgr Charlie Portelli, parish priest of Keilor Downs, Archdiocese of Melbourne, formerly master of ceremonies to Archbishop Pell and a witness in the case.

[7] A Greek word meaning "spiritual teacher".

life proceeds, they tend to be rarer. The refusals, too, are not only more frequent; they become more unmistakable, more emphatic."[8]

He explains we should not draw hasty conclusions if our prayers are sometimes granted. "If we were stronger, we might be less tenderly treated. If we were braver, we might be sent, with far less help, to defend far more desperate posts in the great battle."

I judge this to be an elegant theological explanation by a thinker, a man of faith, and a master of the English language for the Spanish St Teresa of Ávila's lament that it is not remarkable that God has so few friends because of the way he treats them!

Our Lord taught us to pray for our daily bread and that the faith of the suppliant is important. We find an unpredictability in Jesus' miracles, but he acknowledges and rewards faith. I am sure bravery and strength are criteria for those persons who have offices and roles, which cannot be abandoned without capitulating, a shirking of responsibility, or a refusal of duty. To fall, to complain, to denounce bitterly would further damage the Church, so we pray that God does not miscalculate, does not overestimate our strength, but gives all those in the wrong place at the wrong time the muscle and wisdom to hang on, to muddle through, sustained by the prayers of so many of great faith, both young and old. I suspect that many of those who find themselves in desperate posts in the great battle are surprised to be there, given their inadequacies.

Tuesday, 10 December 2019

I continue to ponder the thoughts of St Teresa and C. S. Lewis, which I quoted yesterday, which I accept, but which need to be filled out by other facts typical in the Christian story and by some other teachings of Our Lord. He did encourage us to take up our cross and follow him, but the yoke is easy and the burden is light (Mt 11:30); and he promised his followers a one-hundredfold reward in this life and eternal life in the next (Mt 19:29 and Mk 10:30–31). This has been true for me so far.

---

[8] C. S. Lewis, "The Efficacy of Prayer" (1958).

If I have encountered more than a usual share of adversity, my life has been showered with blessings: a good family and education, many true friends, enjoyable and worthwhile work in three countries, and with three popes. A strong, good father and a loving mother with faith and her sister, Molly, who lived with us, laid the foundations for all this. I cannot pretend my years have been dominated by adversity. By any standards, I have enjoyed the one hundredfold in this life.

Fairly early on, I took to heart the Lord's teaching on the talents, that more was expected of those who had received more. So, I decided to strive to do what I was asked, not just by my superiors, but by those around me who asked for help. This was to be my principal form of penance, as I wasn't someone who fasted much, and I abstained mainly at Lent—from alcohol. My patterns of prayer strengthened when I became seminary rector, a position I had never contemplated before Bishop Ronald Mulkearns (who negotiated the appointment on behalf of all the Victoria bishops) asked me; any more than I had thought of going to Sydney when I was archbishop of Melbourne. As an archbishop, I was often mentioned as a possibility for different Curial positions: probably shortlisted for prefect for the Doctrine of the Faith when Cardinal Levada was appointed, and very nearly became prefect for the Congregation for Bishops. But I never thought before my work with the Council of Cardinals for Economic Affairs under Pope Benedict that I would finish up as prefect for the Economy. It helped that there was not a high-class field of honest alternative candidates.

Cardinal, now St John Henry, Newman's epitaph was "Ex umbris et imaginibus in veritatem" (We come to the truth through shadows and images). The providence of the one true God can only work out in history through the activities of men and women, largely free, who are either saints or sinners or lukewarm and myopic. God knows in his love what he is up to, while our task is to front up to what needs to be done now and tomorrow; certainly, with an eye to the future, but not using a distant future to avoid immediate responsibilities. I intend to keep praying the Our Father and asking for our daily bread.

The temperature did reach 38°C [100°F] yesterday, but in our air-conditioned cells, it is very difficult to judge the temperature outside, although, through the mesh and opaque glass, we can tell whether it is clear or overcast. Today was pleasant, a nondescript day in the low to mid-twenties [mid- to high 70s°F].

A progress report on my slow decline into old age: my general health continues to stabilise, although I was still lethargic (more than usual) during my hour in the gymnasium. My right hip is much better, mainly, I believe, because I am not bending, trying to touch my toes. And I am no longer fretting over the time I still have to pass in jail. As I have found on other occasions, my mood changes are sometimes quite independent of changing circumstances, following no discernible logic. I am not suggesting that bad news is not bad news, but in "ordinary time" between the clear highs and lows, my mood deviations are not always logical. I find the repetition of "Jesus, *pace e bene*"[9]—a hybrid prayer—is good for me.

My letters which arrived today were Christmas cards, and I have moved through the backlog of mail. I phoned the lawyers' office to inform Kartya that I had sent out more than a tub full of mail, a couple of journal volumes, and three *Spectators* to "Property" and to request that she come with a wheelbarrow to collect them.

Tonight, I watched the ABC interview with Lawyer X, Nicola Gobbo, who was a police informer while she defended her clients. This has provoked the Royal Commission, which is now conducting hearings.

I will be interested to hear what my legal team and friends make of her performance, where she claimed all her actions were performed at the direction, or at least with the permission, of the police and, indeed, the commissioner. She claimed to be living overseas with her two children, whom the police are threatening to take from her. She also claimed baldly that she feared the police will kill her and that she had more to say. The interview effectively placed Ashton,[10] Overland,[11] and senior police on notice. Everyone realises that there are police and police, many good police, but the main question now is about how far and how deep the corruption runs (and whether it impinges on my case). Law enforcement in Victoria is poisoned.

---

[9] *Pace e bene* (peace and goodness) is a Franciscan greeting.

[10] Graham Ashton was chief commissioner of Victoria Police from 2015 to 2020 and also served in the Australian Federal Police.

[11] Simon Overland was chief commissioner of Victoria Police from 2009 to 2011.

I conclude by returning to the theme of my earlier reflections on God's providence and our responses by quoting my favourite poem, "Lead, Kindly Light" by St John Henry Newman. Not for a moment do I suggest this is the finest poem in the English language; it is simply the one I love best:

> *Lead, kindly light, amid the encircling gloom,*
> *Lead thou me on.*
> *The night is dark, and I am far from home,*
> *Lead thou me on.*
> *Keep thou my feet; I do not ask to see*
> *The distant scene; one step enough for me.*[12]

Wednesday, 11 December 2019

Today I prayed the office of the feast of the Immaculate Conception of Our Lady, which was displaced from last Sunday and which I should have celebrated on Monday. It is important to give Our Lady her due.

The feast is often confused with the Virgin Birth of the Lord and is a medieval feast, whose central truth was not accepted by St Thomas Aquinas. The sticking point was that Mary could only have been conceived without sin through the action of her Son, the only Redeemer, who was not yet born; but the solution was proposed by the great Scottish theologian Duns Scotus, who taught at Oxford, by explicitly acknowledging the agency of Jesus' redemption in this sinless conception.

Speaking of this valiant woman, Mary, reminds me that on this coming weekend, Sr Mary will complete twenty-five years of service as prison chaplain. She is highly respected and continues to make a wonderful and Christlike contribution in alleviating suffering. Holy Mother Church should publicly recognize her contribution.

A copy of George Weigel's short article in the American magazine *First Things* (4 December 2019) arrived: "A Last Chance for Australian Justice". It is not just overseas and not just among Catholics that many believe, with George, that "the Australian criminal justice

---

[12] John Henry Newman, "The Pillar of the Cloud" (1833).

system has stumbled or failed at every stage of this case", i.e., my case. The complainant and I have a unique advantage in knowing this is true, but my making a claim, such as George does, would avail little. The reputations of the legal practitioners involved have already been enhanced or damaged by their contributions, and the story is not concluded. In few cases has the evidence been subjected to such widespread and detailed scrutiny.

My solicitor Paul Galbally said to me last week that not one learned or semilearned legal writing has appeared supporting the majority position in the Court of Appeal. I have to concede that I have the viewpoint of a participant, but I am capable of clear thought; and George is absolutely correct that "not a shred of corroborating evidence has yet been produced" and that the "crime ... simply could not have happened in the circumstances and under the conditions it was alleged to have been committed".

I am second to none in my admiration of Judge Weinberg's judgement, but I was surprised, and pleased, to hear George's claim that "one distinguished Australian attorney described [it] as the most important legal document in that country's history."

Not all my supporters are theological or ideological allies; I find this gratifying. In his article, Weigel again compares my situation with that of Captain Dreyfus[13] in nineteenth-century France, while for Australian supporters, the point of comparison is Lindy Chamberlain.[14]

A couple of articles also arrived from Rome, including Ed Pentin's *National Catholic Register* story about the Vatican investment in Elton John's biopic[15] and a defiant and revealing statement by Cardinal Becciu.[16]

---

[13] Alfred Dreyfus, a French Jewish artillery officer, was wrongly convicted of treason twice, in 1894 and 1899, based on false evidence. He was finally exonerated in 1906, pardoned, and released from prison.

[14] Convicted by a jury in 1982 of killing her baby at Ayers Rock but released in 1986 and declared innocent.

[15] See note 2.

[16] Archbishop Giovanni Becciu was the substitute for general affairs in the Vatican's Secretariat of State from 2011 to 2018, when Pope Francis made him a cardinal and the prefect of the Congregation for the Causes of Saints. In 2020, after Cardinal Becciu was accused of improperly using Church funds to purchase a London property, Pope Francis requested his resignation as prefect and removed his prerogatives as a cardinal, including participation in future papal conclaves.

[According to Pentin] one million dollars were invested, allegedly from Peter's Pence, in Elton John's story *Rocketman*, which was "the first major Hollywood studio release to include an on-screen homosexual sex scene", which was banned in some countries. The *Corriere della Sera* claimed that many investments were made through the Centurion Global Fund of Enrico Crasso, an Italian financier resident in Switzerland, whose fund's losses at the end of 2018 it estimated at about €2 million.[17]

Pentin also mentioned an earlier fiasco of Cardinal Bertone[18] in 2012, when he pressured the IOR [Institute for the Works of Religion], the so-called Vatican Bank, against the advice of its then director Ettore Gotti Tedeschi, to invest €15 million in an Italian film company Lux Vide, which had to be completely written off, entirely lost.

Cardinal Becciu is unlike most of the other Vatican personalities in the financial dramas, who hunker down and remain silent until the artillery barrages cease and then get back on with their lives. This cardinal often issues a statement. On this occasion, he wrote to Sandro Magister of *L'Espresso*, repeating that he had nothing to do with the IDI hospital[19] financing and explaining that he did not consider "the contrary opinion of Cardinal Pell" on the London purchase because he was never consulted on the matter "since it was not within his competence to control the accounts of the Secretariat of State",[20] an authority the pope had never given him. The Italian phrase used is "controllare i conti della Segreteria di Stato"[21] translated as "control". While I don't have access to an Italian dictionary, the charter of our secretariat explicitly gave us authority to supervise (*controllare*) all the accounts in the Vatican, including those of the Secretariat of State, and purchases of property etc. above €500,000 needed our approval. This was not requested, but the faulty accounting of the enterprise provoked our opposition, where the loan was obscured and balanced out against the value (theoretically) of the purchase, contrary to accounting regulations. Our view did not prevail, but three things are clear.

---

[17] See note 3.

[18] Tarcisio Cardinal Bertone was the Vatican secretary of state (2006–2013).

[19] Instituto Dermopatico dell'Immacolata in Rome.

[20] Sandro Magister, "Becciu: 'Non competeva al cardinale Pell controllare i conti della Segreteria di Stato'", *Settimo Cielo*, 2 December 2019.

[21] Full translation: to supervise the accounts of the Secretariat of State.

1. In the charter, the Secretariat of State was never exempt from the Economic Secretariat's supervision, and

2. Our activities were regularly, but not totally and effectively, resisted by some, but not all, in the Secretariat of State. Elements there were hostile to any outside light on their activities (and we now understand better why this was so), and

3. The *sostituto*[22] cancelled the external audit and forced the auditor to resign. He does not directly deny our opposition and says nothing about the huge losses on the investment (15 percent from the Brexit devaluation and at least 15 percent from the collapse of the London property price bubble, i.e., at least a €60 million loss on the initial €200 million investment), and nothing about the attendant malpractice, such as excessive fees and commissions.

As we remember Our Lady today, we close with one of the prayers of intercession.

Saviour of the world, by your redemptive power you preserved your mother Mary from every stain of sin;
—deliver us from the evil that lies hidden in our hearts.

Thursday, 12 December 2019

A pleasant day for my couple of hours in the garden, almost cool at first until the sun came out from behind the clouds. It was 40°C [104°F] for the opening cricket Test against New Zealand in Perth, while Brisbane received 100 millimetres of rain in twenty-four hours (almost five inches, for my generation) about twenty-four hours after the SBS weather bureau forecast no good rain in South East Queensland for six months. Their relentless propaganda for catastrophic man-induced climate change continues unabashed.

Terry Tobin called to see me on his return from work in Timor for the Order of Malta. The mother superior of the hospital in Dili

---

[22] The deputy secretary of state, then Cardinal Becciu.

sent her best wishes and prayers and expressed her certainty that I am innocent. I continue to receive twenty or thirty Christmas cards or letters every day.

One good friend has again been very generous toward my legal expenses, and the extracurricular activities continue around my case; but we have no news of any knockout blow. A short enigmatic note appeared in one daily, indicating that elements in the police involved in the Lawyer X scandal were pleased that my problems would provide a diversion from theirs. We also briefly discussed Lawyer X's television interview, which Terry had not seen, but many experienced in the law believe her fear of the police is genuine. It would require a brave person to assert it isn't justified.

Yesterday, a letter arrived from Marie Houlihan in Pakenham, telling me of the death of her husband, Michael, described in his son's eulogy as "lifelong servant of the Church, dairy farmer, barrister, and magnificent bastard". I often recall explaining to my old friend "Boffin", the English Jesuit Fr O'Higgins, an Oxford specialist in eighteenth-century unbelief, that the "b" word was often a term of affection in Australia. "Yes," he replied shortly, "I can understand that." The letter had been sent to me in April at the remand centre and turned up back at Marie's place two months later marked "insufficient address". Life in jail is replete with these mishaps.

Michael lived nearly all his life at Nar Nar Goon, southeast of Melbourne, and was the son of old Tom, who had fought in the First World War, and Molly, who died when Michael was fourteen.

I was close to the next brother, Tom, and knew Paul, who was even younger, at St Pat's in Ballarat. After one year in boarding school in Ballarat, Michael stayed home to help his father, "a widower in his 60s, without the big joyful female presence of Molly, in very loose control of three wild colonial boys".

I remember staying in a small, spectacularly old wooden farmhouse, probably the same one Michael's grandfather had dragged by bullocks to the selection he had bought in 1892.

In 1960, Michael met Marie Donahoe, a librarian, whom he married and with whom he produced six children, and then twenty grandchildren followed. He was not only one of the best men among his generation of Irish-Australian Catholics, but certainly one of the most interesting.

He had a cast of mind which could not be anything but Irish; I have met no Irish who were quite like him and his ilk. Even more basically, he was from country Australia, with an edge, a self-confidence, and a set of practical skills which amazed a more comfortable, and ineffectual, provincial like myself.

His son described him as an open-minded ideologue, who, as one of his legal friends, an atheist, explained, "actually acted like Christians say people are meant to act".

After completing year eight at school many years earlier, he was admitted to study law and economics at Monash University in his thirties, graduated, and then spent more than thirty years as "a tenacious advocate", "the scourge of low-wattage magistrates everywhere", who never had "more of a spring in his step than when he had a murder trial on".

Always interested in politics, he supported the DLP [Democratic Labor Party], was immersed in the anti-Communist struggles, and moved on to the Liberal Party.

He was deeply Catholic, developing a love of the Latin liturgy in the latter decades of his life, and said the rosary every day. A granddaughter estimated that he would have asked Our Lady one million times during his life to "pray for him at the hour of his death".

As a child, he would "melt a candle onto his bedpost and read into the night", and he became a learned and wise adult, with a mastery of the magnificent, pithy Australian English which television and debased courses in English at school and university have destroyed. He was formidable and eccentric, but his son conceded that so much of what his father did "that we found painfully unfashionable has now swung into fashion".

People like Michael and myself belonged to a fortunate generation which escaped the World Wars and the Depression and which grew up when there was sufficient anti-Catholicism to keep our community together, when the Catholic schools were producing historically rare social mobility, and the discovery of the contraceptive pill, television, scientific advances generally, and then the Internet had not yet produced those mighty sociological currents which have carried off many of our middle-aged and younger people into confusion, religious muddle, and sometimes serious unbelief, without mentioning damage to the family.

His son's eulogy is a beautiful tribute to Michael, as we see the learning, the faith, the love of language, and the mordant Aussie humour continue in the next generation.

May Michael and his tribe rest in peace.

Friday, 13 December 2019

The best news of the day was that early results and exit polls were giving Boris Johnson a majority of more than 85 seats and predicting Labour's worst result since 1935 with fewer than 200 seats in the 650-seat Parliament.[23] Britain will be leaving the European Union.

Recently I congratulated Tony Abbott on the speech he gave in England in favour of leaving, and he replied that it is one of the speeches which, in retrospect, gives him the most satisfaction and of which he is most proud.

A cynic might say that de Gaulle[24] has been vindicated, as he was always opposed to Britain's entry. But the European elite, who are profoundly undemocratic, with many powers transferred to the non-elected European Commission, and hostile to dissenting views, have brought this result upon themselves. They can now turn their attention to their own profound problems, the contrast between Northern and Southern Europe, and especially the economic problems of Spain, Italy, and Greece. Anti-European feeling has grown in many EU countries, even in France itself, fuelled by large numbers of unintegrated Muslim migrants and terrorist activity. And the European Union is no friend of Christianity, refusing even to mention the Christian contribution in their constitution.

Modern communications and ease of travel have made cooperation easier between Britain and the most distant places, like Australia and New Zealand, and a more Asian world will draw European-style communities closer together. Britain did well when it was on its own

[23] Boris Johnson became prime minister of the UK in July 2019, without a general election, when the Conservative Party chose him to replace Theresa May. In the December 2019 general election, a large majority voted for him to continue in the office.

[24] Charles de Gaulle (1890–1970) led the Free French Forces in the Second World War and the French government afterward. In 1963 and 1967, he vetoed the UK's applications to join the European Economic Community, a precursor to the European Union.

and with the proper leadership will do so again. Whether Boris is the person to provide this leadership is uncertain, but I believe his prospects are good, and he is certainly a better alternative than [Labour leader Jeremy] Corbyn. Any party system needs to be changed when it enables a man to be appointed with views so different from the majority views among his parliamentary colleagues and the majority of the party generally.

Another article by Ed Pentin arrived, giving book, chapter, and verse on how APSA [Administration of the Patrimony of the Apostolic See] transferred €50 million to the bankrupt IDI hospital, first of all to the congregation, the Sons of the Immaculate Conception, then to the Luigi Monti Foundation, and finally to the hospital, against the advice of the Secretariat for the Economy.[25] The Bambino Gesù hospital, like the IOR bank earlier, had refused to cooperate, but APSA so far has refused the hospital directive to transfer their 50 million in certificates of deposit (CDs) from APSA to IOR. Pentin also reported correctly that KPMG[26] refused to sign a report that the loan could be repaid.

Two laymen, Franco Dalla Sega and Carmine Stingone, each received a six-figure commission for their work on the loan, while Dalla Sega was also a member of the intermediary Luigi Monti Foundation: a clear conflict of interest.

From my first meeting, I had not been impressed by Dalla Sega when he responded with a set of problems for every proposal given to him. I closed the meeting early and asked him to return later with a strategy to overcome his problems. His most egregious performance was at a round table meeting on IDI, when he publicly reassured Cardinal Parolin[27] that he did not need to understand the fate of €21 million, as this was a "technicality". It was at this same meeting that Profiti[28] from Bambino Gesù claimed that the bankrupt IDI, then losing €7 million a year, could repay the €50 million loan at the rate of €18 million a year over the next three years.

---

[25] Edward Pentin, "Tangled Web of Transactions Utilized to Fund Bankrupt Italian Hospital", *National Catholic Register*, 10 December 2019.

[26] Klynveld Peat Marwick Goerdeler is a global network of financial services based in the Netherlands.

[27] Pietro Cardinal Parolin became the Vatican secretary of state in 2013.

[28] Giuseppe Profiti, president of Bambino Gesù hospital 2008–2015, was convicted in 2017 for diverting €422,000 of hospital funds.

Two important German-language papers, *Neue Zürcher Zeitung*[29] and *Die Zeit*,[30] with the Italian *Libero Quotidiano*[31] revealed even more lurid details of the Secretariat of State London purchase.

After the initial joint venture with Mincione,[32] his portion passed to Gianluigi Torzi's Luxembourg group Gutt. Soon after signing the contract with Torzi for 30,000 out of 31,000 shares, the Vatican discovered that all the voting rights were with the 1,000 shares they did not own. To remedy this and obtain control of the project, the Vatican was forced to pay another €62 million, much of it to Mincione.

This spectacular loss resembles the IOR property sale scandal in the 2000s, now before the courts,[33] although it is not quite in the league of the Calvi, Sindona, and Banco Ambrosiano losses in the 1980s.[34] It could be said that old habits die hard.

---

[29] Marcel Gyr and Dieter Bachmann, "Der jüngste Finanzskandal im Vatikan erfüllt so manches Klischee" (The latest financial scandal in the Vatican lines up with so many stereotypes), *Neue Zürcher Zeitung*, 10 December 2019.

[30] Julius Müller-Meiningen, "Unter Räubern. Der nächste Finanzskandal: Vatikanmitarbeiter kauften in London eine Luxusimmobilieund veruntreuten Spenden in Millionenhöhe. Jetzt greift der Papst durch" (Among thieves. The next financial scandal: Vatican employees bought a luxury property in London and misappropriated donations in the millions. Now the Pope takes action), *Die Zeit*, 9 December 2019.

[31] Caterina Spinelli, "Papa Francesco e lo scandalo offerte: così il Vaticano ha speso 700 milioni destinati ai poveri" (Pope Francis and the contributions scandal: how the Vatican spent 700 million intended for the poor), *Libero Quotidiano*, 15 December 2019.

[32] Raffaele Mincione, an Italian businessman under investigation, served as financial adviser for the Secretariat of State.

[33] Philip Pullella, "Prosecutor Freezes Accounts of Ex-Vatican Bank Heads", Reuters, 7 December 2019, https://www.reuters.com/article/vatican-bank-accounts/prosecutor-freezes-accounts-of-ex-vatican-bank-heads-idUSL1N0TS0LN20141208. "The Vatican's top prosecutor has frozen 16 million euros in bank accounts owned by two former Vatican bank managers and a lawyer as part of an investigation into the sale of Vatican-owned real estate in the 2000s."

Prosecutor Gian Piero Milano said he suspected the three men, former bank president Angelo Caloia, ex-director general Lelio Scaletti, and lawyer Gabriele Liuzzo, of embezzling money while managing the sale of twenty-nine buildings sold by the Vatican Bank to mainly Italian buyers between 2001 and 2008.

[34] In 1981 Roberto Calvi was found guilty of illegally transferring millions of dollars to foreign countries while he was manager and then chairman of Banco Ambrosiano. Much of the money had been transferred through the Vatican Bank, Ambrosiano's largest shareholder. Ambrosiano collapsed in 1982, and soon afterward Calvi was murdered. An earlier case of fiscal misconduct involving the Vatican occurred in 1974, when the Holy See lost millions of dollars after the collapse of Franklin National Bank owned by Michele Sindona, who died in prison after drinking poisoned coffee.

A friend of mine from Ballarat East, who is dying, sent the following prayer.

> *Not only in extremes . . .*
> *But in some faithful act,*
> *Some scarcely conscious choice,*
> *We find the grace to hear and heed*
> *The bidding of Christ's voice.*

Saturday, 14 December 2019

During this week, I reverted to the habit of a lifetime by taking my shower immediately after I got out of bed and before the roll call. When I came into jail and I had nothing except my breviary, not even a television in the first day or so, no books, no mail, I decided to have my shower around 6:00 pm to provide a break between the lockdown at 4:00 pm and going to bed. As I was able to receive books, magazines, press cuttings, and mail, my daily routine changed, so that now occasionally I seem to be short of time, and I found that on a couple of days I had not taken a shower by the evening. For decades, showers and Mass and basic prayers made up the pre-breakfast routine, so I have returned to these earlier patterns, although I pray more during the day with my rosaries in the exercise pens and in the garden, and I can easily pray sections of my evening prayer during the SBS television advertisements.

As a Christian, I don't regard the hostile verdicts and the months in jail as a brute fact, the product of blind fate from which nothing can be salvaged or gained except my integrity. Christ's teaching on suffering, beautifully spelt out by St Paul, is what sustains me through the quiet and the tedium, although I am not starved, not maltreated, not even living in any special discomfort. But every now and again, I am tempted to be small-spirited, to feel I am hard done by, like the elder brother in the parable of the Prodigal Son. Every now and again, I feel sympathy for Mary and Joseph on their return from the pilgrimage to Jerusalem and discovering that Jesus was still in Jerusalem discussing theology with the priests in the Temple. He should have let them know and saved them the worry and the extra travel before they found him. Or so my mind runs.

My mail regularly helps keep me on an even keel religiously and psychologically, with one brother priest from Ballarat writing, "Christmas means that God is near us, God-with-us, even more when he seems a long way away."

I was particularly encouraged by a letter from a woman in South Australia, whom I did not know, who is in her early forties and had been a "fallen-away Catholic" for twenty years. She had fallen into the vices of "the modern 'woke' world" but my "tragic story, the false charges, the biased trial, the sad verdict, and the disgusting vitriol from the public" proved to be a catalyst for her and "the beginnings of [her] renewal back into the faith".

She has no rosy-eyed view of the Church, which she sees as "infiltrated with evil prelates, homopredators, fraudsters", and thieves, etc., etc., but my problems have led her "to become more serious about my faith, more thirsty for knowledge, and seeking the fullness of the truth, I am happy to say my faith is stronger than ever." She goes on: "Heaven must be rejoicing as their prodigal daughter has returned. And you have helped lead a sheep back home."

These and similar stories are a consolation for me and an encouragement to keep on keeping on, secure in my Christian convictions.

And there is anguish. By a coincidence, I received today a note from Michael Houlihan's daughter, whom I don't know, who wrote to express her support, to tell of her prayers for me, and to say that she was at the wake in the funeral parlour after her father's funeral when the word of my guilty verdict came through. It was, she said, the worst day of her life.

My day passed quietly. When voting stopped, Boris Johnson had 365 seats, Corbyn had 203, with about 40 seats undecided. Typically, Corbyn had announced he would not lead Labour at the next election but was not standing down immediately.

The weather was good, not too hot and somewhat overcast. [In Test cricket] New Zealand was bowled out in their first innings, still 250 runs behind the Aussies' score, and Steve Smith had taken one of the finest catches you will see, diving and taking the ball in his outstretched right hand.

The Holy Father has appointed [Luis Antonio] Cardinal Tagle, prefect of the Congregation for the Evangelization of Peoples, unexpectedly replacing [Fernando] Cardinal Filoni, whose contract did not finish until 2022 and who is only seventy-one years of age. Rumour has it that Filoni did not agree with the secret deal done with Communist China, which has not diminished the harassment and, indeed, persecution of different groups of Catholics.

As Saturday is Our Lady's day, we commend our small difficulties and the mighty challenges to the Church across the globe to her intercession using the words of the hymn "Daily, Daily Sing to Mary", which is set to the melody of Beethoven's "Ode to Joy" and which I use for meditation.

> *When the tempest rages round thee,*
> *She will calm the troubled sea.*
> *Gifts of heaven she has given,*
> *Noble Lady, to our race.*
> *She, the Queen, who decks her subjects,*
> *With the light of God's own grace.*

WEEK 43

A Blessing beyond Anticipation

15 December–21 December 2019

Third Sunday of Advent, 15 December 2019

The alarm continues to work well, so I was woken in time for *Mass for You at Home*, which was celebrated by Bishop Mark Edwards, a philosopher and an Oblate of Mary Immaculate, who is an auxiliary bishop in the Melbourne Archdiocese. He is a devout and prayerful priest, who celebrated Mass correctly and reverently but gave a sermon of record-breaking brevity. Advent is a time of waiting patiently for God. The butterfly only comes out of its cocoon slowly. If we warm the cocoon, the butterfly does emerge more quickly, but with damaged wings so that it cannot fly. We need to model ourselves on God's patience.

He left it to us, his listeners, to develop this basic lesson as we saw fit and tie it all back to Christmas.

Joseph Prince did not make an appearance this morning, so Joel Osteen moved into his slot, giving his customary excellent sermon without any reference to Advent or Christmas.

The typical gospel objection to Osteen is that he appears to preach a prosperity Christianity, where the situation always, or nearly always, turns out well in this life for a believing Christian. He came close to answering this criticism this morning with his theme of "Wake Up to Hope".

Christians need opposition, just as Jesus was opposed; we, too, need the kiss of Judas. In fact, Judas did more for Jesus than any of the other apostles, because he unlocked our salvation. This involved no attempt to distort what he had done, and it certainly prompted me to think about the nature of sin and the sometimes awful consequences of human decisions.

Joel continued. We dislike difficulties, but we should serve the plan of God, who does not take us in straight lines and, indeed, works on us like a piece of sandpaper. If Joseph, Jacob's favourite son, had not been sold into slavery by his brothers, he would have been unable to help, as a high Egyptian official, his brothers in the time of drought.

We don't know what God is up to; often we don't know God's plan, what he is doing behind the scenes, but God's grace is sufficient, and we should strive to stay in peace, to trust God. And we don't grow as persons in the good times; growth comes in times of adversity.

While I continue to have problems with what Joel does not say, with his claim that all our problems will turn out for good, without acknowledging that this is always true only if we include heaven and hell, the afterlife of reward and punishment, I am grateful for what he says about persevering in hope.

On so many occasions, God does give many of us one hundredfold in this life. Even when the returns do not seem as good as this, who doesn't receive human blessings? Not many at all have no reason, or little reason, for gratitude. Osteen's sermons have been good for me, jolting me away from a self-centred pessimism.

A beautiful Advent service of hymns came from Derby Cathedral, a lavishly decorated church, which seemed more like a concert hall than a basilica and was nothing like a Gothic cathedral. We had an explicit affirmation of faith in Jesus' return, his Second Coming, and some traditional favourites were sung like "O Come, O Come, Emmanuel"; "Immortal, Invisible, God Only Wise", and "Tell Out My Soul", which lifted my spirits in my small cell.

The middle hours of the day were used to read the cuttings from Italian papers on the Vatican finance scandals which Fr Mark Withoos had sent me. Not a great deal of it was new to me, but a lot of accurate information has appeared on the unhappy developments, which cannot be twisted or spun into respectability.

It has emerged that Mincione was also involved with Italian Catholic hospitals, some of whom have debts of hundreds of millions of euros (like IDI), including the St John of God Brothers (the Fatebenefratelli) on the Tiber, on whom Mincione imposed a

20 percent commission.[1] The annual Peter's Pence collection has fallen from 100 million euros to less than 60 million (and probably less again this year), which will worsen the annual Vatican structural deficit further. All this must be seeping into the consciousness of Catholic donors as well as Catholic churchgoers and the general public. The notoriety of the losses and criminality should make repetition more difficult in the future, but not if the basic procedures and precautions to prevent corruption are systematically weakened or abandoned. Underlying all this is the necessity to raise more revenue and/or reduce expenses.

Our Lord promised heaven that day to the good thief on the cross, but he could be brutally direct in word and action.

When Jesus entered the temple courts, he began to drive out those who were selling. "It is written," he said to them, "My house will be a house of prayer, but you have made it a den of thieves" (Lk 19:45–6).

Monday, 16 December 2019

Today is the fifty-third anniversary of my ordination to the priesthood in St Peter's Basilica, Rome, on 16 December 1966 by [Gregorio] Cardinal Agagianian, Georgian born, Armenian rite, and prefect of the then Propaganda Fide Congregation. Pope John XXIII used to tell the students at Propaganda Fide College, where I was a seminarian, that Cardinal Agagianian was runner-up when he was elected pope. Newspaper reports claimed that the fact that his sister still lived behind the Iron Curtain in Communist-controlled Georgia, where Stalin was born and where she might be vulnerable to hostile pressure, was one of the factors which militated against his election.

He, too, had been a student at Propaganda Fide College, then in the Piazza di Spagna, with my first Ballarat bishop, Sir James Patrick O'Collins, a clever man who had been a plumber or gas fitter before entering the seminary and eventually finished up as head prefect of the college. He used to insist that Agagianian came to Rome as a "registered parcel" when he was about fourteen and was

---

[1] Emiliano Fittipaldi, "Peccati mortali ..." ('Mortal sins ... '), *L'Espresso*, 20 October 2019.

an outstanding student, obtaining "full marks in every subject" (such was the legend). He was certainly a clever man and a brilliant linguist.

Naturally, no one has mentioned the anniversary to me, and I remembered to pray for my classmates, a good number of whom have died, especially among the Africans.

The highlight of the day was the visit of Jean-Baptiste de Franssu, president of IOR, the so-called Vatican Bank, who came from Brussels to visit me. He had spent a couple of days in Sydney, where Danny Casey had looked after him, before flying to Melbourne. He returns to Europe tonight. The visit is a wonderful gesture of support, which I deeply appreciate.

At a local, diocesan, and national level in Australia, it was always consoling to find so many good and highly competent lay men and women who were prepared to help the Church professionally. At Rome, too, this was the case with men and women like Jean-Baptiste, Sir Michael Hintze, the Australian-born London financier, and Joe Zahra, the Maltese banker who headed COSEA,[2] the committee which revealed the mess and corruption and laid out the remedies we tried to implement, which were so tenaciously and imaginatively opposed for so long.

Jean-Baptiste and I worked together for reform in our different areas. Although he was often maligned and mistreated and physically threatened on at least one occasion, he was more effective in the bank in eliminating corruption than I was across the Vatican, although we were both unable to discover the full truth on some older major scandals, where the facts will probably continue to lie buried.

It was the IOR's refusal to cooperate in obtaining another €150 million for the disastrous London purchase in Chelsea that recently brought matters to a head. I was pleased to learn that it was the Holy Father himself who not only authorised the "raids" on the Secretariat of State and AIF offices but insisted that action be taken.[3] Jean-Baptiste

---

[2] Early in his pontificate, Pope Francis named the Maltese banker Joseph Zahra president of the newly formed Pontifical Commission for Reference on the Organization of the Economic-Administrative Structure of the Holy See (COSEA), which has examined the Vatican financial situation and proposed comprehensive reforms.

[3] Sandro Magister, "Searches at the Secretariat of State. The Pope: 'I Signed the Authorization'", *Settimo Cielo*, 26 November 2019, http://magister.blogautore.espresso.repubblica.it/2019/11/26/searches-at-the-secretariat-of-state-the-pope-%e2%80%9ci-signed-the-authorization%e2%80%9d/.

also agrees that there is *prima facie* evidence of wrongdoing at AIF and that if René Brülhart, the AIF president, did resign, it was because he had no alternative. IOR came under considerable pressure to cooperate, and one of their officials was menaced and threatened, although he wasn't called over to inspect the freshly opened drawer and find a revolver there, as occurred in the good old days.

Mincione was active in many areas, not only with the Catholic hospitals but with [Alberto] Matta in the Budapest Exchange Palace affair,[4] which was never satisfactorily resolved (as I recall). Jean-Baptiste had asked Pope Francis about his trip to visit me and been strongly supported. I hope in turn that he continues to receive the official backing his efforts deserve and the Vatican needs as it slowly digs itself out of its financial woes, out of a hole.

I was gratified to hear that a number of cardinals, not all of my thinking, now concede that what I was explaining years ago was happening and that my, or our, reform efforts laid the foundations for the recent breakthroughs.

Even more pleasing was the news that a decree has gone out that APSA investments are to be consolidated and made in a coordinated way, as COSEA recommended six years ago and we were prevented from implementing. This will be opposed ferociously by the APSA old guard, and it is a moot point whether there is the capacity and a sufficient amount of good will for success.

As Jean-Baptiste is in contact with [Philippe] Cardinal Barbarin, archbishop of Lyon, I enquired how his legal case is going and asked for my best wishes to be conveyed. Apparently the "not guilty" verdict will be announced in the New Year, although the saga has taken its toll on Barbarin's health.[5] Please God the "not guilty" verdict on his handling of a particular case of paedophilia will be confirmed. Jean-Baptiste promised to phone Lyon on his return.

I was able to explain that my health improved when I no longer had the daily pressures of often unsuccessful battling against the forces of darkness in Rome. And I am pleased I am no longer there, although it was my duty to stay while I had a mandate. I commend

---

[4] Matthew Vella, "Vatican Chases Millions to Stop Malta Fund from 'Abusive' Sale", *Malta Today*, 14 December 2019.

[5] Philippe Cardinal Barbarin's conviction for not acting quickly enough to report a paedophile priest was overturned by an appeal court on 30 January 2020.

Jean-Baptiste for remaining to fight the good fight, when he could easily have walked away, and I wish him well in his efforts to consolidate stability and enhance profitability. Please God he will be able to finish his tour of duty with dignity and his contribution will be acknowledged.

The hymn "Thrice Holy" has a couple of wonderful lines to the one true God.

> *Holy, holy, holy, though the darkness hide thee,*
> *Though the eye of sinful man, thy glory may not see.*
> *Only thou art holy, there is none beside thee,*
> *Perfect in power, in love and purity.*

Tuesday, 17 December 2019

Pauline, a good friend and a Scot from London, sent me a Christmas card with a copy of Filippino Lippi's painting of the Madonna and Child with the infant St John, which hangs in the Glasgow Art Gallery. She has been a generous supporter, praising George Weigel's efforts on my behalf, and she wrote, "I hope you are holding up. The problem with being a Christian, of course, is that Jesus ended up on the Cross. What do we expect? But the Cross wasn't the end, and it's not your end, either." And that remains true no matter what the High Court rules.

However, this was a good day despite the fact that the gymnasium was closed and I missed my hour of exercise. Tim O'Leary[6] was interviewed yesterday for an interesting and important position, so I phoned, as promised, to enquire how things went. Last night he was told that he was the preferred candidate and that his referees were being consulted. He should know more clearly on Friday, but the situation is promising. This was a boost to my morale.

The second piece of good news was to hear that the lunch Terry organized for Jean-Baptiste after his visit had gone very well indeed.

---

[6] Tim O'Leary is now a senior executive of the Archdiocese of Melbourne and a friend of Cardinal Pell.

The group, which included a couple of retired senior judges, had clicked. Good and competent people who love the Church have a lot in common, even when they come from different parts of the world. While Terry had prepared Jean-Baptiste for the jail conditions, he had taken it all in his stride, as I would have predicted, and was delighted by our time together. He remarked that it was like chatting in my office in Rome, and I felt exactly the same way. While I am pleased to be out of the financial work in Rome, I am more pleased and proud I was there as we broke the back of the criminal network, although it could have been achieved more quickly and comprehensively. And I made some wonderful friends. None of this means that financial security and probity are assured for the Vatican in the future, but immense progress has been made. And the game is there to be won.

Sr Mary called for her weekly visit with her assistant, Roxanne, who had just returned from the Catholic Youth Gathering in Perth, attended by six thousand young adults, with a thousand coming from both Melbourne and Sydney. Roxanne was very happy with the atmosphere, where she found plenty of vitality. The speakers were good, some of them from the US.

Chris Meney had arranged for me to speak with Archbishop Fisher by phone to exchange Christmas greetings. The archbishop was in fine form, buoyed by the carol services at the cathedral and another epic performance at the Maroubra Catholic church directed by Dr Mark Schembri. He also confirmed Sr Mary's news that they had decided to halve the expenditure for the Australian Catholic Bishops' Conference, a sign of the changing times and different priorities.

Holy Mother Church in Australia and elsewhere has formidable strengths, as is demonstrated by the number of letters and the amount of support I have received, even in a deeply polarised society. But a fundamental decline has to be acknowledged. The challenge is to slow this down and reverse the trend.

Yesterday, one of the antiphons for the evening prayers consisted of those ominous words of Our Lord himself, which I find the most disconcerting in the entire New Testament.

When the Son of Man comes, will he find any faith on earth? (Lk 18:8)

Wednesday, 18 December 2019

A new problem has arisen in my prison life—so many letters that a backlog develops of those which need to be opened, and some tiny pressure is put on my prayer time. This was the story of my life when I was busy, a story written in bold, but I hadn't anticipated so many cards and letters, which are a blessing beyond anticipation. As one female prison officer commented when she enquired about the letters, "It's good; it gives you something to do." The help goes much deeper than this, because nearly all promise regular prayer and many assert their belief in my innocence. In God's providence, this is one of the ways I am being helped, which preserves my equanimity most of the time.

My usual disposition can be found between two extremes described by two of my correspondents: the first a laywoman from Dallas, Texas, and the second a contemplative nun in Australia.

My American friend, who regularly provides food for thought and prayer, uses Advent as a time to refocus. At the moment, she is burdened by loss, so she is working at "a renewal of my awareness of God's goodness and my need to receive what he permits". Our suffering is God's pruning, and she writes: "You are in the midst of a very great pruning." She doesn't quite subscribe to Murphy's Law. What can go wrong will go wrong, but she writes: "I laugh at the presumption that the support I receive is normal, and trials are unjust and abnormal. That 'stinkin thinkin' gets me into trouble."

I don't believe that God prunes throughout the whole year, and for most of my lifetime the cross has not been too difficult nor the burden too heavy; but no pruning means little fruit.

The Australian contemplative nun confesses: "I must say, YES, that I have a holy envy of you. What God is calling you to suffer in order to be conformed to the image of His Son is just so GLORIOUS. I don't mean to be insensitive to your suffering—I feel for you terribly—but what treasure you have been given." My fate is not too terrible or uncomfortable, but for me the glory is well hidden, even as I happily concur that I want to be more closely conformed to the image of the Lord.

Was able to spend my hour in the gym, where I went through all my routines and met my goals, while the bulk of the day was spent reading a couple more articles on my case by Christopher Friel and another collection of Italian articles on the Vatican's financial woes. Sad reading because so many of their financial partners and agents are crooks, who are already on every list of suspects and who plunder the Church without mercy.

One investigator fears the Vatican will default on the Swiss loan for the Chelsea building and that leverage etc. could result in the loss of half a billion euros. Please God this is not correct, as there is quite a distance between 200 and 500 million, but no consolation at all in losing one million, let alone hundreds of millions.

On Monday, Jean-Baptiste had said very reasonably that not only laypeople should be punished as wrongdoers, while, on a happier note, he was able to assure me that the new promoter of justice, recommended by Draghi,[7] and the new head of AIF are well regarded among his peers.

Two verses of Psalm 41 speak to us.

> *With cries that pierce me to the heart,*
> *my enemies revile me,*
> *saying to me all the day long:*
> *"Where is your God?"*
>
> *Why are you cast down, my soul,*
> *why groan within me?*
> *Hope in God; I will praise him still,*
> *my saviour and my God.*

Thursday, 19 December 2019

Today was the storm before the Christmas quiet, one of my busiest days in jail and one of the more pleasant.

When I phoned the lawyers during my morning exercise to tell Kartya I had passed out to "Property" a tub full of letters received, she intervened quickly to explain she was on her way to see me as her message was better delivered face to face.

---

[7] Mario Draghi, European Central Bank President and current prime minister of Italy.

I guessed from the inflection in her voice that the news was not bad, and my best guess was that we had received information about the date of the High Court hearing. Experience had also taught me to be prepared for anything.

The two-day hearing has been set for March 11–12, which is as early as we could have hoped and is another good sign. The team had conjectured months ago that an early date would be encouraging, and Kartya repeated again the party line of "cautious optimism". I totally agree with this both in heart and mind, but both words are important. After three mishaps of increasing gravity, caution is in our bones.

Ruth is in Sydney working with Bret[8] (as she was yesterday), and she and Kartya will come tomorrow for a good long session. I decided to pass out my Friel documents, marked up as they are, for Kartya and Ruth and consigned them in the afternoon with the information that the lawyers would be coming tomorrow. Such a successful transition would be unusually swift.

I was to be out in the garden, but that proved impossible, so I was offered an hour in the gymnasium instead, which I accepted.

I reached my regular goal of an unbroken series of a 100 shots on both backhand and forehand, after a few false starts, and went through all my routines, including a goal-shooting competition (basketball) with a younger warder, who had not played much. I am still reduced to throwing underarm, but my aim has improved a lot. So, too, has my balance, but I don't think it would be good enough to move around a tennis court.

As my gymnasium time finished, I was informed I had another professional visit (to my surprise) and found waiting for me young Patrick Santamaria, the solicitor looking after my two civil cases. His main reason to visit was to bring Christmas greetings, but he confirmed that the first claim had been withdrawn and the second one could well go away also because the plaintiff had already received compensation for the assault of Br X in 2016,[9] and cases after 2015

---

[8] Ruth Shann and Bret Walker, the barristers for Cardinal Pell's appeal to the High Court.

[9] Cardinal Pell explains in volume 2 that he believed he was peripheral to the Br X case because the accused was a Christian Brother in Melbourne at a time when the cardinal was no longer in charge of the diocese.

cannot be judged again following on recent legislation. As he was well represented then and received a six-figure sum, his further progress might be barred.

Fr Michael Mason, my scheduled visitor, was admitted early to obviate my brief return to my cell, and we finished up speaking for more than an hour. He looked well enough but shows his age and laments a slight decline in his memory capacity. I was able to update him on some aspects of my case, and we spent a deal of time talking about the Vatican finance scandals, about which he had heard very little recently.

He is not optimistic about the Church scene in Melbourne but conceded that Anthony Fisher in Sydney was visible in the media and always speaks and writes well. Fr Tony Kelly at Galong had a fall while out walking but has bounced back and is still writing. Nearly all the young Redemptorist priests active in Australia are Vietnamese, just as many young priests in the Melbourne Archdiocese are Indian. As half the population of Melbourne and Sydney are overseas born, or have one parent born overseas, our ethnic priests, provided their English is good, are a natural part of our emerging scene. But we desperately need more vocations from the Anglos and from the Australian-born children of ethnic migrants, who can speak more easily to their Australianizing peers. Grace will need to abound if the weak are once again to make good progress among the strong.

St Columba was the great Irish missionary of the sixth century (521–597) who founded monasteries in France and northern Italy. This was one of his prayers:

> *My dearest Lord,*
> *Be thou a bright flame before me.*
> *Be thou a guiding star above me.*
> *Be thou a smooth path beneath me.*
> *Be thou a kindly shepherd behind me.*
> *Today and forever. Amen.*

Friday, 20 December 2019

A hundred bushfires are burning in New South Wales as well as bad fires in South Australia. Unusually high temperatures are now regularly defined as "unprecedented" (since 1971!), but some or many of the temperatures in South Australia, Victoria, and perhaps New South Wales could well be the highest in the last fifty-plus years. My hazy recollection is that the earliest records are excluded, but the term "unprecedented" is used imprecisely, while extreme bushfire danger is described as "catastrophic", long before the catastrophe occurs.

A couple of firefighters in New South Wales died (RIP) when their fire truck hit a tree which had fallen, the prime minister has cut short his Hawaiian holiday to return home, and protestors are outside the prime minister's residence in Canberra protesting government inactivity on climate change. The point that we can do little to prevent bushfires apart from deterring arsonists and burning off excess undergrowth (often resisted) and that banning coal mining would have no effect on the fires whatsoever has been lost completely on the small number of extremist protestors. When God is out of the equation and hell is banned from the public imagination, catastrophic climate change fills the gap as the current fear, and many are reluctant to concede that we are powerless in the face of the millennial patterns of climate change. An SBS news report showed a human-built barrier, now submerged under the waves on the Israeli coast, which was constructed more than two thousand years ago. It battled ineffectively to resist rising sea levels. Given their evangelical fervour to buttress their claims to unprecedented sea-level rises and temperature increases today, it would have been more in the alarmists' interests to can that news report.

Kartya and Paul arrived with the present drafts of material for the High Court for me to study, while Ruth stayed at home working so that they can be filed either before Christmas or New Year. The material has been reorganized to confront the judges from the beginning and as strongly as possible with the claim that a major injustice has been perpetrated. I had to pass back to the lawyers the material I had cited, so that it will then come to me through the proper channels! Part of the punishment in prison is that all procedures proceed slowly. Prison must be heaven for those bureaucrats who find a special delight in creating difficulties and hindering speedy execution.

A large bag of cards and letters arrived today after fifty to sixty yesterday from many parts of the world and with a variety of messages.

One Asian lady has been a strong fan for many years, believing, as the attacks on me began, "in my heart that you must be a great threat to the devil". She has read my books and heard me speak, but she laments my poor posture, which, she felt, worsened with the years. "I wanted you to stand up straight, for you are a tall man, and at least that height would give you some advantage." She sounds like my mother. She eventually took consolation in the fact that Mother Teresa of Calcutta was short and tough and thanked me for my contribution.

Another lady, this time from New South Wales, began, "I find myself doing something I've not done for a long time", going to Mass. "Your troubles have inspired me back to my Catholic faith. I want to stand with you.... I pray for you often."

She then continued even more controversially, and this time I agree wholeheartedly. "In the future, the Catholic Church will need more men like you. Men strong enough to carry Catholic values forward into the next centuries. I say men, not women. Masculine leadership is seemingly out of fashion and badly lacking."

Leaving aside the point of comparison, the claim must be true of the Catholic Church if she is to go forward, because our leaders are men: pope, bishops, and priests. I only wish that in the Western world today, we had available the leaders who abounded in the women's monastic and religious orders for around 1,500 years, as this contribution complemented the work of pope, bishops, and parishes and was not an alternative, not in competition.

The writer ended, "Stay strong, Your Eminence. Take care of your health. Rest often. Know there are people who believe in you." As I am well aware of many people who use my "guilt" to justify their hostility to, and sometimes departure from, the Church, a story such as this return provides a special balm.

So, I understand the sentiments of the author of Psalm 68:

> *Let not those who hope in you be put to shame*
> *through me, Lord of hosts:*
> *let not those who seek you be dismayed*
> *through me, God of Israel....*
>
> *I burn with zeal for your house,*
> *and taunts against you fall on me.*

Saturday, 21 December 2019

Marvellous Melbourne. Yesterday the temperature was over 40°C [104°F], but today is perfect, with a light breeze and a temperature in the low twenties [68–75°F]. The air conditioning in our cells is effective and shields us from the extremes.

My customary hour in the gymnasium passed pleasantly, although it needed many attempts before I achieved 100 shots on my forehand in an unbroken series. For some reason, I was a bit sluggish, although I had more evidence that practice still improves performance, even at my age. I can handle walking on the treadmill, without hanging on to retain balance, much better than when I started, while my underhand shots for goals with the basketball have also improved. As someone who previously never worked out in a gymnasium, although I tried to swim once a week, my thrice-weekly workouts are a novelty and a blessing. And I am pleased at my capacity to improve various skills.

Earlier this morning, I received more mail, on top of the large paper bagful which came yesterday. So, I am well behind when it comes to opening them.

I spent the middle hours of the day reading the present draft of the twenty-page document prepared by Bret and Ruth, the two barristers, to go to the High Court. It lived up to the praise of Paul and Kartya. In a note, Ruth explained that they set out (1) to produce "an immediate sense of the manifest injustice of the convictions"; (2) to demonstrate "the profoundly inept manner in which the prosecution conducted themselves"; and (3) to show "the flawed judicial method employed by the majority". I am hard to please but was delighted by the clarity and precision of the writing, particularly as it laid bare the obfuscatory ambitions of the prosecution. They set out to confuse the jury and were successful.

No witness supported the complainant, whose evidence was completely uncorroborated. At no stage did the prosecution suggest any of the witnesses were liars, and almost uniformly the prosecution did not challenge them or, for the most part, even suggest, much less demonstrate, that this or that evidence should or could be rationally set aside. This meant that much of the defence evidence remained unchallenged, as though the prosecution feared that direct questioning would provoke further clarification and further weaken the accusations. Time and again, they asserted theoretical possibilities, claiming these demonstrated that the accusations were not impossible. But there are profound differences between possibility and probability and a chasm between a theoretical possibility and a demonstrated fact.

The prosecution successfully enticed the jury into reversing the onus of truth, so that it was enough for the accusations to be possibly true, and the defence was required to prove innocence, to defend impossibility against every possibility. Mr. Boyce, the prosecution counsel at the Court of Appeal, had this mantle thrust upon him. It was the weakness of the prosecution case, the poor cards he had been dealt, which contributed most to his performance. What was most surprising was the fact that the two majority judges accepted these flaws and ineptitude, although I believe the "flaws" were explicitly contrived rather than inept. So far, they have worked.

My case is not a referendum on how the Church deals with the paedophilia crisis, but an act of judgement on a series of allegations. One letter came from a man who was holding me up before God in prayer but was "not even Catholic". He believed in my innocence, explaining that he had been a victim of crime. While his assailant was never caught, he "would be insulted and outraged if an innocent man was convicted of my assailant's crimes". The writer did not give his name, although he is Australian, claiming the country has learnt nothing from the Lindy Chamberlain story. And he promised to make a Christmas donation to Vinnies[10] on my behalf.

The fires were still bad this morning, particularly in New South Wales, but Carols in the Domain[11] was not affected by smoke and a cool change had arrived.

As we are so close to Christmas, we have another reason to remember Mary, Jesus' mother, on this Saturday, and the Marian version of the "Ode to Joy", its first lines, provide a suitable conclusion with one word change:

---

[10] The St Vincent de Paul Society.
[11] An annual Christmas concert held in the Domain Gardens, Sydney.

Daily, daily, sing to Mary,
sing, my soul, her praises due.
All her feasts, her actions (worship) rev'rence,
with the heart's devotion true.
Lost in wond'ring contemplation,
be her Majesty confessed.
Call her Mother, call her Virgin,
Happy Mother, Virgin blest.

WEEK 44

Christmas in Prison

22 December–28 December 2019

Fourth Sunday of Advent, 22 December 2019

The cooler weather brought improvement, but the midday news from the NSW [New South Wales] premier had much of the town of Balmoral lost and homes destroyed in a big blaze in South Australia. The Big Bash cricket in Canberra yesterday had to be cancelled because of the smoke haze. We have an extraordinary start to the summer bushfire season.

Bishop Mark Edwards again celebrated *Mass for You at Home*. Which reminds me that Fr Jerome Santamaria will come with Sr Mary to celebrate Mass for me on Tuesday. The sermon was again short, but interesting, on the theme of putting Christ into Christmas, the same Christ whose mother could not find a place for the birth in the Bethlehem inn. The bishop cited Thomas Merton's claim that the world's biggest problem is efficiency, presumably because so many are so busy that God and important truths are crowded out. Merton must have lived in a world different from mine, although Australia rates well for efficiency. If Merton had claimed being busy was the problem, I would have been more inclined to agree, as I found, even as an archbishop regularly dealing with godly things, it is not difficult to be distracted from Christ and the Transcendent, to become submerged by the daily routine.

Although I did not watch the *Hillsong* program, it was *Christmas at Hillsong*, unlike Prince and Osteen, who did not touch on the feast or the season.

Joseph Prince spoke on the secrets of Jesus hidden in the tribes of Judah, not one of his better performances in my judgement. He was dressed soberly in dark trousers and jacket and wore only three rings. He mentioned that Judah's symbol is a lion, while Benjamin is represented by a ravenous wolf. The one point which struck me was his emphasis on Jesus' kindness and consideration in cooking the fish for the apostolic fishermen, who were wet, cold (this was his claim), and certainly tired after a night on the job.

The three Toakley boys have written me Christmas letters, although their jokes were not as good this time. Joel Osteen always starts with a silly story, which I will be able to use in reply. A self-confident scientist was talking with God, telling him he was no longer needed because of human scientific and technological progress. He therefore challenged God to a man-making contest, a challenge God accepted, and he then bent down to work with the earth. God intervened and stopped him. "No, no," he said, "get your own dirt."

Joel was on song, repeating his regular message about the importance of godly self-affirmation. We should not allow ourselves to be put down by others, given a bad name, but believe in ourselves and do great things. I must say to myself: "I am healthy, whole, energetic, called to be God's masterpiece." Both Jacob and Abraham had received name changes and went on to do great things.

Songs of Praise was the 2011 service of Christmas Readings and Carols from Stratford-upon-Avon, held in Holy Trinity Church. I have read that an atheist is now in charge of religious broadcasting at the BBC, so I wonder whether they still produce such explicitly Christian programs. *Songs of Praise* is a favourite of mine, and this was among the best of the best. It began with the traditional opening hymn "Once in Royal David's City" and concluded with a rousing "Hark the Herald Angels Sing", the melody from Felix Mendelssohn and the words from Charles Wesley (something I learnt).

Spent the latter part of the morning reading the financial news from the Vatican (until December 12, 2019) and was pleased to see Austen Ivereigh quoted in an *America* article of December 12 acknowledging my work of introducing professional accounting standards and dependable budgets and the fact that, in 2017, I was complaining that the proportion of Peter's Pence financing the deficit was too high.[1]

---

[1] Colleen Dulle and James T. Keane, "Is the Vatican Misleading Donors? Peter's Pence, Explained", *America*, December 12, 2019.

The only novelty was the reporting (*Malta Today*, 14 December) of the Malta court case where IOR is claiming it was misled in a €30 million investment by two groups, Future Investment Manager and Optimum Management, which was destined for a purchase of 84 percent of the Exchange Palace in Budapest. Optimum has countersued,[2] although it was identified in 2015 by Italian authorities as fraudulently investing money in itself, on one occasion using Mincione's Athena Global Fund.

Before I came home, the IOR authorities had negotiated a settlement in this dispute, which was ready for signing and implementation, when this was prevented by Vatican authorities. The decision was certainly unfortunate and possibly the result of a self-righteous incompetence; but it is difficult to avoid the suspicion that the forces of darkness were at work for their nefarious purposes.

A little hyperventilation seems excusable. It is fantastic that, thirty years after the Ambrosiano banking scandal, where Calvi was found dead under Blackfriars Bridge in London and the Vatican had to pay out hundreds of millions of dollars, rogue elements in control of some sections of the Vatican have continued to deal with notorious financial agents, who have stripped them of more than €100 million (at least) during the last ten years. Corruption has to be stopped in the Secretariat of State as it has been at IOR and APSA.

The poem "In a Late Hour" was written by James McAuley[3] at a dark time, though he began by insisting:

> *Though all men should desert you*
> *My faith will not grow less.*

Unease runs more widely in church and state today than it did among McAuley's friends and allies, so that we are forced to conclude:

> *Forms vanish, kingdoms moulder,*
> *The Anti-realm is here.*

---

[2] *International Investment*, 30 October 2017.
[3] Australian academic and poet, 1917–1976.

Whose order is derangement:
Close-driven yet alone,
Men reach the last estrangement:
  The sense of nature gone.

Nonetheless, through the adversity and in parallel with the confusion and the lapsing an increasingly strong cohort of young believers is emerging.

While the mystery is enacted
I will not let you go.

Monday, 23 December 2019

A perfect day for my purposes, although we could do with a good rain, while some others might want warmer swimming weather. During my couple of hours in the yard, I was able to sit out in the sun, wearing my wrinkly straw sun hat, which used to upset Fr Mark Withoos because of its lack of style, without getting burnt and enjoying the breeze. The birds are noisy but don't come much into the garden. Many dead and almost dead roses make a sorry sight, as no one is picking their heads and few new blooms are on the way. The red roses are at a better stage, but they all bloom shortly.

Margaret[4] came down for her first visit in her wheelchair, which, she complained, David made her use, as she can walk. I was pleased enough with the way she looked, although she has lost weight, as I have, and has aged a bit. The ulcers on her legs are somewhat better, especially her left leg, and we had a lovely hour. She was intrigued by my prison overalls, which I must wear to prevent or hinder smuggling in goods such as drugs. During the visit, a senior officer interrupted with a photo of a $5 note, which I had left on my shelf, after it arrived yesterday in a Christmas card. I confessed it was mine, explained its origins, adding I had also received a $20 note. I survived to live for another day and was instructed to hand in such notes.

---

[4] Cardinal Pell's sister.

By a strange quirk, when I returned to my cell, the $20 note, which I had attached to the inside front manila cover of my journal, had disappeared. The senior officer knew nothing, but after I had explained that I had told my visitor of its existence, he disappeared into the corridor and then returned to tell me they had already found the missing note. I was beginning to wonder whether someone had taken it as a tip!

A one-page letter came in from Dave and Margaret Forster of Bet Bet, who come down each week for a day's prayer outside the jail. Most of the interactions they have there are positive. They were also kind enough to visit my sister, Margaret, at the Mirridong Aged Care Facility at the suggestion of our old friend Denise Cameron.

Last night I moved through and opened most of the backlog of letters, where only about forty to fifty remain. Five or six cards arrived today, and I sent down to "Property" more than two hundred cards or letters, which I had carefully packed in my plastic tub, before transferring them into a large brown paper bag for Kartya to collect. Many books etc. have arrived, so property personnel will prepare a list so I can decide what is to be done with them.

The letters are many with various messages. The Dominican Sisters at Ganmain have proved to be strong supporters, with someone writing each week. One of them, a younger Sister I presume, began her encouraging note: "I guess if God spent his first Christmas in a feed lot, a cardinal can spend one of his in a clink and feel he is keeping good company." Beat that for an opening line.

Another gentleman with more zeal than clear judgement offered to exchange places with me for a few days so I could take a break.

To return to the Sisters. One of them explained that roses are generally good after a drought, as they prefer a dry winter. She saw this as a symbol of the dry, confusing times in the Church today with the roses as signs of hope.

A close priest friend wrote, "Sometimes we produce our best work when we think we are doing nothing at all", adding that Christmas means that the dark will never overcome the light.

Caterina Pagani from the Way in Sydney kept me up to date with her letter giving news of her fifteen children. Giovanni, who is smallish and whom she described as "a skinny boy" of fourteen, defended me against one of his teachers, a "big man". I am not surprised, as none of the children lack intestinal fortitude.

St Edith Stein didn't emerge alive from her Nazi concentration camp, and she remains one of my heroes. She wrote this about Christmas:

> *In front of the crib you are connected to all those*
> *who are scattered all over the world and beyond.*
> *That's a comforting secret.*
> (A couple from Ravensburg in Germany sent me this quotation.)

P.S. A hundred homes have been destroyed in New South Wales by the fires, and eighty-six in South Australia. Al Jazeera TV announced that the fires covered an area the size of Belgium.

Christmas Eve, 24 December 2019

"Know today that the Lord will come: in the morning, you shall see his glory." This is the opening antiphon in today's Divine Office for Christmas Eve, and it sets the scene well.

I had cleared up opening the backlog of mail last night while watching the Big Bash cricket, which, I explained to Fr Jerome Santamaria, who came to celebrate Mass for me, is like Impressionist painting, inasmuch as it is beautiful and attractive but lacks intellectual rigour and spiritual sustenance, which are found both in classical painting from the fifteenth century and Test cricket. He replied simply by saying he had never heard Big Bash cricket compared to Impressionist painting!

Spent a half hour in the pen around 8:30 am and phoned Terry and Bernadette. To my delight, the phone system still worked although they were in Mornington. Terry was pleased with the High Court dates, and his optimism because of this was comforting. He agreed strongly with the three basic thrusts of the submission, as Ruth had described them and I recounted to him, and was pleased that the prosecutor and the majority judges got what they deserved.

I spent an hour or so rereading the draft submission to be sure that it wasn't too good to be true, wasn't asserting more than the often-unchallenged evidence demonstrated. I have a couple of half questions on "undisputed" evidence (on the rehearsals) and "unchallenged" evidence on when Potter[5] opened the sacristy door, but the document remained as convincing and the evidence as strong as it was on my earlier readings. I am looking forward to discussing the draft with Ruth and Kartya later this week, wondering whether some Friel material can be introduced into the descriptions of the incident itself and whether we should make more of the claimant's initial claims of an internal return through the cathedral to the sacristy.

Two enormous envelopes containing two to three hundred letters were delivered to my cell this morning, which I still haven't started to read at 7:25 pm as I am writing. It is a pleasure in store for me.

The warders were very cooperative, allowing me to stay for nearly two hours with Sr Mary and Fr Jerome as he celebrated Mass for me. Being unable to celebrate Mass and watching the Protestant services, with their often powerful explanations of the word of God, have confirmed me in my love of the Mass and my certainty about its importance. I was a very young seminarian when I read the line "It is the Mass that matters", which might have been in Frank Sheed's *Theology and Sanity*. This line of thought has remained with me unchanged. Sheed was a fine theologian, Australian born, who married Maisie Ward and remained in England, where they founded the Catholic publishing house Sheed and Ward, which did good work for decades.

Fr Jerome brought me up to date with news in the Melbourne Archdiocese, where a couple of good priests are taking leave in the New Year. This is always a blow, and departures have been few since the early years of St John Paul the Great. Jerome brought good wishes from another priest, who had reminded me of our time together in Split, Croatia, where I recounted to him how Diocletian, one of the last great persecutors in the Roman Empire, had resigned his position as emperor and retired to Split to grow cabbages, which, tradition tells

---

[5] Maxwell Potter, former sacristan at St Patrick's Cathedral, Melbourne, testified on behalf of Cardinal Pell.

us, he found more satisfying than trying to run an immense empire, while becoming ever more aware that his persecuting the Christians was proving counterproductive. While I didn't like the comparison, our mutual friend thought I would enjoy growing tulips in Sydney after my release. I hope to concentrate on roses.

Swept and mopped my small cell so that everything would be ship-shape to celebrate the birth of the Lord. Also enjoyed my fifty minutes in the gymnasium, where I realised early on that I was sharper than on my last visit. I arrived at 180 plus shots in an unbroken series on my backhand on my second attempt and early on managed over 100 on the forehand. My underarm goal shooting for the basketball was also OK from three different distances. My balance on the treadmill and stairs is also improving.

Every Christmas as an archbishop in Australia, I looked forward to the cathedral choir carols in the hour before Midnight Mass. This year I had to settle for the Melbourne TV celebration of *Carols by Candlelight* in the vastly improved Sydney Myer Music Bowl. A capacity crowd with many children sang and enjoyed themselves in what I found a surprisingly Christian celebration. I don't know whether my expectations have slipped, but I suspect there was a higher Christian content. We had "O Holy Night", one of my favourite carols, with "Silent Night", "O Come All Ye Faithful", and the "Hallelujah Chorus".

I am sure they would not be giving the people what they felt the people did not want. Are the Christians feeling embattled and making their presence felt? Is violent Islam provoking a reaction, ranging from a deeper interest in Christian answers to a sentimental return to traditional Western rituals?

The reason could simply be a Christian producer who goes to bat for the tradition. But, whatever the reason, I rejoice in the strength of the Christmas carol tradition, although I am not sure how often the modern musical arrangements are an improvement. We must do all we can to strengthen those sociological currents which favour faith, love, and knowledge of the Christian tradition against the powerful tides reducing our social capital, hardening our hearts, and blinding us, making it harder to see and hear God, even when we are interested enough to try. Money, perpetual motion, sex.

But God is always at work. A letter of support came from an Australian, I presume, from St Mary's parish in Dubai (one of the largest parishes in the world), who was received into the Church this year nine days before the feast of St Nicholas. He had been a lifelong agnostic and felt God's presence during a visit to Montserrat in Spain two years ago. "If anyone had told me, earlier in my life," he wrote, "that I would convert in the Arab world ..." *Deo gratias*.

My correspondents from Ravensburg in Germany also sent these lines of Dietrich Bonhoeffer, the German Protestant theologian jailed and executed by the Nazis for his involvement in a plan to kill Hitler.

> *We know your light is shining through the night.*
> *If now the silence is spreading deep around us,*
> *let us hear those full sounds of the world*
> *that is widening invisibly around us*
> *the high hymns of all your children.*

Christmas Day, 25 December 2019

The first of two lines of the most popular carol of them all, "Silent night, holy night, all is calm, all is bright", are not the best lines to begin today, because in every prison, and certainly in Unit 8, the solitary confinement section, all is not calm and bright.

At the quieter Toorak end of the unit, you become used to someone shouting now and again at the other end, except when it is too loud or too frequent. But as I was in the exercise area this morning, two or three episodes of fierce and prolonged roaring and ferocious banging distracted my meditating. I knew neither his voice nor his hands could keep up such a racket for too long, and quiet eventually returned. By a coincidence, he has just recommenced at 5:30 pm as I am writing this. Whatever is in the heart of the poor wretch, it is not Christmas calm, as he is almost certainly damaged through drugs, probably ice [crystal meth]. Quite a few warders have asked me whether we are disturbed late in the evenings or early mornings. But I have never been seriously annoyed then and unable to sleep, so far.

Quite a few parents and grandparents ask me to pray for their children and grandchildren, some of whom have drifted away from regular practice, and one such parent lamented that she herself still found praying hard after many years. So do I, sometimes more than at other times in my meditating, as I don't find praying the Hours[6] too difficult. I have always enjoyed retreats at Tarrawarra, the Cistercian monastery, not least because of the regular round of chant and psalms. However, the suggestion of one of my regular correspondents from Dallas in Texas that I use the words and melodies of favourite hymns as a meditation technique has proved invaluable. It has diminished the number of distractions and enabled me to pass through the dry patches more easily. Ten days ago, I received a couple of pages with the words of favourite Christmas carols, which I am using nearly every day. I am intrigued that I don't remember hearing of such a technique during sixty years of retreats.

One of my failures in Sydney, perhaps more than in Melbourne, was my inability to increase the number of priests making an annual retreat. As an archbishop on retreat, I know how difficult it is to resist taking off an hour or so for urgent business, which was genuinely "urgent". Can godly business make us too busy for God?

A special pleasure was to follow, on Channel 2, the Christmas night Mass celebrated at St Peter's in Rome by the Holy Father with about thirty cardinals, forty bishops, priests, and a congregation which almost filled the nave. The numbers are down from the high points of St John Paul the Great and Pope Benedict.

St Peter's, the second church built on the site, is my favourite church, even ahead of St Mary's in Sydney, as there I was ordained priest in 1966, twice received the pallium from Pope John Paul II, was created a cardinal, and worshipped regularly for the great feasts during my four years' work in Rome. I was also present in the square when we celebrated the four hundredth anniversary of the completion of this second church and the smoke and debris from an enormous fireworks display drifted across to envelop the Santa Cecilia Orchestra and their precious instruments. Only in Italy.

---

[6] The Liturgy of the Hours, the breviary.

St Peter's, this Renaissance and Counter-Reformation master-piece, is a far cry from the stable at Bethlehem, but it represents the best efforts of the Western world, especially during the sixteenth century, although Bernini's contribution came a bit later, to praise and glorify the one true God and his only Son. All around Rome, we find churches from different centuries and sometimes from different countries and cultures giving of their best to glorify God. That is what we did in the restoration of the chapel at Domus Australia,[7] the best we had to offer from the Land of the Holy Spirit at one end of the earth, just after the second Christian millennium. As the Anglo-Saxon pilgrims built their centre in Rome in the eighth century, like the sixteenth-century English College, like the French, the Span-iards, the Germans, and more recently the North Americans—all gathering at the See of St Peter to unite in worship and communion.

I remember hearing of a young Chinese woman with no religion who was told how God sent his only Son to live among us as one of us, poor and vulnerable. "What a beautiful story", she exclaimed; and so it is.

At St Peter's, the feast was solemnly announced with the tradi-tional proclamation.

> The twenty-fifth day of December, when ages beyond number had run their course ...; when century upon century had passed since ... the Great Flood ...; in the thirteenth century since the People of Israel were led by Moses in the Exodus from Egypt ...; in the year seven hundred and fifty-two since the foundation of the City of Rome ... Jesus Christ, eternal God and Son of the Eternal Father, ... was conceived by the Holy Spirit ... and was born of the Virgin Mary in Bethlehem of Judah.

This is our faith. This is the faith of the Church. We are proud to profess it everywhere, in palaces and in slums, in great international cities and in deserts and jungles, in St Peter's, the most famous church in Christendom, and in jail, home of the disgraced and condemned.

St John Henry Newman prayed this prayer at the end of one of his parish sermons.

---

[7] Domus Australia is a pilgrim house in Rome owned by the Australian Catholic Church.

May each Christmas, as it comes,
find us more and more like Him,
who at this time
became a little child for our sake,
more simple-minded,
more humble, more holy,
more affectionate, more resigned,
more happy, more full of God.[8]

Thursday, Boxing Day, 26 December 2019

Today the Church celebrates the feast of St Stephen, the first martyr, an almost brutal reminder of Christian truths and the importance of redemptive suffering. Apart from Christmas, the only other birthday celebrated in the liturgical year is that of John the Baptist, because Church feast days usually celebrate the saint's birth into eternal life, through death.

My Christmas day alone passed pleasantly, with some extra praying. I hope I am not coming to enjoy my own company too much.

I had forgotten to mention that the Salvos[9] had given each of us a bag of lollies, long jelly snakes, and a diary for next year. Unfortunately, the diary did not have any mention of Jesus, not even one page. I am told that in comparison with past times, more and more prisoners don't have many religious ideas, much less convictions. But prison forces most inmates to confront basic questions, and I suspect a higher percentage of prisoners are open to God's grace than in the general population outside.

My nephew Nicholas came to visit me some hours earlier than the set time, but the staff allowed him in, and we met for over an hour. He looked well and happy, and we had a fine time. I twice tried to phone my sister, Margaret, and heard her answer the phone, although she couldn't hear me. A bit distressing to be so near and so far. Spent an hour in the garden in perfect weather with a light

---

[8] John Henry Newman, "The Mystery of Godliness", in *Parochial and Plain Sermons* (San Francisco: Ignatius Press, 1997), p. 1021.

[9] The Salvation Army.

breeze. And Australia had its nose ahead of New Zealand in the first day of the Test cricket with four wickets down for 287. Another 100 to 150 letters arrived, so the backlog to be opened has increased since yesterday, even though I opened letters as I watched the cricket. I am no longer transcribing full addresses onto all the cards and letters, many from overseas, because it will be impossible to reply to so many thousands, presently three thousand plus.

A couple of months ago, Venetia Mackin sent me an account of how the famous French atheist and writer Jean-Paul Sartre had written a Christmas play, *Bariona*, where he himself had played the role of King Balthazar, the old wise man who recognized hope in the newborn child. Sartre was then in the Nazi prison of Trier in 1940 with other troublemakers, including some priests, after the defeat of the French army.

Since I studied philosophy in the 1960s, I have been interested in the intellectual reasons for God's existence and in atheism. As someone who took a couple of units in Fr Cornelio Fabro's Institute of the History of Atheism at my Catholic Pontifical Urban University in Rome, I remember that Fabro thought Western philosophy took an important wrong turn with Descartes' "Cogito, ergo sum" (I think, therefore I am), which placed the foundation for existing and knowing in individual judgement and not in objective truth about the world. I am not sure he is correct, but the flight from realism has gathered pace, arriving at "my" truth and "your" truth and no "truth", prompting identity politics, "no go" areas of discussion because feelings are hurt, outlawing debate and prohibiting robust discussion. We have no objective truth to be found.

Another of Fabro's basic claims was that Sartre honestly presented the extreme consequences of atheism. Without a Creator God, a Supreme Intelligence, existence has no "telos", no point or purpose. For Sartre, existence is a horrible leprosy, so that man's dignity is found in his despair, and to give birth to a child is a monstrous error of tact, telling the God who torments us that we approve of his diseased world where our blameworthy parents have brought us.

Sartre is no Dawkins[10] because he is a fine writer, one of the French "immortals". Forty years ago in Australia, some tertiary colleges had

---

[10] Richard Dawkins (b. 1941), the English evolutionary biologist, ethologist, and author of *The God Delusion*.

departments of religious studies, and I remember one lecturer, who had been a Protestant minister, told me that he had been in the United States when he finished reading Sartre, either *Nausea* or *Being and Nothingness*, closed the book, put it down, and declared, "Now I am an atheist." I did not doubt his story. Sartre is Promethean, a believer in absolute freedom for every person. Hope is forbidden, as an escape from the inexorable harshness of existence.

I believe Fabro was correct in his estimate of Sartre, because if there is no God, human hope is a fiction, and, as Sartre wrote, the lives of a great statesman and of a solitary drunkard are equally pointless. The options are God or blind chance.

The play is not Christian, but it is a world removed from this nihilism and despair. Bariona is the head of a Jewish village, where the Roman procurator decrees an increase in taxes, which Bariona accepts. But he tells his people to have no more children, so that Rome will eventually be ruling a desert. He doesn't yet realise that his wife, Sarah, is expecting a child.

Bariona is then told by the shepherds that a young Messiah has been born in Bethlehem, which he rejects as a delusion, so that he even considers killing the child himself. He goes to Bethlehem as does his wife, Sarah, who wants to see this happy woman who has given birth to a new baby boy. Bariona, too, is moved by the joy and reverence of the group in the stable, and when he sees the hope, the depths in Joseph's eyes contemplating the child, he cannot "find the courage to snuff out this young life between my fingers". Even more than that, when he hears that King Herod means to kill Jesus, he arms his people and leads them into battle against Herod, which he knows can only end in their defeat.

The German guards allowed the play to go ahead, missing the identification of the Nazis with Herod, and Sartre wrote to Simone de Beauvoir: "I have written a very moving Christian mystery, it seems, to the point that one of the actors burst into tears."

The theme wasn't Christian, of course, even though Sartre was reading Paul Claudel and Georges Bernanos, two leading Catholic writers, and admired them. Later in life, he was less enthusiastic about the play than he had been with de Beauvoir.

A baby boom in the Western world occurred during the peace after the Second World War, while no Western country now is producing a sufficient number of children to keep the population numbers stable. Sartre was right about childbearing, which is an act and expression of hope, of confidence in life's goodness and the future, and he was tragically wrong to reject this insight.

Sartre also understood the Christian claims about the Incarnation, about "a little God one can hold in one's arms and cover with kisses, a warm God that smiles and breathes, a God one can touch and who lives".

He has Mary thinking: "This God is my son; the divine flesh is my flesh.... He has my eyes and the shape of my mouth.... He is God and he looks like me."

The Italian author of the article, Massimo Borghesi, claims that Sartre never again wrote like this of God and man (although I have a hazy and unreliable memory of a recent discovery of his flirting briefly with faith late in his life), but that he gave us "one of the most beautiful representations of Christmas in the literature of the twentieth century".[11]

And he wrote it in prison, where he was close to the truth.

Friday, 27 December 2019

The apostle John was unmarried (probably), unlike most of the apostles (certainly unlike Peter, with his mother-in-law), and a special friend of the Lord, the only one of the Twelve to remain with him at the foot of the Cross. It was there that Jesus consigned his mother to John's care, and tradition has it that they came to live in Ephesus together.

John is one of the two apostles, with Matthew, who are Gospel writers. Not only is his Gospel more theological than the three synoptic Gospels, but John is a gifted narrative writer, expert at depicting the different protagonists, the verbal jousting, and the sequence of events which often lead to a dramatic culmination. I love proclaiming the Gospel of the cure of the blind man and recounting how he deals with Jesus' adversaries.

More than the other three Gospels, John's is different even in the events it describes. John is the only Gospel to narrate Jesus' pardon of

---

[11] Massimo Borghesi, "Sartre and the Christmas of Jesus", *30 Days*, no. 1, 2004, http://www.30giorni.it/articoli_id_2867_l3.htm.

the woman who was to be stoned for adultery, and it does not contain a narrative of the institution of the Eucharist.

In John, Jesus' discourses are often less earthy and immediate, but more explanatory and theological. Some exegesis today doesn't require the different Gospel accounts to be grounded too closely in Jesus' own teaching, so that we might have John writing what he would have liked Jesus to say. Such a claim, stated baldly, is not a Catholic option, at least in my view, although each evangelist gives out the good news as he understands it and for the purposes he regards as important.

I believe that John understood Jesus' deeper teachings more adequately because of his intellectual background, which differed from Matthew's and the tradition behind Mark and even Luke.

Let me give an example. I have a good friend in London who is a successful financier, deeply Catholic, and interested in the "God question" as I am. After discussing the pros and cons of atheism and theism, he sent me a large and learned book, even indicating the pages for me to study. However, it was wasted on me because I have no knowledge of tertiary mathematics (and no time or need to master it) and the section required that to be understood.

I believe that my friend's knowledge of mathematics was like John's knowledge of theology and philosophy, so that John was better equipped than the other Gospel authors to understand what Jesus was saying and to spell out the consequences of his teaching. His intellectual interests were different from those, e.g., of a man who had been a successful tax collector. By any criterion, it is appropriate to have John's feast day near the birthday of the man he chose to follow and explained so well.

My day was very quiet (as Fridays are, with no gymnasium or garden), and Ruth and Kartya did not arrive to discuss the legal draft. The day was warmer, perhaps 27–28°C [80–82°F], but still pleasant for the 50,000 spectators at the second day of the Test, who saw Australia grind steadily to a first innings total of around 480 runs. I anticipate the Australian bowlers will continue to do well and, indeed, might play havoc tomorrow unless the pitch quietens and becomes predictable. I spent the day opening about 150 letters as I watched the cricket and have another day's work tomorrow, even if no new letters arrive.

Most are Christmas cards from Australia, rather than letters, although many come from overseas, especially the United States, but also from Britain, Ireland, and New Zealand. One unsigned card with no written message had the colour photo of a man proclaiming emphatically that I was a dinosaur.

The First Epistle of John is a small masterpiece, especially as translated in the Jerusalem Bible (used in the breviary), although the translation of the opening verses in my prison Bible is awkward and ugly, written by someone totally uninterested in the public proclamation of the word of God; or perhaps so interested, but with a tin ear. The principal glory of the King James translation of the Bible is that it was translated to be proclaimed. It is often magnificent.

When I was at Campion Hall in Oxford, I used to go fairly regularly for the sung Evensong at Christ Church, the cathedral and college chapel of what was Cardinal Wolsey's foundation. Once in a while, most of those attending were from Campion Hall. When the Dean of Christ Church, the fabulously learned Patristic scholar Henry Chadwick, proclaimed the Scriptures, it was one small example of Western culture, indeed civilisation, at its best. They used the King James version.

For me, the opening verses of John's First Epistle are among the most powerful in the New Testament, moving me like Churchill's Second World War speeches still move me, but for a much better and more sublime purpose.

> *Something which has existed since the beginning,*
> *that we have heard,*
> *and we have seen with our own eyes;*
> *that we have watched*
> *and touched with our hands:*
> *the Word, who is life—*
> *this is our subject.*

Saturday, 28 December 2019

Today is the feast of the Holy Innocents, who were slaughtered by the tyrant Herod, alarmed by talk of the birth of a baby king in Bethlehem. From the beginning, the forces of darkness were active against Jesus, and these young innocents were the first victims and witnesses of his unique role. Joseph, Mary, and the baby fled as refugees to Egypt, where I have visited the Coptic Christian Church built on the site where, tradition tells us, the Holy Family lived in Cairo. The Copts make up 10 to 12 percent of the Egyptian population, and in these times of Islam militancy, they have suffered from church bombings and regular hostility, even under the present military government.

The Copts and the Maronites in Lebanon are the largest Christian minorities in the Middle East, large enough to have a chance of survival, but elsewhere the Christians are being driven out. Generally, the local Catholic clergy support their remaining, and I can understand this, but who can blame parents choosing to bring their children to the peace and prosperity of Australia or Canada, or Trump's America. Trump is no gentleman and an unlikely champion of Christians, but he is not anti-Christian and, unlike recent presidents such as Obama (of course) and George W. Bush, he is even prepared to wish people "a happy Christmas".

In Sydney, we used to celebrate a pro-life anti-abortion Mass in St Mary's Cathedral on the feast day, with a number of lighted candles brought to the sanctuary, representing the thousands of known abortions in the state. I brought the idea from Los Angeles, where I attended a powerful Mass and ceremony dedicated to the defence of human life, which was performed with impressive faith.

Los Angeles is the largest diocese in the United States and is led by the Latino Archbishop José Gómez,[12] who has not been created a cardinal, despite his effective leadership in a community which is theologically divided and often confused. In some ways, I was surprised and certainly heartened by the size and zeal of the congregation at the pro-life Mass.

Hundreds more letters arrived today and yesterday, so the backlog has increased despite my work. I consigned some hundreds of read and opened letters to the "Property" section to be collected by my solicitor Kartya Gracer.

One of these packages contained the hymn sheets used by the fifteen to twenty younger people who sang carols outside the jail for

---

[12] Archbishop Gómez was elected president of the United States Conference of Catholic Bishops in 2019.

me on Christmas Eve. I did briefly hear some voices singing carols that night; perhaps it was a few prisoners taking up their music and carrying it further. They also sent their greetings and an action-shot photo of the performance.

My reflexes were good for my hour in the gymnasium, after which I returned to my favourite meal—a hot pasty which I warmed in the microwave. Tim O'Leary has a meeting tomorrow which, I hope, will clinch his new job. As with my own case, I urged "cautious optimism".

The fate of the Holy Innocents is terrible; we pray they died quickly. Their life's promise was unfulfilled, but the fate of their parents was (arguably) worse: a life term of anguished memories and permanent loss, until they, too, were healed in a just God's heaven.

The Church, like Jesus, cannot avoid the clash between good and evil, love and hate, faith and darkness. This is what St Ignatius of Loyola describes as the battle between the Two Standards, and the unknowing young baby boys around Bethlehem were caught in it and destroyed. Jesus' life struggle has not begun well.

So on this feast day, surrounded by the peace and hope of Christmas, we pray to the Lord Jesus that we might find joy in his birth, forgiveness through his death, and eternal healing and happiness through his Resurrection.

WEEK 45

Appeal Moves Forward

29 December 2019–4 January 2020

Sunday, 29 December 2019

Uncle Tom was a favourite uncle, one of twelve Burke children, a brother to my mother, Lil, a man I did not know extremely well, as he lived in Melbourne. But he was a pleasant and kindly uncle, who was also a bit of a character. Family legend has it that his wife, Aileen, asked him to buy her some bread, and he arrived in Ballarat to visit us on the next day with the bread still under his arm. He wreaked havoc when he prayed our family rosary at night because of his piety and his invariable habit of praying very loudly and out of time with the rest of us. Even my mother, who was master of ceremonies for the rosary, would be forced to laugh as he just kept ploughing on.

When Tom was dying prematurely in 1959, I came down to Melbourne to visit him in St Vincent's Hospital, and while not being in the cubicle with him, I could still hear him praying loudly and repeatedly: "Jesus, Mary, and Joseph, I give you my heart and my soul. Jesus, Mary, and Joseph, assist me in my last agony."

My uncle Jim died twenty years before I was born, but for ten out of the other eleven Burkes, faith and regular worship were an important part of their lives. The youngest brother had a drink problem, but I would be surprised if he was without faith.

Tom's death affected me, together with the death of another uncle by marriage—who happened to have a son a priest and a daughter a Josephite nun—and the death of Br Ulmer, my year twelve English teacher whom I much admired. Three deaths of people close to me in a month or so. At school I was quite successful, a big fish in a small provincial pond, and dissatisfied. Within the next few months, I decided to try for the priesthood, not because I was much attracted to the idea or particularly generous, but because I reluctantly concluded this was what God wanted me to do. My non-Catholic father thought it a great waste, but I always had the support of my mother, Mum's sister Molly, who lived with us, and my sister and brother.

Every year, the feast of the Holy Family inspired me to preach on the challenges to family life in our society, which has seen such a deterioration over the last sixty or seventy years. The permissive revolution followed the invention of the contraceptive pill; its message spread by groups like the Rolling Stones and the Beatles, and it is still rolling forward, sped on its way by social media and Internet pornography; the latter is an enormous, often undiscussed problem, and not just for Christians.

We always turn to Our Lady when we are in trouble, but St Joseph, too, has work to do, as we need a movement for Catholic men, to provide them with mutual support as the Holy Name Society did for many or most male churchgoers in the parishes of my childhood. Their special focus was to prevent blasphemy, but the challenges are different today. We need more *dikaioi*, strong, just men like Joseph who know and love their faith and who will work cooperatively with women leaders as Joseph worked with Mary. The absence and disinterest of fathers is as damaging for the daughters as it is for the sons.

Bishop Mark Edwards celebrated a Mass for Christmas, not the Holy Family feast. Joseph Prince was again missing, while Joel Osteen mentioned neither Christmas nor the Holy Family, preaching well on the theme "Wake Up to Hope". We have to outlast our problems, trust God's timing, and persevere as Moses did when he escaped with his people from Egypt. God wants stubborn people, like Paul, because anyone can give up. Joel often speaks a word which helps in my situation.

Most of the letters I opened today were from overseas, from the US, Britain, Ireland, and quite a few from Germany. They were uniformly supportive, but their messages were more various than usual.

A Polish card opined, "German cardinal said that Australia now is like England under Henry VIII", while the traditional Roman rite community from Berlin, Germany, quoted the last letter from jail of the provost of St Hedwig's Cathedral, Bernhard Lichtenberg (1875–1943), a champion of the persecuted Jews in Nazi Germany:

"Everything happening to me, the joyful and the painful, I want to look at in the light of eternity. I want to suffer everything out of love."

A woman from Seattle wrote, "Francis George foresaw the future with his favourite quote" about the fate of his successors,[1] although I could be said to have broken ranks in the procession. A Polish parish priest from Grodno explained that at the solemn Christmas Eve supper, which is a highlight, they always leave an additional place prepared for an unexpected visitor, for someone who is lonely. But he assured me I would "remain spiritually present" at his parish table.

A card from Ireland promised that "you have the love and prayers of all the little ones, especially here where the mountains of Mourne sweep down to the sea."

Another ally wrote from Saffron Walden in Essex, UK, in very supportive and somewhat apocalyptic tones. He calls a spade a spade, except when it is a shovel, and has little enthusiasm for "Ressourcement" theologians such as Hans Urs von Balthasar. He quotes approvingly an American journalist on Balthasar: "I found myself praying for at least one verb", and he supports Arnold Lunn, who denounced the weird "cult of softness—which is at best an ignorance of God's exact and inevitable justice".

I don't like the notion of God with an iron rod, but Jesus did denounce hypocrites and the corruptors of youth as well as promising heaven to the good thief, who had repented. Both the gate and the road to life are narrow, and many go through the broad gate to destruction (Mt 7:13–14). It is not difficult to seal yourself into a quiet routine, which underestimates evil and humanly induced suffering and which then makes it easier to ignore what is necessary from a just God confronting unrepented evil.

My friend emphatically rejected those for whom hell is an empty metaphor and heaven is "a (shoo-in), free-for-all", and those for whom "the concept of authority that could punish evil was abhorrent".[2]

---

[1] Francis Cardinal George of Chicago (1937–2015) said in 2010: "I expect to die in bed, my successor will die in prison, and his successor will die a martyr in the public square. His successor will pick up the shards of a ruined society and slowly help rebuild civilization, as the Church has done so often in human history."

[2] The letter writer could be alluding to Hans Urs von Balthasar's book *Dare We Hope "That All Men Be Saved"?* yet misrepresenting the subject of the work, which is the hope that inspires the Church's prayers and sacrifices for the salvation of all souls through their repentance and acceptance of God's forgiveness.

Over the centuries, the practices of the Church have waxed and waned on guilt and punishment, but for most centuries, the practice was stricter than it now is in the Western world. The roots of our answers can only be found in the New Testament, first of all with Jesus himself.

But on this feast of the Holy Family, one clarifying question, perhaps not the last word, is to ask:

What would Mary and Joseph think?

Monday, 30 December 2019

Thirty thousand people have been ordered out of East Gippsland as two of three huge bushfires, which have been burning since November, threaten to merge. In the southwest of the state, near Lorne, the nine thousand fans who had already arrived for the Falls Festival were ordered to leave, with about 20 percent of them being too drunk or drugged to do so immediately. Life is cruel.

While the sky was covered with cloud as I took only an hour in the garden, it was hot, but not above 40°C [104°F]. The peak was due to arrive in the early evening, to be followed by a cool change with an estimated temperature of 21°C [70°F] tomorrow.

One large, beautiful red rose, just about to pass its best, and one perfect gold and yellow bud made up for the dead and dying roses, victims of the heat and time. A little more human intervention would have improved the rose display dramatically, so I regret again that my gardening career was ended so prematurely, despite the fact that news of my gardening exploits spread to most parts of the Anglosphere.

My brother, David, his wife, Judy, and my niece Sarah spent a happy hour with me, although the Christmas rush of visitors had exhausted all the drinks for sale. I settled for a Mars bar. My great-nephew, Sonny, and his exploits and eloquence took up a lot of the time, so I regret not having directed more attention to Sarah, whose birthday we were celebrating.

Ruth and Kartya arrived with the next and close-to-final draft of our twenty-page submission to the High Court. I began by asking whether Ruth was responsible for thinking of the unchallenged pieces of evidence as the key to explaining what the prosecutor was attempting. He did not want clarity about the accusations, which would only lead to my exoneration, but to obfuscate, generate doubt and confusion, by outlining possibilities whereby what we claimed as impossible was not that entirely.

This comes nowhere near where a prosecutor must arrive to prove guilt beyond reasonable doubt, and it reverses the onus of proof.

Ruth pleaded guilty to devising this key which reveals the prosecution strategy, which might be described as both inept and infamous. I explained that I had counted fifty-one such references in the draft to unchallenged evidence both generally and particularly, for people and events. This outstrips even the twenty-four changes in the complainant's story.

I suggested inserting the words "not even a credible witness can be in two places at the same time" at the end of paragraph 26, promising they would be taken up by every paper or magazine which was not hostile to me. Ruth replied that she was attracted to the idea and would suggest it to Bret for inclusion, adding that they hoped to inject some humour, some derision about the legal lapses, into the address to the court.

For the first time in ten months, I joined in a friendly conversation with my neighbour in the next exercise pen, who insisted he knew who I was and had gone to school at St Joseph's. "Are you talking about Joey's in Sydney?", I asked. "Yes" was the answer.

We had a good chat, and it emerged that I knew both his father and his grandfather, whom I know better. He claimed to have seen me at St Joseph's, which I visited each year for a boarders' Mass and for the rugby union game against Riverview.

He is blind as a result of a bashing in jail by a group of prisoners and as yet has no Braille books and was even without a chair for his first few days. He, too, is at the Toorak end of the unit, but in the middle, and finds it very noisy, explaining that the loss of sight is accompanied by greater powers of hearing and touch. I remarked that neither of us when at the school would have anticipated meeting in our present circumstances.

Australia again crushed New Zealand in the Melbourne Boxing Day cricket Test by 247 runs. The summer season has been more successful than I had expected for the team.

Tonight I pray especially for all those in jail with me at the Melbourne Assessment Prison, whether they be here rightly or wrongly, and for their loved ones.

Lord Jesus, you came into our world to bring light into our darkness, joy into our sadness and pain, and peace into our restless hearts. Bring healing to those in prison, especially when they are wounded in heart, mind, and spirit. Help those without faith to see your light, and strengthen your hope in all of us.

Tuesday, 31 December 2019

I couldn't say the day, or the even the times, were "out of joint", as the arrival of a cool change meant my unanticipated hour in the garden was very pleasant and brought some improvement to the immense bushfires in East Gippsland. And my day was disjointed.

In the early morning, the second draft of my legal appeal, which I had reviewed yesterday with Ruth and Kartya, was delivered to my cell, so that, after I had finished my morning prayer, I began to examine what changes had been made. Experience has taught that if this prayer is displaced, it can be hard to get back to it. Earlier in the morning, another 150 letters had been delivered, like yesterday, so I am seriously behind in my letter opening.

Once again my newly found companion was next door for my time in the exercise pen. I asked him what his first name was, only to be reminded that he had told me yesterday: Joseph, but he is usually called Joe. He wasn't too worried by noise last night, although on one of only a few occasions, I had been briefly awakened in the early hours of the morning by shouting. We chatted about many things, including restaurants and food and his love of red wine, especially Australian reds. I didn't confess fully that my recent years in Italy had meant that I now find many classic Aussie reds too heavy, too much.

Tuesday brings an hour in the gymnasium, where all went well, as I quickly ran up a series of over 200 shots on my backhand and around 140 on my forehand. My basketball shooting from three different spots was as good as I can manage, and my balance on the treadmill continues to improve. I now enjoy my gym workouts, although before coming to jail I had scarcely ever entered a gymnasium.

Sr Mary arrived to pray and give me Communion, but not long after we sat down, we were told that a difficult prisoner had to be removed and taken to hospital, so the meeting might have to end. Sr Mary said she could wait, even if an hour were needed, so I returned to my cell.

When I tried to push out my canteen order from under the door, I realised the space was blocked, so I concluded they were proposing to use gas to compel the prisoner to leave. In fact, they did use capsicum, and Sr Mary said that even the dog squad was present for the operation, although she was not permitted to reenter.

I was asked if I would like time in the garden, which I always enjoy, and they proposed Sr Mary would join me there for my Communion service. It was a pleasant setting, free from noise and interruptions. Mary herself is to have a knee replacement on January 22, and she asked my advice. "Do exactly as the experts tell you, and make sure you go into a centre for a period of rehabilitation." She had no problem with either proposal. She is a force of grace and nature in our land, not to be trifled with and much respected.

As 2019 comes to an end, I thank God for what has been, for the grace and strength I have received to enable me to cope, to cooperate with grace, and I ask the good God through his Son and with the help of Mary, Our Lady, Jesus' Mother, that next year, 2020, might be an easier year for me and, more importantly, for the Church; but still fruitful and life-giving and, above all, in conformity with his will.

Wednesday, 1 January 2020

Already twenty years into the twenty-first century. It only seems yesterday that we celebrated entry into the third Christian millennium with St John Paul the Great. Wonderful memories.

The feast day celebrates the solemnity of Mary, Mother of God, and it is appropriate to start a new year under her protection and patronage. While the Church's liturgical year begins when Advent commences, I have long thought that we should have tried harder to encourage the faithful to start the New Year with Mass, and in Melbourne I introduced a New Year's Eve Mass in the evening. We didn't make great headway, although I am no longer (if I ever was) an enthusiast for fireworks displays: once you have seen one, you have seen them all.

At the start of a new year, it is not unusual to pause and look backward, especially if you are not spending time devising New Year's resolutions. I have never been an enthusiast for such promises, which belong at the start of Lent and, as I get older, at the start of Advent, too.

Today I received from Ian Smith, a longtime friend I have known since my days in Mentone, an article he had posted on August 26 entitled "The Narrow Gate: Unfashionable Causes". He wrote with insight of the prevailing cultural hegemony, which is anti-Christian, and where "all of us—judge, juries, and police included" are "like proverbial frogs being boiled in the constantly rising temperatures of ideological stridency".

Wikipedia defines cultural hegemony as the domination of a culturally diverse society by the ruling class, which manipulates the culture of that society to justify the status quo as natural and inevitable, perpetual and beneficial for all, rather than as artificial social constructs that benefit only the ruling class.

Wikipedia acknowledges that this is a Marxist definition, and the left-of-centre cultural elite have not conquered most of the Australian parliaments, except in the Australian Capital Territory and Victoria, although they are everywhere influential. And they dominate in most of the university humanities faculties, in the ABC, in what used to be Fairfax Press, in the world of entertainment, and everywhere in the middle and lower ranks of the journalists.

But their unreflective stridency and their arrogance as they attempt to rule out of discussion many foundational topics have produced a strong backlash, such as Trump, Brexit, Boris Johnson's thumping victory in the UK, and even the return of the Liberal government under Scott Morrison in Australia.[3] The constituencies are changing, as Christianity recedes in the middle and upper middle class and social conservatism persists in ethnic groups, among blue collar workers and

---

[3] Scott Morrison became prime minister of Australia when he was elected leader of the Liberal Party in 2018. He continued in the post after he led the Liberal-National Coalition to victory in the 2019 election.

many voters in country areas (but not always in the National Party). It will be interesting to see whether the Tories in five years' time can retain their gains in Northern England in what was the Labour heartland for generations. I am convinced that Tony Abbott would have a better chance of election in a Western Sydney seat than in his own posh and pagan Warringah.

Ian feels that my advocacy of unfashionable causes has provoked the guardians of the hegemony of political correctness, and many of my correspondents from Australia and overseas see the hostility as specifically anti-Christian. He quoted at some length a paragraph from the *Melbourne Age* of 2012, which was reprinted there last year in 2019:

> Pell seems to see it as his task to keep the rest of us on the right path— not just Catholics but society in general. In speeches, newspaper columns and pronouncements from the pulpit, he delivers judgment on the big issues of the day, denouncing the Greens party as "anti-Christian" and dismissing climate-change concern as "a symptom of pagan emptiness" with the same conviction that he preaches about the sinfulness of contraception, abortion and sex outside marriage.[4]

The paragraph is unusually well written to slant the discussion by the topics chosen and omitted, and my first instinct was to reply "guilty as charged". But I was never naïve enough to believe I could get many on to the right path, while the author shows herself vexed, and even somewhat outraged, that a Christian leader would be pronouncing and "judging" on the big issues, obviously an uppity deplorable.

In the old days, I wrote more than a few pieces for the *Melbourne Age*, and I was twice asked to become a regular columnist for the *Sydney Morning Herald* when I was archbishop of Sydney. I was happy to be asked, but never seriously tempted, because I was well pleased to have a column with the *Sunday Telegraph*, which lasted for thirteen years and was read by more of "my" people. I would never have enjoyed security of tenure with Fairfax.

Every war has casualties, especially if it is the culture war for traditional Western civilisation (which won't be successful without Christian participation) or for Catholic truths and practices. Even

---

[4] Jane Cadzow, "Our Man in Rome", *Sydney Morning Herald*, June 16, 2012, https://www.smh.com.au/lifestyle/our-man-in-rome-20120611-204wh.html.

when you are outgunned and the strategies are ineffective, it is a start to recognize that the war is on and to be able to find the main battlefields, one of which is not climate change.

We still live in a democracy which allows free speech, political action, and (so far) ample religious freedom. Christians have as much right to participate in public life and discussion as any other group, and we need to be active and vocal. To be cowed into silence would be shameful, and to be drowned in political correctness would be worse.

Obviously, some approach my court case as though it were a referendum on how the Church has dealt with the sex abuse scandal. They want scapegoats and leaders to be punished. While we clergy made the rod for our own back through the sins of the fathers, the rod is heavier than it might have been because of our silence over the way this criminal and spiritual cancer in Australia has been radically reduced for more than twenty-five years. Even many Catholics are surprised to hear how low the number of incidents is since the mid-1990s. When courage accompanies truthfulness, we have the foundations for wisdom.

Al Jazeera was correct, or at least their estimate has been accepted, because one Aussie news channel claimed that an area equal to Belgium had been burnt out and around one thousand homes destroyed in the season's bushfires. The cool has brought a respite, but the conditions on Saturday threaten to be bad again.

The usual goals were met during my forty-five minutes in the gymnasium, as I felt quite sharp for someone my age. Another seventy-five letters arrived, so I must attack the backlog tomorrow, and I enjoyed the Royal Edinburgh Military Tattoo[5] this evening, which I manage to watch on most New Year's Days.

Mary, Mother of the Church, we seek your intercession for the whole Church, but especially for lay leaders and the pope, bishops, and clergy.

Strengthen our faith; help us see the light of Christ in the apostolic tradition so that we can show and teach it to others through our deeds and words.

We make this prayer in the name of Christ your Son.

---

[5] A ceremonial concert and marching display by bands from Britain and around the world at Edinburgh Castle in Scotland.

Thursday, 2 January 2020

It was warm for my run in the exercise pen in the morning, but perfect for my couple of hours in the garden, where the light breezes could enter, before the visit of Toto and Rita Piccolo.[6] Both Rita and Toto were well and brought me up to date with news from the communities. Many members of the Neocatechumenal Way from around the world are praying for me.

I spent most of the day opening and reading Christmas cards and a few letters. Only about ten arrived today, so I have made good progress in dealing with the backlog.

Dr George Mendz from the medical school at the University of Notre Dame in Sydney was surprised by the amount of interest in my case in Europe, which he visited recently. His friends informed him of my successful plea for the High Court to hear my appeal. He went on, "At the same time, I have heard many unfavourable comments about the justice system in Australia, and I had to make clear the difference between the State of Victoria and the country as a whole."

Andrew Bolt[7] has said that the Victorian criminal justice system is on trial in my case, but more of my overseas correspondents make this point than Australian writers. One Chatswood man who has been active in my defence is dismayed that "this injustice could occur in our justice institutions" but was kind enough to recount that he had seen me in a dream walking in a nice city park "and admiring the trees with a warm half smile on your face". He hoped this would soon be my situation. I have done well out of my too brief gardening career.

I was honoured to receive a supportive note from Michael O'Brien in Canada, who is not only the best Catholic novelist writing in English today and a fine painter but a believer with remarkable powers of insight and spiritual perception. I am pleased and grateful that he and his family are also praying "that you will have peace and total trust in the Lord".

Deacon Nick Donnelly from Cumbria, UK, one of my foremost champions in social media, told me he is walking beside me in my

---

[6] The founders of the Neocatechumenal Way in Australia.

[7] Andrew Bolt writes social and political commentary for Australian newspapers and hosts *The Bolt Report* on Sky News.

sufferings, while I also received a kind message of support from Caroline Farey in Worcester. It was my privilege to support both of them in their brave attempts to set up the School of the Annunciation for catechesis at Buckfast Abbey in Devon.

Recently finished *Decline and Fall*, the first published novel by Evelyn Waugh, which is beautifully written, both brilliant and inconsequential. Or so it seemed to me, at least by itself. So many of Waugh's characters are remorselessly caricatured, exquisitely reduced to absurdity. It is more interesting when a writer is prepared to be cruel, especially when the cruelty is accurate and penetrating, delighting in the foolishness revealed. Waugh had all these gifts and more.

Time magazine is quoted, explaining that Waugh developed "a wickedly hilarious yet fundamentally religious assault on a century that, in his opinion, had ripped up the nourishing tap root of tradition and let wither all the dear things of the world".

Decline and Fall was published in 1928 and therefore written before Waugh became a Catholic. He was well and truly in demolitionary mode, certainly "wickedly hilarious", although the unfortunate central character, Paul Pennyfeather, who was "reading for the Church" at both the beginning and end of the novel, seems to be the story's principal and unfortunate victim, not revealing but concealing any religious ambitions Waugh would later develop.

A month or so ago, I finished C.J. Sansom's *Tombland,* the last of a series of murder mysteries, in this case 860 pages long, set in sixteenth-century England during the Reformation. The central character is Matthew Shardlake, a hunchback Protestant lawyer, who began his career as an agent for Thomas Cromwell in the closing down of a large Benedictine abbey. His novel *Dissolution* is still my favourite.

Shardlake, naturally, was born Catholic, and we learn in *Tombland* that he contemplated becoming a priest and that when he lost his faith in the Old Church he felt "uprooted, like a straw in the wind". Now he can no longer pray.

Shardlake is a recognizable twentieth-century figure, finishing as a humane theist: part agnostic, lamenting the religious violence, but with a conscience formed by Christian moral teaching. I don't know enough about the period to estimate how many establishment lawyers were like this in sixteenth-century England.

This novel is set in the peasant rebellions of 1549, about which I knew nothing. Sansom is rated well as an historian. I enjoyed the seven novels in the series for their insight into the controversies and daily life of that tumultuous time rather than the murders. We have fascinating glimpses of Elizabeth and Mary, a good picture of Queen Catherine Parr, no idealization of Thomas Cromwell, and a terrifying encounter with Henry VIII. Sansom is no great admirer of Thomas More, but does not demonise him à la Hilary Mantel.[8] I cannot recommend the series too highly for anyone who likes a good murder mystery and is interested in the religious and civic tumult of sixteenth-century England.

Some months ago,[9] I made an uncertain reference to stars, galaxies, and the Milky Way. A professional astronomer, with his own program on the ABC, today brought light to my confusion by explaining that there are 200,000 million stars in our galaxy, the Milky Way. And only the Lord knows the number of galaxies.

Despite decades of searching, scientists have no evidence of any other intelligent life in the universe. What was the good God up to in creating such an immeasurably huge and expanding universe, and so many stars, some of them with planets?

Amos had no Hubble telescope, so he had little idea of what was hidden in the night sky, but he was still full of awe.

> *It is he who made the Pleiades and Orion,*
> *who turns the dusk to dawn*
> *and the day to darkest night, . . .*
> *the* LORD *is his name. (Amos 5:8)*

Friday, 3 January 2020

Tens of thousands of tourists and residents have fled their homes in southeastern Victoria and along 200 km of the south coast in New

---

[8] The well-known English author of *Wolf Hall* (Picador, 2010), *Bring Up the Bodies* (Picador, 2013), and *The Mirror and the Light* (Henry Holt, 2020), which depict Thomas Cromwell sympathetically while painting Thomas More in an unfavourable light.

[9] See *Prison Journal*, volume 2.

South Wales, at government direction, to escape the disasters which threaten in tomorrow's heat. It could be worse than the New Year's fires. Today the Navy's *HMAS Choules* has evacuated one thousand people from Mallacoota, while three thousand remain. A smoke haze covered much of Melbourne, and the two new high buildings which have crept up during my ten months in jail (one is the new police headquarters) were also obscured but recognizable.

The prime minister was insulted in one New South Wales town, but what he or anyone else might have done to prevent or diminish the fires (except through more early burning of excess vegetation) has never been explained. When the electricity supply is gone, bank cards are useless, cash registers are down, and petrol cannot be pumped. We are vulnerable in new ways.

Kartya called to inform me that the twenty-page High Court appeal document has been lodged and the prosecution has twenty-eight days from today to respond. My suggested inclusion that even the complainant could not be in two places at the same time was not put into the text but might be used orally. The text will be emailed to my team and eventually will be on the High Court website. I believe it important that we encourage its circulation because of its fidelity to the truth and the quality of its argumentation as it reveals the basic legal issues and the strategy of the prosecution.

Today's second reading in the Office of Readings was an outstanding piece by St Augustine, commenting on John's Gospel and explaining the importance of the two great commandments of love and their interconnectedness. These two commandments ought to be most familiar to us and never blotted from our hearts. They should be pondered, retained, and practiced, he explained.

Augustine then tells his readers: "You do not yet see God, ... [but] by loving your neighbour you gain the sight of God." By loving your neighbour "you purify your eye" for seeing God. So, he urges them to begin to love their neighbours by feeding the hungry, welcoming the homeless into their homes, clothing the naked, and not despising servants or slaves. Our journey to the Lord is of first importance, and while we have not arrived, we do have to support those travelling with us.

Our Lord has taken over these perspectives from the Old Testament; as the psalmist told us, the man with clean hands and a pure heart climbs the mountain of the Lord (Ps 24:4).

If Indians are the most religious people on the planet, the Swedes are the most irreligious, and the United States is a nation of Indians often ruled by Swedes, where in Augustine's exhortations do we obtain help to understand why irreligion is stronger in the Western world than in other cultures? Why is the faith in decline among us, in a way that it is not occurring in Africa or Asia or even in South America, where the mass movement is from the Church to evangelical Protestantism? Is there a lesson in the fact that in great cities, because of the light they generate, you cannot see many stars in the sky at night?

Jesus extolled simplicity and poverty, saved us through his suffering, and warned frequently about the love of money.

I spent most of the day opening my Christmas mail, and the backlog is much reduced. Australia again had a good first day in the cricket against New Zealand, which made five changes in their team. Steve Smith made sixty-three, but the magic is still missing.

Those who love the Church and want her to flourish and expand often define her differently, espousing alternative models, e.g., a community of faith and individual service or a political group working to reform the structures of society or one great river of natural religion like a number of others or as a network of unstructured gospel communities. Not all the models are mutually exclusive, but even when our definitions are Catholic, we can mistake both the sources of spiritual energy (grace) and the activities that are more likely to constitute genuine growth in God's Kingdom.

A woman from Wisconsin sent me a small poem, which I did not know, by George MacDonald, whose first verse now follows:

> *They all were looking for a king*
> *To slay their foes, and lift them high;*
> *Thou cam'st a little baby thing*
> *That made a woman cry.*[10]

Saturday, 4 January 2020

The threatened fire catastrophes have not occurred, as far as we know in the early evening. However, the day has come but is not gone,

---

[10] George MacDonald (1824–1905), "That Holy Thing".

although the cool change with its unpredictable winds has arrived already in Melbourne and parts of Gippsland. A couple of towns there were blacked out by smoke during the afternoon, dark like the night, and in one place a huge fire was generating its own weather and raining light mud. Please God, the worst has been avoided, but the absence of bad news might be partly caused by ignorance. Dozens of fires are burning.

I phoned Terry and Bernadette and was surprised to hear the High Court had already posted our appeal document on their website. I was delighted. Terry did not wax as enthusiastic as I anticipated, although I had extolled it lavishly to him. He was disappointed that the text did not say that (in the complainant's scenario) the altar servers must have arrived before the complainant, travelling twenty-five to thirty metres from the glass doors to the sacristy against the alleged two hundred metres plus of the complainant and his companion as they doubled back to the same spot. So, too, if the claimant arrived before sacristan or servers, the sacristy door would have been closed. These are two more demonstrations, not of the implausibility, but of the impossibility of the complainant's own story.

Both of these are strong points, different aspects of the situation described in the last paragraph of the appeal, and I defended the submission by saying our team probably wants to keep some cards up their sleeve, at least for the present.

Also spoke to Margaret, my sister, after a break of some days. She was pleased to hear I was well, and vice versa! I was a bit sharper than usual at the ping-pong, and the warmed pasty on my return from the gym was as good as ever.

Also scored a bonus mid-afternoon with the main meal, because my salad was not available and I was asked whether I would prefer sweet and sour pork or something else (I can't remember what). The pork with boiled rice was excellent, and it was hot when it arrived. Joe, who chats to me from the neighbouring exercise pen in the morning, explained that our food is much better than the food in the New South Wales jails, where he has also spent some time. Certainly our regime could be much harsher, and the medical care is excellent, but slow, unless you can convince them you need prompt assistance.

Australia made a first innings score of 455 with Labuschagne scoring a double century,[11] although our last wickets fell cheaply. New Zealand had lost no wickets at stumps for 63.

More letters arrived, and I again spent the afternoon opening cards as I watched the cricket, further reducing the backlog. Most of the mail now are Christmas cards from overseas, but the letters come from a wide variety of places with a similar wide variety of themes.

My first letter arrived from the Faroe Islands, between Scotland and Norway and an autonomous part of Denmark. The writer, a Catholic convert, is a carpenter, historian, and vice president of the Catholic community, who invited me to visit "after you have been liberated" to see the old Catholic sites and celebrate Mass for them.

A French missionary priest in Taiwan told me of his hope for my "fast liberation", mentioning the spread of confusion and even doubt in the Church as well as the increasing difficulties in mainland China.

A Japanese layman from Miyakonojo in Japan also wrote (once again a first), and, to balance out the China missionary, a group who had been members of the underground Church in Czechoslovakia (1968–1989) sent their love and prayers.

A Canadian priest from Port Perry in Ontario explained that he had met me and that he and his friends held me in the highest regard. He must have been reading Christopher Friel, because I can't believe he had read Louise Milligan,[12] when he printed across the top of his card "Veritas, filia temporis" (Truth, the daughter of time).

A Slovakian priest who had studied in Rome at the Lateran University and every day passed the ancient Egyptian obelisk nearby reminded me of the words inscribed there: "Per crucem victor" (Victor through the cross).

A Spaniard in scarcely legible handwriting (in Spanish) sent me personal greetings from the president of the Catalan Assembly(?), who like me is being persecuted, but for different reasons.

A German Catholic now working in Papua New Guinea told me the encouraging story of his great uncle Fr Martin Utsch, MSC, who

[11] Marnus Labuschagne is a Test cricket batsman for Australia. A double century refers to more than 200 runs.

[12] Louise Milligan is an investigative television reporter and the author of *Cardinal: The Rise and Fall of George Pell*, which was published in 2017 and fostered a negative view of Cardinal Pell before his trial.

had been the superior of the North German MSC [Missionaries of the Sacred Heart] Province before World War II. He was imprisoned by the Nazis and prevented from celebrating Mass until a Protestant guard smuggled in bread and wine. The guard converted, and Fr Martin was later freed by the Nazis, due to the vocal support of friends and especially of the "Lion of Munster", the outspoken opponent of euthanasia and defender of the sick and feeble, Cardinal August von Galen, another one of my heroes, who made nearly as much trouble for the occupying British as he did for the Nazis.

"Why am I writing this story right now?" wrote Chris Adam, my correspondent. He then replied to his own question. "I am absolutely positive of a similar 'outcome' in your case."

All these messages support me and my faith, but the most poignant came from a mother in Hopetoun Park in Victoria. She wrote, "My youngest child suffered a serious injury (compartment syndrome). In the midst of her suffering, I asked her if she was offering her pain. She said, 'Yes, for Cardinal Pell.'" I cannot think of any more effective spur than this to remind me to persevere manfully in faith through my present difficulties.

In this incident, we understand why Jesus taught that young children are better suited to his Kingdom than we are. G. K. Chesterton understood this too, as we see in his "A Christmas Carol".

> *The Christ-child lay on Mary's lap,*
> *His hair was like a light.*
> *(O weary, weary were the world,*
> *But here is all aright.)* ...
>
> *The Christ-child stood on Mary's knee,*
> *His hair was like a crown,*
> *And all the flowers looked up at Him,*
> *And all the stars looked down.*

WEEK 46

A New Jail

5 January–11 January 2020

Feast of the Epiphany, 5 January 2020

Today is the feast day of my seminary on the Janiculum Hill over-looking St Peter's in Rome, Propaganda Fide College, the missionary seminary for the universal Church, founded in the 1620s by Pope Urban VIII, a Barberini. His brother was an early prefect of the Propaganda Fide Congregation for the missions. Both are remembered in two splendid marble busts by Bernini.

The college was originally housed in the palace near the Spanish Steps in the Piazza di Spagna, designed by Borromini, but was transferred by Pope Pius XI in the 1920s to its hillside spot above the Jesuit Curia building (the only spot in the world where the diocesan clergy look down on the Jesuits, according to the Jesuits). My four years there were a blessing, not without difficulties, but a liberating and enriching experience among the sixty-three nationalities present in my time. I pray for all those in the college with me between 1963 and 1967 and especially for my classmates.

Cynics claim that you can tell a Rome-trained priest anywhere and tell him nothing. In fact, the opposite is closer to the truth, as a Roman priest knows the universal Church is like a lifetime, full of surprises. In the bad old days before the Second Vatican Council, ex-student bishops were listed, when appointed, on the notice board under the heading "La Gloria della Famiglia".[1] And quite a few of us became bishops; some bit the dust spectacularly, but the

---

[1] The glory of the family.

97

overwhelming majority served their people well. And over the centuries the college has produced many martyrs.

Naturally, I was not able to have any elaborate crib in my cell for Christmas, but different people sent me a triptych card of the *Adoration of the Magi* by Gentile da Fabriano (ca. 1370–1427), an early Renaissance masterpiece now housed in the Uffizi Gallery in Florence, which I balanced on my wall above the box of teabags. The painting is a work of faith, spectacularly beautiful with multiple figures, human and animal, reverencing a surprisingly upright Christ Child with Mary and Joseph. The Magi are dressed, not as shabby philosophers or other-world astrologists, but as splendidly costumed Renaissance princes in richly decorated brocades. I suppose the manger in Bethlehem would not have been as grand as this, with three additional portraits in the frame and three scenes from Jesus' early life in the predella. But it is a genuine tribute to Emmanuel, the Transcendent God who has come among us.

The Indian-born priest Fr Kaniampuram of the Melbourne Archdiocese celebrated the *Mass for You at Home* this morning in an imperfect, somewhat stilted English, but his sermon was the best in my ten months of listening. He explained that the ancient world of the East was a star-gazing civilisation, both in Babylon and then in Persia, the traditional origin of the seekers who left home to follow the star. These men searched for the will of God in the stars, and he described them as symbols of the best of the human condition, who learnt from the monotheist Jews they consulted to identify what they were seeking. God's only Son came as a baby, the full manifestation of Divine Love.

Joseph Prince's official theme was "Positioned for His Provision" about the Shabbat, the Sabbath [that coincided with the Passover during the Passion]. The nine plagues have come and gone, and while there is darkness outside, light shines in God's houses. The Jews were entitled to plunder the Egyptians, who had forced them to work as unpaid slaves for generations.

He was quite clear that the Gospel is not about health and wealth, that he doesn't preach prosperity, but a gospel of grace. By his suffering on the Cross, Jesus took away our sins. Indeed, Jesus became our sin, according to Joseph, and we are now candidates for the rapture. He wore a dark suit and tie with white stripes on the suit collar and on his sleeves. Three rings with bracelets on both wrists.

Joel Osteen was in top form on "The Smile of God" by urging us to return good for evil and forgive our enemies, because God is testing us to discover whether we are worthy of promotion. Just as Esau later forgave Jacob for stealing his birthright, so Jacob's son Joseph of Egypt, who was aware of Esau's magnanimity, was able to forgive his brothers who had sold him into captivity. Children follow what their parents do even more than what they say, and if we are the smile of God, God will smile on us. Bad and sad events can produce unexpected good fruits, and he recounted how a bad accident put the mother of an estranged family into a coma. Gathered around her, all eventually reconciled with one another. Joel is like Job, as he only paints on a this-world canvas, but it is effective and challenging Christianity as far as it goes. Joseph Prince grapples with all the New Testament evidence, painting on broader themes than Osteen, but with less charm.

Tim O'Leary received word on New Year's Eve that Archbishop [Peter] Comensoli had appointed him as chancellor of the Melbourne Archdiocese. I am delighted, as he will make a fine contribution and provide strength and wisdom to the archbishop.

The first priority today of the authorities in the bushfires crisis was to save lives. While the hectares destroyed are enormous, Victoria suffered only one death when a firefighter had a heart attack. Three thousand Defence Force personnel were deployed with a couple of naval vessels and a number of helicopters. The damage is worse in New South Wales, while one-third of Kangaroo Island in South Australia has been burnt out. God has no hands but ours, but we should be thanking him for more than small mercies, including the cool and the rain.

Despite the bushfires and the violence between the US and Iran (with the possibility of worse to come), we are still able to pray the first verse from the hymn of morning prayer.

Songs of thankfulness and praise,
Jesus, Lord, to thee we raise,
Manifested by the star
To the sages from afar;
Branch of royal David's stem
In thy birth at Bethlehem;
Anthems be to thee addressed,
God in man made manifest.

Monday, 6 January 2020

The highlight of the day for me, apart from the third consecutive crushing of New Zealand in the cricket, was the visit of Chris Meney's daughters Jessica Phillips, Jane, and Bernadette. Two are teachers, and Bernadette is a business executive. I have watched them grow up in Melbourne and then in Sydney when Chris came up to work for the archdiocese. They are wonderful company, strong and informed Catholics actively involved in the "culture wars", wonderful loving cousins. Their visit gave me a good psychological boost as well as a deeper consolation.

The second reading in today's Office of Readings was by one of my favourite preachers, St Peter Chrysologus, and speaks in his treatment of the Incarnation of the visit of the three wise men: "Today the Magus, the wise man, finds weeping in a crib him whom he sought for shining in the stars.... Today the wise man ponders in profound amazement over what he sees there: heaven on earth, earth in heaven, man in God, God in man, and him whom the whole universe cannot contain, confined in a tiny body." Nobody has expressed this better, and, of course, I have used the passage in Christmas sermons. It is such a help to understanding and devotion to be able to draw from the best that has been written or composed, painted, or sculpted during two thousand years to praise God and his only Son.

The day was showery, cool, overcast and had the smell of smoke in the air, especially in the early morning. I received a dozen letters and spent the afternoon watching the cricket while opening the backlog of letters and cards. Only a dozen or so remain to be dealt with (at 9:00 pm), and I consigned about three hundred, which had been read and sorted, to the jail's "Property" section for Kartya to collect them.

Most of the cards were from the United States: very supportive and often from large families. There was more of a spread in the letters.

Bernadette Tobin sent me half a dozen cuttings, mainly from the opinion pages of *The Australian*, analysing what is happening, which is badly presented to us in the news, never without a smaller or larger dose of propaganda. I miss reading *The Australian*'s editorials, Greg Sheridan, Paul Kelly, Dennis Shanahan, and Henry Ergas.

Michael Heinlein, biographer of the late Francis Cardinal George (from Chicago), wrote a kind note, telling me that I have been in his prayers for some years and that he is imploring the good cardinal's intercession for me. I certainly hope to be able to take up his invitation to speak together about the cardinal, an outstanding John Paul the Great archbishop and a good friend, whom I admired greatly.

Two letters were written in starkly contrasting styles, but not expressing contradictory views. The first was from an eighty-three-year-old Catholic widow from country Queensland, who still grieved at the loss of her husband but has "had a simple but wonderful life". Dr Austin Woodbury, the distinguished Marist priest, had been a family friend and a yearly visitor, and two of the widow's sisters were nuns, one a contemplative. Unexpectedly after her husband's death, she had been asked to become president of the local St Vincent de Paul group, which she rejuvenated so that it became the biggest conference in the Toowoomba Diocese.

Without any comment, much less bitterness, she said that in their local Catholic primary school, the children were "nice mannered", but hardly any of them came to Mass, and most of the teachers don't go to Mass. Unfortunately, I cannot claim that her experience is unique, especially in Australian country areas, and she quoted the spiritual adviser to the visionaries at Medjugorje, who has written that the question most frequently asked by pilgrims is for help and advice to "get their offspring to return to the faith". I remember nearly thirty years ago a Bulgarian bishop, who had been working under Communist rule, mischievously asking me how I could live in such an anti-religious society as Australia's. We had been together at a Roman Synod and become friends.

My Italian correspondent from Brescia wrote rather than typed his letter in good English but using an untidy scrawl. He has only become interested in my case in February, was scandalised by it and the false accusations of the Billy Doe story in Philadelphia and the allegations at the heart of Operation Midland in the UK.[2] He confessed he was a sixty-year-old Anglophile "coming from an ancient but corrupt and cowardly country like Italy", who had only recently become "aware of terrible cultural and social flaws (sins) in the Anglophone world".

---

[2] Two widely publicised and lurid cases of abuse of young people that turned out to be completely false.

The "old world" UK is "less crazy", the new world US is "more crazy", and "the very new world Australia" is "the craziest of all".

While he regards me as "a real Christian martyr of our time" and is a bit sceptical of our Australian capacity for renewal, he suspects that pride in our own Australian tradition "will prevent the Australians from destroying their reputation throughout the world".

My instinctive reaction to such a flamboyant criticism is to become defensive, but a better response is to wait and ponder, which doesn't require us to agree completely. I think of Australian pagans as solid performers, sometimes dull and truculent, but not as crazy as the Californians.

To round out the picture, my correspondent says he is "keen on Winston Churchill" (as I am) and recommends that I read the "Christian masterpiece" Manzoni's *The Betrothed* (*I Promessi Sposi*), something I haven't done but agree that I should do.

Psalm 36 today reminds us that corruption will not have the last word, although it can wax eloquent for too long.

> *Calm your anger and forget your rage;*
> *do not fret, it only leads to evil.*
> *For those who do evil shall perish;*
> *the patient shall inherit the land.*
>
> *A little longer—and the wicked shall have gone.*

Tuesday, 7 January 2020

Today 190 letters and cards arrived. I counted them for the first time, disregarding the good God's displeasure at King David for conducting a census. Most are from the United States, and I will move through them as I watch the Big Bash cricket after the evening TV news.

After some weeks of comparative quiet, we have a couple of knockers who break out in short bursts in the evening. Last night we had a noisy flurry around midnight, but they don't persevere. For nearly a week we have heard from some poor wretch who breaks out into abuse every now and then, sometimes unprovoked by any human agency. His abuse is not poetic, but repetitive across a limited range of obscenities, as he discharges an explosive rage. He is badly damaged, and it is sad because Francis of Assisi would find it difficult to help him. While he does not continue for hours, by some mischance he is in the Toorak end of the unit, a couple of cells from me and next to my friend Joe. I am not absolutely sure he is still with us, as the inmate from cell 12 (my cell is number 11) was transferred this afternoon, taking the opportunity to attack the warders and provoking an enormous racket, while Sr Mary was with me. She was outside watching the fun, but I was returned briefly to my cell for the move. We prisoners in Unit 8 never see one another.

Dave the liaison officer made his weekly visit, and I asked for my Thursday half hour to be extended to an hour. He asked me to write my request to the governor, which, Sr Mary explained, would be a bonus (if accepted), as the regulations allow only two visits a week totalling one and a half hours.

Spent my usual Tuesday hour in the gym, where I was sluggish and needed multiple attempts before I achieved a hundred unbroken shots on my backhand and forehand in the ping-pong.

One hundred fires are still burning in New South Wales, and government efforts are intensifying during this cool lull to continue clearing up, opening back roads, and restoring electricity. One estimate set the length of all the fire fronts at one thousand kilometres; 125 homes were destroyed in New South Wales. Naturally many, too many, see the fires as conclusive evidence of climate change, which they believe we can modify by eliminating coal-fired power plants. I am not sure how many community leaders, including the politicians, know the basics of the history and science of climate change, understand the uncertainty of the diagnoses and the uselessness of the proposed remedies, but maintain a prudential silence when faced by the vigilantes. There must be some, but they are hoisted on their own petard by their silence.

A recent article by Bjorn Lomborg (*The Weekend Australian*, December 28–29, 2019), who is less sceptical than I am, listed some of the futile responses. When Sir David Attenborough was asked what he could do as an individual to combat climate change, he promised to unplug his phone charger when it was not in use. An electric car with a range of 400 km has a huge carbon deficit when it hits the road and will only start to save emissions after 60,000 kms.

Every battery-powered electric car is subsidised to the tune of US $10,000, and today US $129 billion a year is spent subsidising solar and wind energy, yet these sources meet 1.1 percent of global energy needs. And Lomborg gave other examples.

The average world temperature has been increasing in fits, starts, and stops since the Little Ice Age and over the last two hundred years. No computer model so far has predicted accurately future temperature changes or patterns. Billions of dollars are expended on the climate change academic-industrial complex, one of the most expensive follies in history. Somehow it is symbolic that children are not being led up the garden path by the Pied Piper; rather, gullible or cynical adults are being led by a sixteen-year-old girl. What cost increases for electricity, how many power blackouts will be needed before this madness is curbed? The pagan Greeks were onto something when they claimed that those whom the gods wanted to destroy they first made mad (but I am not suggesting the one true God intervenes in this way; he doesn't need to do so).

Our Christian faith reminds us of the existence of another higher plane of existence beyond the beauties and travails of our world, a point acknowledged in the hymn for Wednesday's Office of Readings.

O God, Creation's secret force,
yourself unmoved, all motion's source,
who from the morn till evening ray
through all its changes guide the day.

Grant us, when this short life is past,
the glorious evening that shall last;
that, by a holy death attained,
eternal glory may be gained.

Wednesday, 8 January 2020

Catholics everywhere are instinctively universalist, and it is not because the Greek word *katholicos* means "universal", but because of regular practice and because we are aware of the spread of Catholic communities around the globe. We had many Irish-born priests in the Ballarat Diocese when I was growing up, we collected money for "the missions" overseas, schoolmates regularly joined the Irish-founded Columban Fathers to work overseas on missionary work for a lifetime, the pope was in Rome. It was entirely natural to help overseas and to receive help from overseas. This dimension of Catholic life struck me in a new way when I travelled as a bishop in Eastern Europe, encountering many good members of Orthodox Churches. Their world was regularly confined by their national boundaries, and they worked happily enough within these limited horizons.

Therefore, I was not surprised when I received some messages of support from overseas, but I have been overwhelmed and humbled by the loyalty, the prayers and penance, and messages from many corners of the earth. The new social media have transformed the scene, not so much by spreading news of my fate, but by informing supporters of my address.

Pride of place among these blessings belongs to the cards and handwritten message from Auxiliary Bishop Athanasius Schneider of Kazakhstan and his Metropolitan Archbishop Tomasz Peta. Bishop Athanasius is well-named, as he grew up under Communist persecution and is now an outspoken and fearless champion of Catholic truth. I was touched by a card from a Malaysian woman, who thanked me for my story, which gave her "a reason to remain in this Church, despite it all".

There were messages from a Dominican priest in Sweden, a prayer group in Belgium, the German Capuchin Sisters (the Clarissas), who are contemplatives in Assisi, Italy, the former South Korean ambassador to the Vatican, whom I know, and from Geneva, Switzerland.

A couple from Auckland, New Zealand, wrote, "We pray that you get a better hearing in the High Court than St Thomas More had", and last, but not the least in this list, a gentleman from Michigan in the US promised he would "write to President Trump so this horror will end soon". Regular mail comes from England, Ireland, and Scotland, although most now is from the United States.

One unhappy theme runs through many of the letters, as the writers are worried by the confusion and scandal in the Church today. While my writers are a self-selecting group, they are often but not always politically conservative and almost universally doctrinally faithful; others inform me they belong to St Pius X communities.

One writer from Birmingham, who recently attended the canonisation of St John Henry Newman in Rome, stressed the optimistic tone of Bishop Schneider's interview, but she still felt the whiff of "an almost demonic presence" at the Amazon Synod. A woman from Cumbria spoke of "this utter confusion in the Catholic Church".

In Australia, opinions also varied, with one woman from George Town in Tasmania claiming that "it seems as though we are living through the Reformation times again", and a gentleman from Boyne Island in Queensland explaining, "There are many people here hungry for God." He was also encouraged that a former Anglican chaplain to the Queen, Rev Dr Gavin Ashenden, recently came into the Catholic Church, quoting one contributor to Twitter: "This is at once gratifying, mystifying, and consoling, if he has chosen this poor shipwrecked Church at its very worst moment, it should give us heart."

The twentieth-century popes spoilt us, and a knowledge of Church history quickly demonstrates that now is not the worst of times, least of all in Anglophone Catholicism. We have the great scandal, unease, and worse about the Church's leadership, and a decline of faith and practice in many places, but we still have formidable strengths, and our decline in no way matches the collapse in Belgium, Holland, and Quebec. A medical doctor from Vienna, Austria, wrote, "We as Christians are living in a dark time, God has been banned from our society, and we are witnessing the extinction of the flame of faith." I hope she exaggerates, but Catholics in Austria, Switzerland, and many parts of Germany face much deeper challenges than we do, and often there the Church leadership is not just rattled and immobile, but resolutely heading in the wrong direction.

Many of these great matters are far beyond our control and in distant parts of the world. Our task is to concentrate on the work at hand, continue to pray, serve, support one another, and rally around our bishops and the papacy. God hasn't forgotten us, and unconsciously exaggerating our troubles can be used as an excuse for our mistakes and inactivity.

Not surprisingly, St John Henry Newman struck the right note in one of his sermons:

When the Eternal Son came on earth in our flesh, men saw their invisible Maker and Judge. He showed Himself no longer through the mere powers of nature, or the maze of human affairs, but in our own likeness to Him.[3]

Thursday, 9 January 2020

The day was hot, with temperatures in the low thirties; it was pleasant for my one and a half hours in the garden. Tomorrow is supposed to be hotter, so the bushfire danger in Victoria at least will be extreme. Rain and a cool change are estimated to arrive in Victoria later on Saturday, and the cyclonic rain in Western Australia might even make it to the east coast in some much diminished form. The threat of a cyclone around Darwin has been downgraded.

Twiggy Forrest, the mining billionaire from Western Australia, has donated $70 million to the Bushfire Relief Program. Our paths had crossed in Sydney and more frequently in Rome through his work against modern-day slavery, which the Australian ambassador to the Vatican, John McCarthy, also supported strongly. It is a wonderful cause, meeting a dire need to help men and women trapped in poorly paid work, who are unable to leave their positions because, e.g., their passports are confiscated or they are threatened with physical violence if they try to escape. In the Vatican, we committed to supporting international efforts to ensure that the supply lines for our goods and services did not employ forced labour at any stage.

Another item of big news was the announcement by the Duke and Duchess of Sussex, Harry and Meghan, that they were retiring as "senior royals" to help the institution of the royal family in a "progressive" way and work toward financial independence. The Palace responded by issuing a statement that discussions on this matter were still at an early stage and that many details needed to be clarified. The royal family let it be known that they were disappointed by the lack of any warning.

---

[3] John Henry Newman, "A Particular Providence as Revealed in the Gospel", *Parochial and Plain Sermons* (San Francisco: Ignatius Press, 1997), book 3, sermon 9.

One feels for Prince Harry, who suffered so drastically through the death of his mother when he was still a young boy. He is well loved by the public, and his fear of the tabloids is well-based.

However, they celebrated a lavish public wedding as recently as 2018, and both would have known what was entailed in marrying a prince and living and working as a princess. Therefore, the timing and manner of their retirement are unfortunate.

I recall reading months ago that Germaine Greer had described Meghan as a "bolter" some considerable time before that. Germaine now expresses a thoroughly un-Christian set of principles, but she thinks clearly and with insight and common sense. She is proof that a Catholic education (in this case, at Star of the Sea College in Gardenvale, Melbourne) is never completely wasted. She has also been courageous and correct in what she has said on some gender issues.

I wish the Sussexes well, but remain sceptical that their escape will bring them peace, which is more usually achieved through embracing duty rather than rejecting it, after you have put your hand to the plough.

The normal run of prison life has continued with its small ups and downs for the past week or so, with my daily routine clearly established. My blind friend, Joe, whom I had never seen in the next exercise pen but with whom I had been chatting for five or six days, has been shifted elsewhere, either in this prison or to some other. I am delighted for him but will miss our chats, which I increasingly enjoyed as I refined my capacity for small talk, which had atrophied even further in ten months of solitary confinement and after decades of absorption in my work.

We had talked a couple of times about whether it is worse to be deaf or blind. I made the tentative case that deafness would be worse because of the difficulties in communicating, while Joe pointed out that an implant and medical intervention can reduce deafness, but there are no such possibilities to replace the cornea, which is connected to the brain, etc., by ten thousand nerves. The eye and, indeed, the human voice box, which enables us to communicate our ideas, would be quite an achievement for blind chance; and these are only two particular human attributes.

Staff are rotated around the various parts of the prison, and yesterday two novice warders (at least to Unit 8) were on duty. This meant that I missed my afternoon outside in the exercise area for the second day in a row; and they refused to open the door so I could pass out my brown paper bag containing a lot of rubbish. They promised to come back; they didn't.

My initial paranoid reaction was to wonder whether this was part of a new program, so that I might have problems with registration of my two visitors. No such confirmation had come through, but it was there in the unit when I went out to exercise at 8:30 am today.

The old patterns recommenced, and I was given some extra time when Kevin Andrews, still in Federal Parliament, a former minister and a stalwart defender of common sense and Christian values; and Fr Tony Percy, rector at Good Shepherd Seminary in Sydney during my time as archbishop and now vicar general of the Canberra-Goulburn Archdiocese, visited this afternoon. We spent some of the time discussing the Vatican finances, then outlining features of my prison life. The late Tim Fischer, formerly deputy prime minister, received a richly deserved honourable mention. I am deeply grateful for the visit.

Yesterday I opened a card from a woman in New Jersey, US, who was "praying daily that God will give you the strength to surrender completely to his will". She continued,

The blood of the (white) martyr is the seed of the Church. The harvest has dwindled. How the Church needs new seeds.

She prayed well. Amen.

Friday, 10 January 2020

Life changed today. It all began ordinarily enough with breakfast while I watched Channel 7's *Sunrise* and a half hour in the small exercise pen, when I managed to phone Margaret.

After my morning prayers, I was settling down to do my meditation when there was a rattle of keys at the door, and the warder explained that the acting governor of the jail was there to see me. He gestured for me to take a seat with him at the table, was amiable, and then explained that I would be shifting to a new jail. "This is a surprise", I remarked. "Yes, but that is prison life" was his response, going on to say that Barwon would be my new destination.

It would be an improvement: living in a newer building, with a more spacious room, access to common areas, and three prisoners for company some of the time. The transfer would take place today, and I should start packing immediately, taking what I needed for tonight, while the remainder of my goods and chattels would be delivered after the weekend.

The transfer party of four warders arrived before my packing was complete, the compulsory strip search was completed, my wrists were handcuffed, and I was off. I thanked the young senior officer for looking after me, shook his hand and that of the friendly female officer who had informed me that my appeal had been accepted for consideration by the High Court, and nodded to the other two, whom I didn't really know.

In the van, my ankles were also padlocked in the largest size manacles (so I was informed), which were slightly tight. My status as a prisoner necessitates those indignities, apparently, which I don't like, as there is no remote possibility of my trying to escape.

The van had three seats, all obscured to anyone outside, but it had three windows, nine inches by three inches (I still think in imperial measures), which was a psychological boon and enabled me to watch a small slab of the outside world as we went west. We departed at 11:09 am and arrived at 12:17 pm.

On arrival, warders and nurses were affable, and in a splendid irony I discovered that in the Acacia HSU (High Security Unit)[4] where I am placed, prisoners wear a uniform of almost exactly cardinal red. I suppose this is progress from the darker green of MAP, the Muslim colour.

My quarters are about four times the size of my MAP cell, and I have my own yard attached. The main door to my cell opens onto a common internal area, with a kitchen and refrigerators at one end and some gym equipment, including a treadmill, at the other. Moving farther, we find a common outside exercise area devoid of any plants or trees. Everything is recently painted and clean and less tense than Unit 8 was.

The shouter who had somehow landed in the Toorak end of Unit 8, a few cells away from mine, had already gone by this morning,

_____
[4] Within Barwon Prison.

although I was wakened by some poor wretch around 3:00 am, who was shouting and crying, which is rare. I still haven't heard any blasphemy and am not sure whether this is a good sign or not from a religious point of view.

Visits take place on Friday, Saturday, Sunday, and Monday, and I have yet to discover my status so that I can learn of the frequency of the permitted visits. The regulations limit books and magazines to two. I might have to be more focused and disciplined in my reading!

Certainly today is a day of fasting, as I missed lunch and didn't dispatch all my baked beans. None of my food has arrived (I don't know whether it will), and my phone account hasn't been switched here, so I can't phone my brother to spread word of my change of residence. Nor have I contacted my lawyers.

The cool change has arrived, and it was raining an hour ago, but it doesn't seem to have continued.

I introduced myself briefly to my two new companions, who were in the outside exercise area, and chatted with Abdul, who is not a Christian but attended St Leo's School in Altona North. He was certainly friendly.

I gave up the chocolates on Fridays (so that was not a problem), but tonight I won't be able to have my nightcap of chamomile tea, much less wash down the baked beans with Coca-Cola. A bit of useful penance, imposed by circumstance.

Sunday celebrates the Baptism of Our Lord by John the Baptist, which took place thirty years after Jesus' birth, so we are dangerously close to the end of the Christmas season and, therefore, to one of the last opportunities to use a Christmas prayer.

Robert Louis Stevenson, one of the best-known writers in the nineteenth century, the author of *Treasure Island* and *Kidnapped*, emigrated to the South Pacific for health reasons and while there publicly defended St Damien of Molokai against the attacks of a Protestant minister. He also wrote a Christmas prayer.

Loving Father, help us remember the birth of Jesus, that we may share in the song of the angels, the gladness of the shepherds, and the worship of the wise men.

Close the door of hate, and open the door of love all over the world.

Deliver us from evil by the blessing which Christ brings, and teach us to be merry with clear hearts. Amen.

Saturday, 11 January 2020

The Stockholm Syndrome is when a captive adopts the creed of the captors and changes sides. That didn't happen to me in MAP, although I was surprised and encouraged by the general decency and prudence of the warders, after encountering the "enthusiasm" of the East European guard who brought me from court to jail. When the governor thanked me for my cooperating and I remarked on the effectiveness of the warders, he asked me to spread that word outside, and my reply was that I would be pleased to do so.

However, I did become attached to my tiny cell with its almost blocked sink and a floor where in too many places the three layers of paint had been chipped away. But my TV and kettle worked, and the bed was comfortable with the usual reading light. I am pleased that I didn't ask to be moved, despite ten months in solitary, and grateful to the good God that I survived intact, spiritually and psychologically, sustained by so many prayers and good wishes.

Whereas I was given a small mirror (which I had to purchase myself) for the period when I was shaving, I now have two large mirrors in my luxury suite, four times the size of that of MAP. Two doors are clear glass (with bars) rather than one small long window of two layers of opaque glass. Initially at MAP, I found it hard not to be able to see the sun or anything outside or even hear the rain.

Unlike the other prisoners, I will keep my door open to my own exercise area, so that I can step out when I please and get fresh air into the room. I could hear and see the rain falling yesterday evening and hear the birds early this morning.

My first impressions of the outside area were inaccurate as it is a long space, approximately thirty-five metres [thirty-eight yards] by fifteen metres [sixteen yards], with a lawn in the middle, surrounded by a concrete pathway. The lawn is not exactly like the lawns of an Oxford college. A dear friend of mine, an Aussie whose husband was taking out a D.Phil researching the human eye, once asked one of the gardeners at Christ Church how they kept the lawns so perfect. "Quite simple, ma'am," he replied, "just keep cutting and rolling it for three hundred years."

But ours is a real green lawn, and there are eleven boxes where seedlings have been planted and green shoots are emerging. I believe we once had a marijuana plant growing briefly in the back quad-rangle at Aquinas College, Ballarat, now part of Australian Catholic University, unrecognized by naïfs like myself, but I don't think we have any of that medicinal weed in our small boxes here at Barwon.

The food is different from MAP's, but certainly adequate, and we have access to a kitchen, when I am outside my cell in the internal area. While I have no ping-pong table or basketball, all the other equipment I have been using (only three) is available. So after walk-ing for half an hour outside, when it was clear and cold, rather than cool, I took only six minutes on the treadmill. When my program of phone numbers still hadn't been transmitted by early afternoon, I mentioned to the senior warder that it was against regulations to be in a new jail and unable to contact anyone for twenty-four hours. He agreed and put me through to David in his office. They will come down at 12:30 pm on next Monday.

Spoke briefly with the two other prisoners, Derek and Paolo, who gave me some useful practical information and were both cor-dial. Derek has been in jail for nineteen years for the murder of two policemen; he insists that his innocence has now been demonstrated as the police changed the evidence. I wished him well in his appeal hearing in February and insisted with some vehemence that I thought it very wrong for innocent people to be imprisoned.

While I am tempted to bewail my situation, imagine being sen-tenced to twenty-four years in jail, aged twenty, and spending nine-teen years wrongly imprisoned. Peter Kidd was the junior prosecutor in his case, and he is not a fan of the judge.

God the Father, one of our foremost consolations is the knowledge that you are just, that in the afterlife the scales of justice are balanced accu-rately. We know you are a God of love and mercy, that your Son's sufferings and death weigh the balance in our favour, and that you are never unjust, never punish sinners beyond what we deserve.

We ask you, through your Son, to bless those who work for justice in this life and to take particular care of all those who are imprisoned unjustly, especially those wrongly jailed for years and those who do not have the support of family and friend, or enough money and good law-yers as they struggle for justice.

WEEK 47

Solitary No Longer

12 January–18 January 2020

Sunday, 12 January 2020

Without any alarm clock, I woke at 5:40 am, which was perfect timing for the start of *Mass for You at Home* at 6:00 am—a coincidence, certainly a happy coincidence, which I would dub as providential, but requiring nothing beyond what is normal.

Fr Andrew Jekot was the celebrant for the feast of the Baptism of the Lord, the beginning of his evangelical work and, therefore, the first of the Luminous Mysteries of the rosary launched by St John Paul II. This religiously significant beginning bookends and complements Jesus' natural birth in Bethlehem.

The sermon was sound and Scripture-based, where Andrew recounted the deep religious experience he went through when he bathed in the Jordan. The most striking and impressive aspect was that the homily was explicitly God-centred, calling us to reinforce our personal faith. The sermon even claimed that we cannot live without faith.

Joseph Prince started from the story of Elisha to develop his theme, "Overflowing Life and Health". He was dressed in a light grey leather jacket with manifold zips, black shoes, and a couple of rings. As always, the sermon was well prepared with content that stimulated religious reflection. He contrasted the way of the world with God's way. When something bad happens, the world strives to remove the badness. God's way when confronted with badness is to add something, as Elisha added flour to a pot of food that was poisonous and set it aright.

Kiko Arguello[1] is probably the only contemporary preacher I have been tempted to follow closely, although he preaches at extraordinary length. Community meetings of the Neocatechumenal Way, in which I participate regularly, are also conspicuous for their length and not famous for starting on time.

Kiko claims that the main difference between Christians and secularists lies in the response to suffering. Secularists strive often to eliminate the sufferer, e.g., by abortion and euthanasia, or avoid the suffering, e.g., by not visiting loved ones in homes for the elderly or by "quickie", early divorces. The Christian response is to treat the suffering and help the sufferer, to see Christ in those who suffer, by supporting unwed mothers and their children, palliative care, and genuine community for the old and the sick, perseverance for the sake of healing in marriage. This runs parallel with Prince's teaching today, and both explanations are rooted in Jesus' teaching in the Beatitudes.

Joel Osteen returned again to his strength and to his fundamental weakness. When things go badly, according to Joel, God is "doing this" to stretch us to enable further achievement. God wouldn't have "caused it" if he didn't have something better to come. Here we have a couple of problems. God doesn't "do" or "cause" evil; he allows it, respecting human freedom and the laws of nature. And Joel never deals with the fact that the "something better to come" sometimes does not come in this life. Nor does he grapple with the Lord's teaching that riches are not a sign of God's blessing, but a disadvantage, especially for the very rich, while it is the poor who are blessed. When the Jews came to the borders of the Promised Land, the manna stopped falling from heaven and the Jews had to cook their own food. We should not become too comfortable but must be able to say goodbye to old mindsets. As always, Joel's teaching is true as far as it goes.

Songs of Praise came from Fife in Scotland (a 2011 BBC program), featuring the ancient abbey and Gothic church consecrated in 1173 to commemorate Margaret, Queen of Scotland and saint (d. 1093). We saw a number of beautiful medieval churches and ruins, and for some reason I felt a deep sadness for the almost complete elimination of Catholicism in Scotland by the Reformation, before it was revitalized by nineteenth-century Irish migration.

---

[1] Kiko Arguello (b. 1939) is the Spanish cofounder of the Neocatechumenal Way.

One of my great grandmothers was Scottish, Elizabeth Adamson, and I sometimes wonder how, when, and why my Protestant ancestors, such as the Pells, the Berkeleys, the Thompsons, separated from the Catholic Church. When I visited the National Portrait Gallery in London to view the portrait of a distant relative, Sir Watkin Owen Pell, who had been a one-legged admiral in the Napoleonic Wars and later a commissioner at Greenwich Hospital, the curators showed me a drawing of an eighteenth-century Pell woman, who had a Catholic name or names. Her religious allegiance was not certain, and she had not featured in the Nethercote-Pell lists I knew.

The program also spoke of the locally born Andrew Carnegie, who emigrated to the US, went into steel, became richer than Bill Gates, and believed, to my surprise, that "the man who dies rich, thus dies disgraced." By his death, he had given away $319 million, while today the Carnegie Trusts established in a number of countries still distribute on average a quarter of a million dollars a day. I loved the hymns.

The *Herald Sun* today had a front-page reference and an article on page 5 about my transfer to Barwon jail after a drone was seen above MAP on Thursday. I saw nothing when I was in the garden. MAP leaks regularly, as the Abbott visit demonstrated, and I remember the photo of the warder standing side on, rather than square, so the press at the end of the lane could photograph me in handcuffs returning from court.

Kartya and Paul called in unexpectedly to see how I was and learn of my situation. I was able to reassure them with the claim of inmates Derek and Paolo that this high-security accommodation, with semi-isolation, was the best place to be in Victorian prisons. I told them to tell family and friends: "So far, so good, and I do not smell trouble." They had heard of Derek's appeal and thought he had a strong case.

I was grateful for their visit. As early as the seventh century B.C., the prophet Isaiah had taught that those the Lord had called to serve the cause of right should strive

> to open the eyes of the blind,
> to free captives from prison
> and those who live in darkness from the dungeon. (Is 42:7)

Monday, 13 January 2020

The highlight as I settled into my more humane daily routine was a two-hour visit from Margaret, Judy, and Rebecca. I am now permitted two contact visits a month and two box visits a week, each of one hour with a possible extension of one hour.

The time passed quickly as I reassured them and explained the basics of my new life, before we moved on to recap recent family history. Margaret's recall was not perfect, and she will have her hearing tested, as she complained that I was mumbling with my hand over my mouth. She has aged, as we all do at our time of life, but was happy, interested, and alert.

They were interested in the identity of my companions, while Rebecca and Judy know of Derek's case and told me this is the jail where Carl Williams was murdered,[2] something I did not know. David returned to work today after a bad dose of influenza or some debilitating sickness. They, like my other family and friends, had been disconcerted by my sudden transfer and worried that my situation might have worsened. I recounted the verdict of Paolo and Derek that we are in the best accommodation available in a Victorian jail, and this pleased them a lot. My niece Rebecca, a senior high school teacher, summed it up: "They would know."

The weather warmed as the day progressed, with a pall of smoke about in the countryside while they drove down from Bendigo (a two-and-a-half-hour journey), but the dew was still on the grass as I began my walk at 8:30 am; always a beautiful smell in the clear Victorian air, especially when we have a nip of cold. Summer generally comes to stay in Sydney, and the weather is less capricious and changing; but Sydney never has those clear, nippy mornings, least of all in summer, when humidity is never absent, although it is not as regularly oppressive as the weather in Brisbane, without mentioning Cairns and the far north.

Another reassuring detail yesterday was seeing Derek throwing portions from a couple of pieces of bread onto the lawn. Within minutes, a dozen or so sparrows had descended through the wire apertures covering the area. In less than half an hour, the bread was

[2] By a fellow inmate in 2010. Williams was in jail for drug trafficking and several murders.

gone completely. I was encouraged by this humane gesture. While it wasn't on the scale of prisoner X's animal-welfare activities, especially with wounded sparrows, it was an act of simple kindness. And we jailbirds regularly appreciate this.

Part of my baggage arrived from MAP, so tonight I will be able to treat myself with my nightcap of chamomile tea and chocolate. A weekly purchase from the canteen is allowed where the list of goodies is more extensive and daily papers can be bought. However, if I purchased *The Australian* six days a week, two-thirds of my monthly stipend of $140 would be consumed! I intend to buy *The Weekend Australian* and a couple of *Herald Suns*, especially Wednesday's for the weekly television programs. I am probably able to access a wider range of TV channels also.

The regular visitors' room where we met has two white boards, and Margaret was much taken by an inscription from "Lexi" saying he loved his father. A couple of other children had left similar messages, and someone else had written, "Dad is a real ..." The last word was half-erased. It might have been "devil", and I couldn't think of another more benign word with similar letters. It is sad, but good for the dads.

The first reading today was from the Book of Ecclesiasticus on the wisdom which comes from the Lord. Ours is godly wisdom. "There is one who is wise, greatly to be feared, sitting on his throne."

I could never title my life's story "The Getting of Wisdom". But I value wisdom, respect the limited number who are truly wise, and have worked hard over the years not to be foolish too often.

The response to this reading is from the first chapter of Sirach:

> *All wisdom comes from the Lord Our God; ...*
> *It was he who created her through his holy spirit ...*
> *and showed her to those who love him.*

Tuesday, 14 January 2020

Naturally there was no visit from the chaplain Sr Mary O'Shannassy, and I missed Communion, her chat, and Sr Mary McGlone's sermon on the previous Sunday's Gospel. I think the chaplain in this area has just retired, but I look forward to meeting her successor. Mary will soon be having her knee replaced. Please God that goes well.

We prisoners in this Unit 3 make up a quartet. Two are Muslims, and three of us have been educated in Catholic schools. Both the Muslims have already spoken to me about religion. Paolo gave me a copy of "An Explanation of the Last Tenth of the Noble Quran" to read (and I intend to dip into it) and asked me to explain the Trinity, the "only difference" between us, he claimed, as Islam builds on Judaism and Christianity.

I stated that I certainly would not be able to explain this Mystery, as God was spirit, beyond all creation. He had wondered whether we regarded God the Father as being like an earthly father of Jesus, the Son of God. The Holy Spirit was God's presence in the world. So God was one, but like a community of love, I added. I regretted the inadequacy of my explanation, but he seemed pleased enough as the last Christian he asked could not give any explanation at all.

The chat with my other Muslim friend was quite different, because he was upset at the sudden death recently in Lebanon of his young nephew in a sporting accident. His father had died last November, and he was unable to attend the funeral, although his father had visited him in jail a month before his death and the authorities had allowed many meetings through Skype during his father's sickness.

He also enquired about my views on exorcism and whether we had such a rite in the Catholic Church. I explained that there were a few official exorcists in Australia, who would only pronounce the solemn prayers of the rite to drive out the spirit of evil after the subject had been psychologically assessed. In most cases, the disturbance was explained naturally as examples of mental illness. However, I made it clear that I believed in the reality of demonic possession, which, I suspected, was becoming more frequent in Australia. I didn't add that this was a consequence of the decline of Christianity, of evil moving into the vacuum, but did express my view that exorcisms could be violent and exhausting for the exorcists and that this often takes a toll on their health.

My friend's own story was even more unusual, as a village sheik in Lebanon had claimed to exorcise him by attaching a written

Quaranic text on his arm, which he was to wear. After there was no improvement over the months, despite objections, they opened the text to discover it was a curse, which they photographed and then burnt.

My friend was then exorcised in a traditional Sunni exorcism ritual, through prayers and physical beating, which they filmed. He does not remember the event, which was spectacular, as he discovered later through watching the film. All this occurred before he began to use ice for some months.

I am struck by the fact that both Muslims, in different ways, are discussing religion with me. Neither claims to be particularly devout, and both have serious criminal records (whether they are fully deserved is another matter). What does it mean? Are both examples of religious self-confidence, still interested and puzzled on some points? Is there an element of masked doubt?

The first point to recognize is that they have not yet been Australianized into religious reticence, and they still have a religious curiosity and sensitivity so many of the Anglo-Australians have lost or discarded. They are self-consciously ethnics in a contentious religious minority, and they have taken up the Australian ideal of standing up for their rights. Many in Europe claim Australians don't know their place. When something is wrong, Aussies believe they are entitled to complain and are much less inclined to "know their place", shut up, and put up with injustice. At one stage, when I was involved with the Congregation for the Doctrine of the Faith in the Vatican, a disproportionate percentage of the complaints about doctrine and liturgical practice from around the world came from Australia.

St Basil the Great was a fourth-century bishop, born in Cappadocia (modern Turkey), a defender of Christ's divinity against the Arians and author of many of the rules for the daily life of Eastern monks. He wrote: "Now what is more marvellous than the divine beauty? What thought has more charm than the magnificence of God? What yearning of the soul is so keen and intolerable as that which comes from God upon the soul which is cleansed from all evil?"

I suspect that the two Muslims here would have more idea of what Basil is discussing than many good true-blue Aussies, men and women. It is as though they are tuned in on a different frequency, on different wavelengths.

Wednesday, 15 January 2020

Close to fifty years ago, a farmer from southern New South Wales, just over the Murray River and not far from Swan Hill, told me how he loved to sit up at night listening to the heavy rain drumming on the tin roof of the old family homestead after a serious dry spell. He didn't have that experience every year.

One of the advantages of being at Barwon is that I can hear the rain and wind and thunder and see the rain falling in my own exercise pen.

At MAP, all the windows were opaque, and in my narrow cell window, we had two or three layers of opaque glass or plastic. You could not hear the rain and could not see it. Once in a while, after particularly heavy showers, large droplets clung to the windows, but this was rare. I could hear the New Year's Eve fireworks before they came up on the television but could only hear the loudest thunder. Most of the changes in Melbourne's quirky weather were lost on me there.

I heard and saw the change come into Barwon about 3:30 pm today. One of the warders remarked that she loved the smell as rain settled the dust. I don't particularly, but I knew exactly what she was saying. Summer is more interesting in Melbourne than in most other temperate spots on mainland Australia; but it is also more frustrating and sometimes disappointing. Once at Torquay in January, we didn't have one good beach day for nearly three weeks, although in fairness to Torquay that was rare, indeed, unique in my experience.

This morning I was asked by Derek, who has been in this unit for seven of his nineteen years in prison, if I could empty a watering can onto his eleven containers of young plants when I was out at 8:30 am, as it was going to be hot. I waved away as superfluous his enquiry whether the can would be too heavy for my heart; and I again marvelled at what he knew about me. I was delighted to help and hope my assistant's role lasts longer than it did at MAP. And I was to fill the watering can again when I finished.

Paolo knocked on my door this morning and gave me another classy pillow and a fine blanket. ("They don't issue such blankets here", he said.) I was keen about the pillow and unsure whether I needed the blanket, but he insisted. He then left outside my door a bucket of hot water with disinfectant to mop my cell. I suspect that it is a semipagan and English Protestant myth that "cleanliness is close to Godliness", but who am I to condemn such a sensible point of view? It seems that different prisons have different ways to remind you that you are in prison, although so far there has been less of this at Barwon.

When I arrived on Friday, I filled in a form ordering a newspaper three times a week. Budget limitations prevented more. This morning, I pointed out this fact, explained that I had received nothing on Monday and hoped to receive a *Herald Sun* today. As is usual, the warder promised to enquire, and the word came back that my request is being processed and my first paper will come next Monday.

I have to commence my outside time at 8:00 am, rather than the 8:30 I suggested, so I will be missing *Sunrise on Seven*, which I enjoyed a lot.

The treadmill has been fixed, no longer roars and bangs, and, more importantly, does not stop suddenly every now and then. The belt was frayed, so it was replaced, and I completed my seven and a half minutes without any incident.

A couple of days ago, Tim O'Leary mentioned on the phone that emeritus Pope Benedict and Cardinal Sarah had coauthored a book defending priestly celibacy. On the SBS news tonight, it was announced that Pope Benedict was withdrawing his name from his contribution, lest it be seen as opposing Pope Francis. I would begin by noting that I don't know the facts of the situation, but I don't support such interventions by a retired pope, although I anticipate that I would approve of his theologizing as I favour maintaining the discipline of priestly celibacy in the Latin Church.

This strengthens my conviction that the Church should promulgate regulations or conventions about the activities of a retired successor of St Peter. This could only be done by a pope contemplating his own future. The first role of the papacy is to protect and enhance the unity of the universal Catholic Church around the apostolic tradition, which reveals Jesus the Lord.

The Church is disturbed; many good Catholics are disgruntled and dismayed. The stakes are high, because very few know the real agenda of the Spadaros[3] of this world, particularly when they claim that in theology two plus two can equal five. Communion for the divorced and remarried is a distraction, the tip of an iceberg where different factions want different rewrites on sexual morality, and the Pachamama[4] is for some the opening shot in a move to recognizing Christianity as one of the four great rivers that feed the oceans: Hinduism, Buddhism, Islam, and Christianity. We could do with Elijah coming out of retirement to proclaim the one true God of Abraham, Isaac, and Jacob, and his only Son, Jesus Christ, the Alpha and Omega.

Tomorrow's second reading is from St Athanasius, the frequently exiled archbishop of Alexandria in Egypt, one of the most important sees at the beginning of the fourth century, and contains the following beautiful passage:

The all-holy Father of Christ, beyond all created being, as supreme steersman, through his own Wisdom and his own Word, our Lord and Saviour Christ, guides and orders the universe for our salvation, and acts as it seems best to him.... And the universe is good, as it was so created and thus we see it, since this is what he wills; and no one could disbelieve it.

Thursday, 16 January 2020

I am still learning the ropes at my new jail, as after submitting my requests for visitors, I discovered that these must be made by the Wednesday before the week of the visit, because both the visitors' list and the particular individuals need to be approved by the authorities. Therefore, David, Judy, and Sarah have "provisional" approval for Monday.

My mistake, or one mistake, was to assume that the practice at MAP would be the practice here, after I discovered that Fr Victor

---

[3] Jesuit Fr Antonio Spadaro, editor of the prestigious Roman journal *Civiltà Cattolica*, a priest known to be close to Pope Francis.

[4] An idol from the Amazon brought to Rome for the Amazon Synod.

Martinez and Dr Fogarty were not on my list. I had thought they were and had even written up a request for them not to be de-listed after their visit. My first reaction was to surmise that my application to register them had been lost somewhere at MAP. On reflection, it is also possible that I was confused, because while they had been listed, this had been discontinued. Now, forewarned is forearmed, and five days' notice, at least, is needed.

On the property front, all my letters, cards, and books have been passed to me, even the hardcover copies: volume 3 of Margaret Thatcher's biography, the life of Governor Macquarie, and Geoffrey Blainey on his early life. St Thomas More's *The Sadness of Christ* turned up yesterday. Tim O'Leary's bundle of articles also arrived, the same which had been described as not being at MAP.

Aileen, the local Catholic chaplain, called to bring me Holy Communion and for a brief chat. Sr Mary's knee replacement is on the 22nd of this month.

Heavy rain has covered most of the state, except for East Gippsland, and moved into New South Wales. This is good news for the bushfire areas. Cyclonic rain from the northwest has contributed to demonstrating once again that weather predicting is not an exact science for the weeks or months ahead and even more uncertain when we speak of "climate changes", which are constituted by blocks of weather for thirty years.

SBS has been running a series by the English actor Tony Robinson: *Down Under*. I had enjoyed him crossing England on the traditional walking paths and travelling here and there by train. I was sceptical and a tad apprehensive about what he might do with Australia and our history, but it is excellent: sensible, a bit irreverent, and informative for one like myself, who knows something of Australian history.

Last night, Sir Anthony was at Port Arthur, the infamous penal jail in Tasmania. He was talking about the grim practice of solitary confinement as it was practised around the 1840s, a state of the art program following "scientific penal theory", where prisoners were completely isolated from one another, only able to communicate with the hostile warders. The stone cells were bare, with little or no light, and in Tasmania, when prisoners left their cells, they had to wear masks. Their main outing was to Sunday Anglican Chapel, where they were locked into tiered stalls, able to see the parson, but not one another, although here, as elsewhere, they could communicate surreptitiously. Not infrequently, rude faces were made at the celebrant (followed by the requisite punishment). For at least a couple of the first decades in the colony, Catholics, too, had to attend the Protestant services.

When I visited the jail in Cork, Ireland, where most of the Irish convicts were held before they left for Australia, I had learnt that they, too, had followed this barbaric practice of scientific penal theory. I remember seeing the exercise yard where they were forced to walk in complete silence. I wonder how many cracked.

As someone who has survived ten months of solitary confinement with luxuries undreamt of in the old Port Arthur, such as a decent bed, hot water in a shower, a modern toilet (some Victorian jails thirty years ago were still using buckets), a kettle, and a television, I have developed a new interest in the topic and its history.

I thank God I wasn't confined in the old conditions, and I wonder when the major improvements were introduced in Victoria, and in Australia more generally. One prisoner, speaking from years of experience, claimed jail conditions were harsher in New South Wales. Certainly as archbishop of Sydney, it was very difficult to gain entry to a jail to celebrate Mass for prisoners. In Victoria, every jail has at least an annual Mass by a bishop as well as regular priestly Masses.

I will investigate whether any or many improvements were made after the Victorian Council of Churches Report in the late eighties, in which I participated as a panel member. I am not an enthusiast for the People's Republic of Victoria, much less for their systems of law enforcement, but their prison system functions pretty well (in my limited experience). One important criterion for evaluating a society is to assess how it treats its prisoners.

A final digression. Not long after Pol Pot's overthrow, when I was in Cambodia about thirty years ago, I asked a cynical elderly Cambodian judge how well political prisoners were treated in that country. "There are no political prisoners in Cambodia, because political prisoners have rights" was the reply. The same Hun Sen still leads the country today.

Books and articles are also modern blessings in jail today, unlike the situation in Port Arthur, when the vast majority of prisoners were illiterate.

Some of Christ's teachings are hard, tough to follow, e.g., the command to forgive always, the rejection of divorce and remarriage after divorce, the constraints on sexual activity. These demand sacrifice and only pay off for society and individuals in the longer term.

However, I have been pleased for many decades and certainly before my incarceration that at the Last Judgement, at the final separation of the sheep from the goats (a notion which is intolerable for "autonomous" secularists), the criterion for judgement will be whether we recognized Christ in those who were suffering. And even more pleased that all those who have prayed for me in jail, sent me letters and cards and visited me, will be rewarded on the Last Day (Mt 25).

Friday, 17 January 2020

When I went out to the lawn soon after 8:00 am, the air was fresh and clean, with no clouds. A magnificent morning. A covering of light cloud had arrived when I came inside at 10:00 am for an hour in the kitchen area. The timetable was varied because the prison went into lockdown for some hours after 11:00 am. Margaret answered the phone, although I rang earlier than the agreed 11:00 am. She was well, but a bit forgetful.

Heavy rain has arrived in many parts of New South Wales and should continue for days. It is doing a lot of good.

Unfortunately I forgot to phone the Tobins, who leave tomorrow for Europe, although I will try as soon as I have access. A note arrived from Bernadette with about a dozen newspaper articles, all of them interesting and varying from articles on China's island building in the South China Sea to the benefit of controlled burns in the bush and the proposed religious freedom legislation. Kevin Andrews opined that the legislation draft should be okay, but the challenge will be its passage through the senate, where the attitude of the ALP will be crucial.

When I left MAP one week ago today, I was about to put together a few thoughts on St Thomas More's *The Sadness of Christ*, his unfinished meditation on the Passion of the Lord, written when he was in the Tower before his execution in 1535. My property arrived days after I did, and originally the More volume was banned because it had a "hard cover".[5] This difficulty has now been surmounted, and I have more hardcover books than at any time in the last ten months.

As a devout Catholic, More had a lifelong devotion to the Passion, which, not surprisingly, only intensified in the Tower. When Cromwell was quizzing him about his attitude to the new statute nominating Henry as supreme head of the Church, he replied that he was not going "to study or meddle" with any such matter as his "whole study should be upon the Passion of Christ and mine own passage out of this world".

I found the English difficult, with very long sentences that were often convoluted, consoling myself that this was pre-Shakespearean. However, More wrote the text in Latin, which was the common language of the educated then in Christian Europe, and the translation was done much later by his granddaughter Mary Basset.

English then was underdeveloped in comparison with today, and Basset often used a couple of English words to translate a single Latin term. Because of its immense vocabulary, English can now be very precise. On a number of occasions at various Roman synods when I was on the committee preparing the texts for the final message, the English version was always shorter than the Italian, French, and Spanish equivalents. The official Latin version was generally written afterward because so few Synod Fathers now know Latin, although the propositions for voting were in Latin. From the point of view of accessibility and understanding, Latin as the official Church language already presents significant problems.

Italian is the working language of the Vatican Curia, although in the Secretariat for the Economy we were allowed to have English as a second working language. This enabled us to employ young experts from many countries, who served us magnificently. Few economists, except Italians, know and understand Italian.

St Thomas More knew himself well and worked to control his fears, so that when confronting suffering, he was like neither a block nor a madman. He recognized that it was better to flee than overestimate his strength, not because this world was better, but "to avoid the risk of losing heaven".

---

[5] And therefore required a scan to make sure there was nothing concealed in it.

Only one bishop, St John Fisher, joined More in his ultimate stand against a national church, so it was logical, although I was surprised, to read how hard More was on St Peter for falling asleep while Our Lord was in agony in the garden of Gethsemane. This granted, I was better prepared for his comparison of the sleeping apostles with sluggish bishops and not at all surprised by his condemnation of the "lewd examples of naughty priests" and of sacrilege, when "his [the Lord's] blessed body in the holy sacrament is consecrated and handled of beastly, vicious and most abominable priests".

St Thomas More's reputation has again been battered by Hilary Mantel's attacks, the devil's work. He would not be surprised and not much disturbed by this. He believed he died testifying to the truth and did not believe in, much less die for, the primacy of conscience. Consciences often come into conflict. Tolerance is now the preferred solution or option, but tolerance collapses when the concept of truth is destroyed or rejected.

I conclude with another beautiful prayer of the saint.

We pray for pardon for what is already past, grace to go through what we have in hand, and wisdom warily to foresee what is to come.

Saturday, 18 January 2020

No letters or cards arrived today, but fifty to sixty came in yesterday, and I went through them last night. It made me realise once more how consoling they are and how they have been part of my daily routine. I still have a backlog of about a hundred, which had arrived at MAP and then been held up for a time in the property department at Barwon.

It is warmer today, although each day when I am let out into the lawn area at 8:00 am, Daylight Saving Time or Eastern Summer Time, the morning freshness is always there, and so, sometimes, is the dew. Heavy rains continue in many parts of New South Wales and Queensland, often the best rain for ten years, with some local flooding.

I was rather pleased to see David Attenborough on television telling the world that South East Australia is on fire, when in fact it was raining heavily through all the mainland Eastern states. SBS carried a report that the German government has announced that it will eliminate all nuclear and coal-powered electric generators by 2038, not quite far enough away for them to do absolutely nothing now. A spectacularly expensive and silly decision, typical of a people that has lost its way. Britain has done well to leave them, although we cannot be sure they won't make the same mistakes, as they certainly would under any Corbynite government.

The letters arrive from many countries and most parts of Australia with different messages of encouragement. Of the 3,500 letters I have received, only half a dozen were critical. I don't know whether more hostile letters were censored, although the authorities are supposed to inform me of any mail they prevent from arriving. However, different staff had different interpretations, and long delays sometimes occurred. Two large collections of articles have emerged since my arrival here.

One regular correspondent is genuinely concerned for my well-being and assured me that God would be annoyed by what is going on. I am sure the good God knows I am not guilty of those accusations and that he expects me to respond as a Christian; but beyond that point is beyond my knowing.

An eighty-year-old great grandfather wrote to me from St Marys in Kansas, US, to boast of the strength of his parish,[6] where they are building a new church to accommodate the number of worshippers. All his eight surviving children and their families are Mass-goers, together with his 550 employees. But he concedes they are "an oasis in the desert" and laments the decline since Vatican II, especially in the number of priests and religious.

He himself, who had spent seven and a half months in jail for pro-life activities in 1981, promised me his continuing prayers and thought the Church would do much better if she returned to the Tridentine rite.

A mother from Mt Gambier in South Australia gave birth to a beautiful baby girl on Christmas Day and offered up her "painful labour" for me and the Holy Souls.

An acquaintance of Franciscan University of Steubenville whom I had come to know through the School of the Annunciation catechetical

---

[6] This parish is run by the Society of St Pius X and is further described on pp 134ff.

project in Devon, UK, told me that his daughter had given birth to Miriam Guadalupe Rose on last September 10th and that I was one of the people she prayed for during the birth.

Many writers refer to the difficulties the Church is experiencing. A woman from Arkansas believes "the Lord is pruning His Church." She went on: "Pruning is painful, but results can be fantastic."

John Burke (an uncle of mine had that name) believes the Church follows a five-hundred-year cycle. He wrote, "The Church has the sources of life and renewal within it. If used, we can begin the next 500-year cycle. If not, then governments and outsiders will painfully do what we ought to have done. But God's will will prevail."

A Dominican nun from Linden in Virginia turned my thoughts in a new direction. She pointed out that I had enjoyed "good fortune to meet and work with saints. Therefore I trust your memories of them and all the holy writings you have read will also help to sustain you in your sufferings."

I have drawn heavily on Cardinal Thuan;[7] St John Paul the Great is one of my heroes, and while I regret never meeting Mother Teresa (and I tried, although I saw her a number of times), her biography is with Kartya to be delivered to me.

I will conclude with a few commonsense reflections from Ronald Reagan, who was an outstanding orator. His speech at the Brandenburg Gate in Berlin, before the Wall came down, is a masterpiece. There, and in this small excerpt, I suspect the hand of Peggy Noonan, Reagan's best speechwriter, whom I met at one of the series of splendid dinners hosted by Vatican Ambassador John McCarthy in Rome.

We can't expect to have it both ways. We can't expect God to protect us in a crisis and just leave Him over there on the shelf in our day-to-day living. I wonder if sometimes He isn't waiting for us to wake up, He isn't maybe running out of patience.

---

[7] Francis Cardinal Nguyen Van Thuan (1928–2002) was bishop of Nha Trang in South Vietnam (1967–1975) and was appointed co-adjutor archbishop of Saigon in 1975. He was jailed by the Communist government of Vietnam in 1975, spending nine years in solitary confinement before his release in 1988. He was allowed to leave Vietnam for Rome in 1991 and was appointed president of the Pontifical Council for Justice and Peace in 1998.

WEEK 48

Our Unusual Situation

19 January–25 January 2020

Sunday, 19 January 2020

Once again I managed to wake up about ten minutes before the 6:00 am *Mass for You at Home,* again celebrated by Fr Andrew Jekot. I know that habits of sleeping and waking develop with time, so that early risers regularly wake in time. My father was an early riser, but my mother and all her Burke sisters never rose early unless they had to do so. In this respect, I am like my mother, although I was always able to rise early when necessary, and over the years morning Mass before breakfast has brought me closer to the Pell pattern. I am also blessed by the fact that I can sleep well on most nights, even in times of turmoil (like my father), whereas Mum claimed she would often worry rather than sleep. However, I don't know whether you can develop a habit of waking once a week at 5:45 am rather than your regular rising time of 7:00 or 7:15.

Fr Andrew preached simply and briefly on the theme that Jesus is the Lamb of God who takes away the sins of the world. The Exodus, facilitated by the sacrificial blood on the doorposts, was given as a precedent. He cited the prohibition of alcohol in the US in the 1920–1930s and the Communist movement as two unsuccessful alternative attempts to take away our sins. I am not sure either example was useful; sin runs much farther than the drunkards, while Communism was a scourge, bringing death and imprisonment to millions. All those of us who acknowledge the Spirit are chosen, which brings responsibilities, not rewards, Andrew concluded. All the preachers followed the Lamb of God theme.

Joseph Prince, who was wearing a dark suit with blue stripes and blue and white sandshoes, explained that the Old Testament lamb was like a credit card, which only paid out the requisite amount when it had access to the amount earned through Jesus' death and suffering. According to the Law, a person touching a leper became unclean, but Jesus laid hands on the leper and cured him.

For Joseph, Christianity can never become a religion (whatever that means for him and his immense congregation); it is a relationship. In life, when we do the crime, we do the time; but Jesus intervenes to take our place.

Joel Osteen preached on the Samaritan woman for whom Jesus was waiting, as he is waiting for us in our difficulties and as the father was waiting for the return of his younger prodigal son. We should not rebuke or condemn, but wait for Jesus to come, as he did when he called Zacchaeus. Although we sometimes cannot see it, God is still acting. Then Joel promised something to his congregation which he cannot always deliver: that they would see all their loved ones come to the Lord.

Songs of Praise was a 2011 program on St Andrew's, the birthplace of golf and home to the third oldest university in Britain, after Oxford and Cambridge, which celebrated its sixth centenary in 2011. We saw the ruins of the ancient cathedral which used to be home for the relics of St Andrew, and a fine selection of hymns were sung by an excellent university choir and a packed congregation. I am intrigued by the number of programs from distant times.

One of the pleasant surprises at Barwon was to find quite a few good books in our small Unit 3 library. In a few days, I moved through a first-rate politics murder story, *The Aachen Memorandum* by Andrew Roberts, one of Britain's best public intellectuals. About fifteen years ago in Sydney, I attended a small dinner and discussion evening where he was the speaker. His theme was that China was the main game and the emerging challenge, rather than the forces of Islam, which would never be able to bring down the Western world. This provoked a stimulating discussion with little dissent from his basic proposition. One participant thought that war between China and the US was inevitable. The only touch of acrimony came from a brief skirmish over republicanism in Australia. I cannot remember how we arrived at that topic!

In the novel, the United States of Europe rules as a police state through comprehensive surveillance and state violence (similar to what is now being introduced in mainland China). Britain has been broken up, ruled regionally from Cardiff and Edinburgh; London has been downgraded, the Mountbatten-Windsors are gone, although the heir survives as King of New Zealand. The hero is an unfit, asthmatic Fellow of All Souls at Oxford, Dr Horatio Lestocq, who succeeds in having the visiting King announce to the world that the British vote approving their entry into the European State has been rigged. There had been no majority approval. Wave after wave of violence envelops the narrative, where loyalty often pays a price and many of the characters are not what they seem. It is a marvellous escapist read, almost plausible, much faster moving than Le Carré, with a dash of James Bond.

It was published in 1995 and makes fascinating reading now so soon after Boris Johnson's electoral victory ensuring Britain's exit from the European Union. The novel is entertainment, but has a high political purpose. It wasn't only [Nigel] Farage who worked for decades so that Britain could decide its own future.

I was intrigued to find that the London Catholic church of the Oratorian priests in Brompton Road, down from Harrods, was one locale in the narrative. It, too, was a victim or example of the new order, where "Jesus the Significant One, who sits at the mighty hand of God, the Father-Mother", was invoked by the priest following a Vatican Three liturgy.

As the story moves toward its chaotic but victorious climax, our hero prays in the Oratory church a prayer similar to that of Sir Jacob Astley before the Battle of Edgehill[1] (both references outside my ken).

O Lord, thou knowest how busy I must be this day; if I forget thee, do not thou forget me.

I certainly wouldn't and couldn't use this prayer now, but once or twice in my busy life, such a prayer would have been helpful.

---

[1] Jacob Astley (1579–1652) was a Royalist commander in the English Civil War, the first battle of which was fought at Edgehill, near Kineton, South Warwickshire, on 23 October 1642.

Monday, 20 January 2020

The extreme weather conditions continued with a heavy storm development from the Yarra Valley, with high winds, heavy rain, and damaging hailstones. Forbes and Parkes in New South Wales were enveloped in fast-moving eerie clouds of dust, while Parliament House in Canberra, with its lawns, were white, covered by ice. Some areas in Western New South Wales have missed out, but many regions continue to receive good rain. Here at Barwon, it was cool to cold and overcast when I was outside for breakfast, and it is raining now around 7:30 pm as I am writing. The other three prisoners in my section are having their usual shouted dialogue from their cells. They continue to be very cordial. Paolo is interested in religion, enquiring why I became a priest, how long I had been a priest, and what was my work in the Vatican. He is the most vocal of the group and enjoys stirring up the other two in the evenings, he explained, but in a good-natured way.

Monday is the pie or pasty lunch day, with a sausage roll, not Saturday as at MAP. I keep my lunch, distributed at 11:15 am, until I come out to the common area at midday, where I can use the microwave and can access my Coca-Cola and chocolate from my section of the refrigerator. The food is better than at MAP, although we have no tinned fruit, jelly, and cream! One cannot have everything.

I had packed up carefully two large brown paper bags with cards and letters, probably more than three hundred, and passed them out to "Property" for collection by Kartya. She has yet to be "approved" as a visitor.

David, who had largely recovered from a debilitating virus which put him into bed for some days, came down with Judy, and Sarah came from East Oakleigh, where she lives and takes care of Margaret's place. We both enjoyed the extra time, about two hours, which is a vast improvement on MAP's half an hour for a box visit for all visitors, even if they had come from interstate.

In the previous Saturday's journal, I quoted from the letter of an octogenarian correspondent from St Marys in Kansas boasting about his parish, which he conceded was "an oasis in the desert". By a coincidence, Tim O'Leary sent me an excerpt from the January/February issue of *The Atlantic* magazine, which is devoted to St Marys, a largely

St Pius X enclave![2] My correspondent certainly regarded himself as Catholic, but his relationship with the Church or the breakaway group was left unspecified.

I was aware that some letters of support came from members of the St Pius X community and was pleasantly surprised by this. I lament the break and have been in contact over the years with their clergy and a couple of their bishops. Pope Francis is, or was, said to be open to reunion, but expert opinion wondered whether their leadership would be able to bring back all their flock into communion. In St Marys, Kansas, they anticipated Rod Dreher's *The Benedict Option*, seeking support together in a community separated in different ways from the mainstream culture in the US. I will return to them when I finish the *Atlantic* articles. It has to be conceded that developments in the Church in the last few years, especially around the Synods for the Family, would not be encouraging them to return.

Neither are the Vatican financial scandals helping. One of my most regular and interesting correspondents from Dallas, Texas, told me that she and her husband have decided to make no further monetary donations to their local church or the Vatican because of the unaddressed scandals. I was a bit surprised when my brother exclaimed that this was "fair enough" when I told him the story.

A recent article on the Vatican finances by J.D. Flynn, posted on the Catholic News Agency on 16 December 2019,[3] is probably the best I have read, among many good and informative English-language pieces, for its understanding of what has been happening, its accuracy, and its value judgements. It is still somewhat understated.

Another well-wisher for Christmas from the United States, a housewife who had converted to Catholicism from irreligion at college, was fascinated by the fact that in my debate with Richard Dawkins about God, most of the audience questions were directed to me. She belongs to a group of thirteen women who are praying for me, and she sent a quotation from "our very old priest".

---

[2] Emma Green, "The Christian Withdrawal Experiment", *Atlantic*, January/February 2020, https://www.theatlantic.com/magazine/archive/2020/01/retreat-christian-soldiers/603043/.

[3] J.D. Flynn, "Analysis: The Vatican's Finance Scandal, and Faithful Stewardship", Catholic News Agency, 16 December 2019, https://www.catholicnewsagency.com/news/43103/analysis-the-vaticans-finance-scandal-and-faithful-stewardship.

He said, "I am not anxious about all the corruption in the Church. I am anxious to see how Christ is going to work and save his Church despite all the corruption."

She commented, "What hopeful words!"

Tuesday, 21 January 2020

Sometimes, but not too often, young Catholics at university or in a seminary have longed to have been born and lived as Catholics before the Second Vatican Council. I appreciate, better than many, the strength and fidelity in Irish-Catholic Australia (and, indeed, throughout the English-speaking world), but I regularly explained to today's youngsters they would have been in a different world before the council, where so much we now take for granted did not exist. They would have loved the high rates of religious practice; community solidarity; a multiplicity of priests, Sisters, and Brothers to love, revere, and sometimes criticize; Benediction and the dialogue Tridentine Mass (perhaps); etc., etc. But ...

While it is one thing to attend a beautiful Tridentine Mass, especially when it is sung and celebrated correctly and with reverence, we enter a different world when every Mass (and in small suburban and country parishes) and all the sacraments were celebrated in Latin, when there were no parish councils or school boards, when ecumenical cooperation was discouraged when not forbidden, when there was no interfaith dialogue, when teachings on sexuality were regularly Puritan or Jansenist (before the sexual revolution of the sixties), and when unwed mothers were encouraged to give up their babies, not even allowed to see them, much less hold them. It is difficult to compare apples and oranges, but they are different. And I am not for a moment denying what we have lost, how much weaker we are.

My generation has lived through a period of exceptional religious change in the Western world and a collapse of faith, practice, and devotion without any parallel in history, except perhaps in France after the 1789 Revolution. The Communist assault on Christianity in Russia and Eastern Europe is also different, sometimes disastrous, but nowhere complete, and sometimes, as in Poland, they were ultimately defeated. Post-Reformation Europe was also different because the Protestants were fiercely Christian, not unbelievers.

I once urged the English Catholic writer Piers Paul Read to produce a novel that might illuminate our unusual situation (which he had already done to some extent in *Monk Dawson*), but he was not attracted to the idea. The Catholic Church in Australia before the invention of the contraceptive pill and the Second Vatican Council was already a different world from ours. It was a period of change across the decades, with mighty forces at work, the failure of transmission across the generations, the departure of thousands of priests and religious which provides rich pickings for those writers capable of collecting and sorting the fruit.

All this was prompted by my reading of Emma Green's *Atlantic* article entitled "The Christian Withdrawal Experiment" for the online edition[4] and "Retreat, Christian Soldiers" in the print version.

The article is fair-minded and not a hatchet job, which recounts the story of an increasing number of good families who have moved to the town of St Marys[5] in Kansas, close to the centre of the US, during the last forty years. Most belong to the Society of St Pius X, which formally broke from the Church under Archbishop Lefebvre,[6] although the canonical situation of their lay members is opaque as far as continuing membership in the Catholic Church is concerned. I remember receiving a delegation from them about twenty-five or thirty years ago who were very keen to hear that they were not excommunicated.

Their numbers in the town have doubled and continue to grow, as most of the children continue to practice the faith as adults. They do represent a type of "cultural secession", where they build strong, mutually supportive communities, follow a classical educational curriculum in single-sex schools, and compete locally in baseball and basketball competitions. Their lifestyle and dress are conservative, not antiquarian.

The "townies", those who were in the town before the arrival of the St Pius X Catholics, no longer feel as welcome as they once did.

---

[4] Green, "The Christian Withdrawal Experiment".

[5] The name of the town does not have an apostrophe.

[6] French archbishop Marcel Lefebvre founded the Society of Saint Pius X in 1970. When he consecrated four bishops in 1988, in defiance of Pope John Paul II, the Holy See declared that he and the other bishops who had participated in the ceremony had excommunicated themselves.

The newcomers have all the voted places on the city commission. Traditional Catholic penitential discipline is administered strictly, and the occasional child who is intellectually rebellious or kicks over the traces doesn't find it easy to leave or even to return.

The author mentioned isolated examples of anti-Semitism elsewhere in Europe but provided no evidence of this in St Marys.

Big families are common; mothers don't have paid work outside the home and regularly support one another in a thousand practical ways. Their vibrant community life, Communion and baptism celebrations, their lived Christianity are sometimes envied by the "townies", the outsiders.

The author feels that melting-pot America, the "e pluribus unum"[7] democracy, is weakened by withdrawals like St Marys, by their insularity. They oppose marriage outside their communities. She also wonders about the consequences for the Catholic Church, not simply in a theological or canonical sense, because of the formal separation, but because she sees St Marys "more like a haven for those retreating from the culture wars than a training ground for battle". So the Crusaders are not an indication, but a somewhat misleading mascot for their school (in her view).

I have come to realise that a strong community of believers is the best context for living and handing on the faith. Families can't go it alone. This community can be found in a variety of ways, certainly in strong parishes. My own preference is for a strong community life lived in the usual suburbs or rural towns in the style of the Neocatechumenal Way, one of the best fruits of the Second Vatican Council. They, too, want to fight but not through flight.

Formal schism, canonical separation, is always a big mistake and one that is damaging. Every effort should be made to heal this.

But I have to concede that building a community of believers such as St. Marys is what St Benedict proposed for his monks 1,500 years ago, and over the decades and centuries they preserved faith and civilisation, converted Western Europe, and founded Christendom. The Benedictine houses not only welcomed pilgrims but became powerful centres of learning, social welfare, and health care. When Henry VIII dissolved the monasteries in sixteenth-century England,

[7] "Out of many, one."

he destroyed the only social welfare agencies, with disastrous consequences for the poor, including many deaths. I don't know how much the Pius X communities reach out beyond their own.

If the Vatican Secretariat of State can reach a secret accord with Communist China (admittedly with no visible beneficial consequences), then reunification with the Society of St Pius X must remain a possibility.

In the meantime, we can all follow St Benedict's maxim: "Ora et labora" (Pray and work).

Wednesday, 22 January 2020

Today began differently. The warders liberated me into the garden area around 9:00 am, one hour after the usual time, providing no explanation when I cheerfully asked whether they were on strike. The delay suited me, giving time to take my breakfast of Weetabix and toast in my cell. Outside, the sky was overcast, heavy winds were blowing, while the atmosphere was warm and slightly humid. Not the usual fresh morning, even though I was an hour behind schedule, and not pleasant.

Sr Mary is due to have her knee replacement today, so I hope and pray that all goes well. I will miss her weekly visits.

She sent me a copy of a sermon for last Sunday's Gospel, where Jesus was defined by John the Baptist as "the Lamb of God who takes away the sins of the world". The anonymous sermon writer set out to explain what John the Baptist meant and in a comprehensively laid out and well-prepared homily mentioned most elements of the answer except that Jesus was able to forgive us when we repent, the most basic explanation for "taking away our sins".

Today we are often encouraged by silence to ignore the fact that we must repent. If we define sins out of existence or omit to be "sorry" or say "sorry", then the good God's activity is constrained. In some cases, only God can forgive, because, e.g., the victim is dead (in a murder) or the victim refuses to forgive.

Crispus, the son of the first Christian Roman emperor Constantine, died in mysterious circumstances, and Constantine was suspected of ordering his execution. His pagan adversaries spread the word that Constantine became a Christian because a pagan could not be forgiven for killing his son. If Christianity continues to decline as an influence on minds and hearts, the society of the future will become less and less merciful, less forgiving on many fronts. This is already obvious in the attributes of the "woke" generation, in identity politics.

The flood of letters has slowed, with twenty to twenty-five arriving on each of the last two days, and none were delivered today. Most are from the United States, cards without too much theology or reflection on the Church and society.

One exception has been in the "to do" file for weeks, coming from my regular correspondent from Dallas, Texas, who is in her sixties and still runs marathons. She worries about the traditional problems and includes a piece she wrote in February 2016, when Obama was still in power and Hillary Clinton's election seemed inevitable.

She began with Francis Cardinal George's grim prediction about the fate of his successors and then: "Something made me leap: an end to the acedia, that hypnotic inertia that keeps the world quiet and docile in the face of the most egregious injustices."

She cited the magnificent prayer book which tells of the martyrdoms performed across the ages by a ruling class or party, not by "underground thugs out of sight". She is not convinced that our society has sunk so low that such activities are presently conceivable, much less feasible. Everyone would agree with her on that point; the concerns are for the future.

Practical conclusions should follow from the present situation, conclusions to be drawn by the Catholic quarter of the population, which constitutes part of the declining, but still majority, Christian group.

My feisty friend wrote, "Have we sunk so low? Some days, I fear we have. But I am more and more convinced that now is the time to kick up the fight, not accede to it." She quotes Steve Ray,[8] whom I don't know: "If enough of us swim hard enough against the tide, we can change the direction."

---

[8] Steve Ray is a convert to the Catholic Church, a contributor to Catholic Answers, and the author of three books published by Ignatius Press: *Crossing the Tiber, Upon This Rock,* and *St. John's Gospel.*

I'm not sure we can, but I am sure we must try, as citizens who still enjoy the right to free speech and public action, who have the right to vote in a society where legislation is decided by elected representatives. I am also quite clear that if our religious freedoms were to be lost or seriously curtailed, this would demonstrate not only a deep spiritual malaise, a loss of faith, but also a political ineptitude of epic proportions for the Christian community, without mentioning our Jewish and, indeed, Muslim allies.

My friend's views about the necessity of struggle have not weakened over the last four years. She wrote recently, "In prayer, I trust God to lead me and let me know how I may fight for goodness, in myself and my family and friends or in a more public way." She believes "one of our best offensive games is the Theology of the Body.[9] The essence of TOB is joy, truth, love, happiness, communion, and fruitfulness. It's all the good stuff. The Devil in the Big City has none of these things."

She claims, "One generation can change a culture." I suppose the sixties are an example of this. More strength to her arm.

I conclude with her words from 2016. "If an age of martyrdom comes, then I pray the Church will be ready, but with Aragorn, I believe it is not yet time."

A day may come ... when the age of man comes crashing down, but it is not this day! ... This day we fight! By all that you hold dear on this good earth, I bid you stand, Men of the West![10]

Thursday, 23 January 2020

A few news items today. When I went to bed, the rain was falling, and I was delighted that I could hear it and see it. In previous times, I might have fretted about the broken drainpipe and the consequent noisy waterfall. But not after being insulated for ten months against such sights and sounds.

---

[9] Developed by Pope John Paul II in a series of 129 talks given over the years 1979–1984.
[10] From *The Return of the King*, the third and final volume of J. R. R. Tolkien's novel *Lord of the Rings*.

It was raining when I was wakened at 7:15 am, and the warder said the rain had continued all night so that we received thirty milli-metres, well over an inch of rain. Aileen, the chaplain who visited today, stated that already we have received twice the average January rainfall. She also reported that Sr Mary's operation had been successful.

A couple of the garden's pots must be poorly drained as the plants were swimming in an inch of water. I exercised my initiative and emptied them and was commended by Derek. It was so windy yesterday that the bread he threw onto the lawn was still there this morning, but around lunchtime the birds arrived finally and consumed all of it.

Chattered through the glass with Paolo and Derek. We agreed the warders were decent and reasonable, and Paolo claimed the difficult few, those who were depressed, were atheists. Derek agreed strongly. I found this pleasantly surprising, but (I reflected) Christ's message is offered first of all to the poor in spirit, to the battlers, not the sophisticates.

On another side of the ledger, Aileen recounted how impressed one prisoner had been by the booklet of simple Gospel teachings and stories prepared by the Geelong Baptists, which she had given him. He thought it was written for him, while insisting he couldn't forgive "the way you people do". He didn't agree on that point.

About fifty letters were given to me today, and my visitor lists were approved. Therefore Daniel Hill, with his parents, Sue and Peter, will visit tomorrow.

I saw something of the other parts of the jail when I walked over to the infirmary for my monthly cardiograph. A couple of other nurses had to be called to encourage the machine to work, but work it did eventually.

Fr George Rutler, the well-known New York convert, writer, and parish priest, has written a book on coincidences, and even he is not certain that it was Einstein who explained that coincidences are God's way of remaining anonymous.

In the light of my reflections yesterday on anti-Christian pressures, changing social mores and the decline of faith, it was a happy coincidence to have a news report in Melbourne's *Herald Sun* and a sermon from St Augustine, both from yesterday, throwing different lights on our situation.

It is a commonplace opinion, at least among my fellow "oldies", that we are pleased that we are not growing up today. Hostile pressures are so much stronger, which goes a long way to explaining why the best of the youth are better than ever (and often when they are young) and more of them are casualties, not just religiously, but in a human sense, as the *Herald Sun* piece reports.

Teenagers are experiencing a sex recession, the page 4 article recounted, with teenagers getting 50 percent less action than their parents. "Sexologists" reported that pornography and video games are being used as substitutes for human contact. Even the condom business has been damaged, so they are urging parents to talk to their children about how to have good sex, presumably to redirect or resurrect their children's promiscuity. Online pornography has changed the landscape, and not just with young adults. Marriages are being wrecked by pornography addiction.

The article made the astonishing claim that 40 percent of young adults aged eighteen to twenty-four have never had sex, not because they are Christians waiting to give to one another in marriage, but because they are unable.

Christians in the future will be distinguished from many of their rich, secular counterparts by the fact that they will produce their own children by an act of parental lovemaking. We can easily forget that people, especially young people, without religious knowledge or principles are more vulnerable to damage than their religious peers, especially those from loving families, to damage from pornography, alcohol, drugs, violence, loneliness.

If the *Herald Sun* article and its "Australia Talks" survey are correct, and those trends are not reversed, then Christians of the future could also be distinguished from many others by the fact that they are able to enjoy the physical pleasures of lovemaking (between spouses in a relationship which at least aspires to permanence and exclusivity).

For all these reasons, the enthusiasm of my Dallas letter writer for the Theology of the Body is wise and, let us pray, prophetic.

St Augustine famously prayed to God to make him pure, "but not yet". He would certainly understand our times, and young people of today certainly understand his story, his struggle to liberate himself.

In Sermon 276 from yesterday's readings for the feast of the Spanish deacon and martyr St Vincent, who died around A.D. 300 under

Emperor Diocletian, Augustine reminds us of the necessity of relying on God's power and not striving to go alone and unaided. For Augustine, the attacks of the world need not subdue us as Christ comes to our rescue. He explains:

The world has a double attacking strategy against the soldiers of Christ: it flatters to deceive—and it frightens to intimidate. Let our own pleasures not capture us, let the cruelty of others not frighten us, and then the world has been conquered.

Friday, 24 January 2020

The Hills arrived early, so we spent more than two hours in lively discussion, where I caught up with their family news and we covered the Church scene in Sydney and more widely. Sue and Peter were in court for both days of the appeal and were amazed by the result. So, too, were my opponents, who were planning to appeal to the High Court. Sue spoke with the unusual man with the placard condemning me to hell and said, "What if he is innocent?" They are great people, loyal friends, and supporters who flew down from Sydney, after driving from Culburra.

Another cool, fresh day; indeed, I came in at 10:30 rather than staying out until midday as I was cold.

I learnt that I had been accepted to do the computer course and placed on the waiting list. They couldn't inform me when I would graduate into the course.

Another twenty letters arrived today, from various places and usually on very different themes. A priest from the cathedral in Kingston, Ontario, in Canada, commended my book on Luke's Gospel as offering "much food for thought", while an elderly lady from North Balwyn was kind enough to describe *Be Not Afraid* as "my best spiritual book and I have many!" This is consoling.

A meditation group from Kostelany nad Moravou in the Czech Republic assured me that "all things work together for good to them that love God" (Rom 8:28). A woman from Michigan (US) wrote that God has a plan for each of us. Her husband has struggled with Parkinson's disease for almost twenty years, and she has been comforted by knowing that "offering up [her] sufferings and trials can help save souls and make expiation for sin."

Much closer to home in New South Wales, a prolife activist from Emu Plains thanked me for my part in bringing University of Notre Dame to Sydney, where she occasionally goes for lunch after praying publicly nearby against abortion. During these prayer sessions, she wrote, "I experienced the vicious scorn, derision, contempt, and hatred directed to us just because we were witnessing to the truth. And that is why I understand somewhat the hatred shown to you."

A priest from the Archdiocese of Detroit (US) sent a couple of excerpts from his books, listing the false accusations for many different offences made against saints and Church leaders over the centuries. These came as no surprise, because I knew also of the accusations that have been made against good priests and then dropped because they were false. This is only one smaller part of the picture, but it is real and painful, as Billy Doe in Philadelphia and Carl Beech in the UK have demonstrated.[11]

A married couple from Oregon in the US wrote that "when you are exonerated, it will be the sign for us the Church is returning and will be renewed." This Church dimension is more important than my personal story, because my exoneration will lift the spirits of loyal Catholics and those who are zealous for the good reputation of the law in Australia. This is one black mark the Church does not deserve. How much this will contribute to renewal is a further question. (And exoneration is yet to happen.)

But even on this last point on renewal, we are not without Christian hope, which is not coterminous with human optimism.

I will conclude with a quotation from Fr Kentenich, founder of the Schoenstatt Sisters of Mary,[12] sent by one of his Sisters in New York.

---

[11] Daniel Gallagher of Philadelphia in 2011 accused several priests and teachers, some of whom were jailed. Englishman Carl Beech in 2014 accused a number of prominent people, many of whom had their reputations destroyed. Their extreme and lurid allegations received wide publicity for years; both men eventually admitted to lying and fabrication.

[12] Fr Joseph Kentenich founded the Schoenstatt Movement, for the moral and spiritual renewal of Germany and beyond, in 1914. From this grew the Schoenstatt Sisters of Mary, the first of which arrived in the US in 1949.

If God wants to use a soul in his special service, he must first make it useless in the eyes of man.

I meet this criterion.

Saturday, 25 January 2020

Today is the feast of the conversion of St Paul, one of the saints I most admire for his gospel zeal, enthusiasm, and perseverance, and his intellectual contribution in spelling out theologically how Jesus is the culmination, the high point of the history of God's Chosen People, and spelling it out in a way that laid the foundation for its explanation in terms of Western thought, more Greek than Roman. I remember the then Cardinal Ratzinger pointing out how providential this marriage of Jewish revelation and Western thought was, and how well-suited these traditions of Plato and the Stoics, and later of Aristotle, were for Christian purposes.

Not only is Christian revelation essentially rooted in the Jewish, or Old Testament, Scriptures, but Greek philosophy has a unique place in our tradition and Magisterium that could never be replaced by the thought of Confucius or Buddha or Marxism, or any other "ism".

For Ratzinger, inculturation means the injection of Christian teaching into these other traditions, into, i.e., their principal trunk so that new fruit can be produced in addition to the old fruits. Inculturation does not mean wholesale rejection of areas of Christian teaching, to be substituted from a different tradition. The interplay between Christianity and Asian philosophy and religions is only in its early stages, but it is never without dangers. In India, one might see the persecution of Christians, severely unprotected under the Modi government,[13] as a useful antidote to the Hindu agnosticism, the relativizing of Jesus and his message, which is such a temptation among some Indian Jesuit thinkers. But it is an interplay, a dialogue which must and will continue as the centre of the world shifts from the Atlantic to the Pacific Ocean.

---

[13] Narendra Modi became prime minister of India in 2014. He is a member of the pro-Hindu Bharatiya Janata Party.

Paul was not always my hero, as I remember ignorantly and pompously pronouncing in year eleven or twelve at secondary school that Paul boasted too much about himself. Certainly he wasn't an old-fashioned, buttoned-up Anglo.

Roland Rocchiccioli was a well-known radio announcer in Melbourne when I was archbishop there, and he asked me to draw up a dinner party list of twelve characters from history. St Paul was close to my first choice (I didn't include any of the Holy Family). St Mary MacKillop, St Catherine of Siena, and Maggie Thatcher were three of my six women, although I am not sure St Paul would have been interested in sitting down to dinner with such a disparate group, not all of them religious, including Winston Churchill. It would have been a great evening, provided it didn't get out of control. I don't think I invited Mary Magdalene. And Paul might have thought it was too frivolous.

A mild and pleasant morning, with no breeze and light cloud cover for my half-hour walk during two and a half hours outside. A brief news report in yesterday's *Herald Sun* announced that the drone above MAP had not been searching for me, but that I would be remaining at Barwon. The drone could not have made a better contribution to my welfare, short of freedom. My companions tell me Unit 3 is the best spot in Victoria's prisons and that the prisons in this state are better, more humane, than in any other Australian state.

I managed to get through on the phone to Margaret, who told me she is worried about David's health. I am, too, as the doctor can't identify the virus and he has been given sick leave until February 14th.

A couple of days ago, Ruth's letter informed me of the death of Sir Roger Scruton, Britain's leading public intellectual, a champion of the best traditions in our culture and of Christian values. The news came as a surprise and a shock, as I did not know he was ill with cancer and I thought of him as considerably younger than I. Ruth thinks I was wrong on that point and that he was only a few years younger. He was a genuine polymath who wrote fifty books, the Andrew Bolt equivalent among English-speaking philosophers.

I admired his contribution, read a deal of his work, but followed him from a distance. A friend gave me his book on wine, but most of it was lost on me. Neither did I like his music, his opera, which I attended, as I am very attached to melody. No one would have mistaken his composition for Puccini's. I was once on a panel with him during one of Prof Claudio Véliz's *conversazioni* in Oxford,[14] where he publicly insisted that those in favour of late-term abortion or infanticide should be forced to look into the eyes of the baby before its execution. He did fine and courageous work for intellectual freedom before the fall of the Iron Curtain in the then Czechoslovakia by organizing an underground network of dissidents.

I felt that, with his views, Scruton belonged in the Catholic Church, but he settled for Anglicanism. He was too English to cross the Tiber easily.

He was no St Paul, but I am pleased to write a few words about him on one of Paul's feasts.

And I will conclude, not with a prayer, but with some words he wrote about Britain which apply equally to us:

We in Britain are entering a dangerous social condition in which the direct expressions of opinion that conflict—or merely seem to conflict— with a narrow set of orthodoxies is instantly punished by a band of self-appointed vigilantes. We are being cowed into abject conformity around a dubious set of official doctrines and told to adopt a world view that we cannot examine for fear of being publicly humiliated by the censors.

---

[14] Claudio Véliz is an economic historian and sociologist. From 1962 to 1966, he was a senior research fellow at the Royal Institute of International Affairs, Chatham House, where he began the Conversazioni on Culture and Society, which spread to Boston, Melbourne, and Vancouver.

WEEK 49

Australian Sympathies

26 January–1 February 2020

Sunday, 26 January 2020

We celebrate Australia Day today, 232 years after Captain Arthur Phillip, with his sailors, soldiers, and convicts, set foot at Botany Bay, before quickly moving on to claim Port Jackson (what we now know as the magnificent Sydney Harbour) before Lapérouse's[1] French ships, which had just arrived, discovered it and were tempted to claim it. As Geoffrey Blainey put it in this *Weekend Australian*, Britain and France were two superpowers then dividing the world between them, pushing aside the Dutch, the Portuguese, and the Spaniards when they were able. In 1788, Britain's rise was more advanced than China's now is, while the Dutch were similar to the Russians today (despite a completely different geography), as their "best" colonial days were behind them.

Ironically, many of the countries which suffered under the Japanese in the Second World War in their Greater East Asia Co-Prosperity Sphere[2] will be looking to Japan as an essential balance to Chinese ambitions. We can only hope and work to discourage Japan and China from getting together, as Japan did with Germany. Japan's conquest of Manchuria will militate against this for many decades among the Chinese people and leadership.

---

[1] Jean François de Galaup, comte de Lapérouse (1741–1788?), was a French naval officer and explorer. The year of his death is unknown because neither he nor any of his ships or crew returned to France.

[2] The Greater East Asia Co-Prosperity Sphere was a Japanese policy during World War II by which the Japanese increased their control over occupied countries by means of puppet governments that worked for the economic benefit of Imperial Japan.

The taxpayer-funded SBS gives a deal of time to those who call this "Invasion Day", which mildly irritates me. I have no "black armband" view of Australian history, which I regard as a great achievement, but we have to face the truth, the considerable dark side of the story. The contest between the British and the original inhabitants was the most unequal in colonial history, and while the British instructions were to foster peace and benevolence, trouble was inevitable and crimes were committed. I am proud of the statements of Archbishop John Polding, the first Catholic bishop in Australia, to defend the Aborigines and of the work of William Ullathorne, later bishop of Birmingham and the key man in the reestablishment of the Catholic hierarchy in Britain,[3] for his outspoken denunciation of transportation, although I suspect the convicts and their descendants turned out much better than he anticipated. Irish Catholic clergy after the 1829 Catholic Emancipation generally followed British imperial expansion, and I am one of the millions across the globe who benefitted.

The series of coincidences, providential or otherwise, came to an end when I awoke at 6:28 am, too late for the TV Mass, if it was shown. Australia Day ceremonies and discussions took the place of Joseph Prince and Joel Osteen.

The *Compass* program featured six Australian survivors of the Holocaust and their special items donated to the Sydney Jewish Museum. Olga's story and donation were both remarkable and disturbing. She told of the young British soldiers who liberated her from Belsen,[4] fainting, vomiting, and crying over what they had discovered. It was a terrible shock. Her donation was a shawl given to her at the liberation by a guard, which was made of human hair: Jewish hair. Jacqueline was shown in a beautiful photo with her three successive generations of descendants. She stated simply, "Whatever Hitler intended, he didn't succeed."

---

[3] William Bernard Ullathorne (1806–1889) was a descendant of St Thomas More. He was a cabin boy before joining the Benedictines at Downside Abbey in Great Britain in 1823. He was ordained in 1831 and volunteered the following year to serve the convicts in Australia. He later returned to England and became the first bishop of Birmingham in 1850. He was a key figure in accomplishing the final abolition (1857) of the British practice of transportation, i.e., sending convicts to Australia.

[4] Bergen-Belsen concentration camp in northern Germany was liberated by the British 11th Armoured Division on April 15, 1945.

Evil is a mystery, and the crimes of the Nazis were instigated by Germans, a people who had produced many of the best philosophers and scientists, fine poets, and the greatest composers. If this evil occurred in such an educated nation, no society is immune.

We pray for Australia today, where so much is seen to be changing and much more is changing under the surface, often unnoticed. We pray for our leaders, political and intellectual, because especially in a "can do" society which disdains ideas, ideas still rule: in media, in the social media, in universities, in schools, and in families.

Give Christian thinkers wisdom and courage to help fill the vacuum caused by Christian decline, to continue the debate in our time of trigger warnings and safe spaces, of "woke" intolerance and identity politics. May they be able to convince those in the middle that the stakes are high and that the consequences for society are often incalculable.

May they be able, like the author of the Old Testament Book of Wisdom (6:9–11), to demonstrate to our leaders that easy options are not always available.

> *Yes, rulers, my words are for you,*
> *that you may learn what wisdom is and not transgress,*
> *for they who observe holy things holily will be adjudged holy,*
> *and, accepting instruction from them, will find their defence in them.*
> *Look forward, therefore, to my words:*
> *yearn for them and they will instruct you.*

Monday, 27 January 2020

Today is a public holiday for the Australia Day which we celebrated yesterday. It was a pleasant morning, although the dew was almost gone and there was light cloud as I began my time outside.

The *Herald Sun* arrived for me, with its usual "very easy" Sudoku, which I completed successfully, and an excellent article by Andrew Bolt on global warming, which was logically impeccable and factually accurate.

He acknowledged that warming is slowly occurring and (to the gentleman's dismay) quoted Professor Andy Pitman, director of the Australian Research Council Centre of Excellence for Climate Extremes, on a couple of points. The first is that climate scientists do not know of a link between climate change and drought; secondly, Pitman admitted that carbon dioxide causes "greening", i.e., increased agricultural yields and forest growth. NASA has found that an area twice the size of the US became greener between 1982 and 2009.

Bolt also mentioned that the number of cyclones has diminished and that only half the area (recommended by the Royal Commission after the 2009 fires) has been cleared by early controlled burning, which the Aborigines used regularly. Five such fires were noticed by Joseph Banks, who was on the *Endeavour* with Captain Cook in 1770. I intend to recommend the article to my niece Rebecca, who is interested in these issues.

I was blessed with a long visit from my good friend and cousin Chris Meney, my indispensable support during this last year, and my good friend Fr Brendan Purcell, Ireland's loss and Sydney's gain, who was with me at St Mary's Cathedral and continues there, technically in retirement, as the cathedral's most industrious curate. He lectured for decades at University College Dublin in philosophy and anthropology, was active in the public struggle for life and family, and is the best type of priest, unfailingly charitable, kind, and among the most quirky and interesting conversationalists I have encountered. It is symptomatic of the Church leadership in Ireland that they made no attempt to entice him to stay there.

We discussed the Vatican and China, Ireland and Australia, the new book on celibacy by Pope Benedict and Cardinal Sarah (life would have been very different if His Holiness had not resigned), the Vatican finances, and the alienation of many devout Catholics in the United States. Brendan confessed that Archbishop Charles Chaput of Philadelphia was well pleased with his nominated successor, Archbishop Nelson Perez.

Just after Christmas, *First Things* posted an article on the Church in Ireland, "The World Will Whimper", by John Duggan, an England-based writer. The first paragraph concludes, "Catholic Ireland, as we knew it, has fallen." Not yet. The death notice is premature. According to Duggan, the Ireland of the 1937 Constitution has been "in full retreat for decades", and he quoted the Irish poet Patrick

Kavanagh, who intuited that Catholicism's banishment to the margins had begun in the 1950s.

He features J. B. Keane's 1972 fictional *Letters of an Irish Parish Priest* and centres the action around the theme of contraception, Pope Paul VI's *Humanae Vitae*,[5] the sensitive and excellent letter in response by the Irish bishops, and the accounts of how the younger and older clergy strove to help their people.

Two points in particular struck me. Heinrich Böll, the German novelist and Nobel Prize winner, loved Ireland and passed the summer there for many years on Achill Island, and in 1967 he updated his 1954 *Irish Journal*. For him, Ireland had "now caught up with two centuries and leaped another five", and the reason was contraception.

The prospect that fewer children might be born in Ireland filled him with dismay. "Nowhere in the world have I seen so many, such lovely, and such natural children," he wrote, "and to know that His Majesty the Pill would succeed where all the Majesties of Great Britain have failed—in reducing the number of Irish children—seems to me no cause for rejoicing."

Böll, like me, is an outsider, and he, too, believes the faith will persist. The Catholic community in Ireland, even more than in Australia, has been damaged enormously by the paedophilia crisis. Priestly vocations are low, nuns' vocations almost non-existent, the faith of many of the young is weak or extinguished, especially in Dublin; but Sunday Mass attendance is around 30 to 40 percent, perhaps three times the Australian rate of practice. Knock[6] is thronged, traditional pilgrimage sites are still visited, many still pray, and strongly. The troops are there for a revival. What is needed is leadership, discernment, and courage.

The poet Kavanagh and John Duggan are Irish and pessimists; but Duggan might be tempted to hope against hope. He quotes the fictional Fr Martin O'Mora from J. B. Keane's 1972 novel, one of "the old, frosty fellows":

We are the hard core, Joe, brought up on the Code. Our mission is to stand fast and to hold on no matter what. We may seem out of step right now, and there are many who would say that the world will not

---

[5] His famous 1968 encyclical restating the Church's teaching on contraception.

[6] Knock, the site of an apparition in Ireland in 1879.

look upon our likes again. They are wrong, for believe me, Joe, the
world will whimper for the likes of us in the fullness of God's time.

That was fifty years ago. The world is now whimpering. And Ireland
is waiting.

Tuesday, 28 January 2020

Today is the feast of St Thomas Aquinas, born in Roccasecca, a
southern Italian town, of a German-Norman family. His brother
had fought against the papacy, and, to his family's dismay, Thomas
joined the recently formed Dominican Order. An outstanding student, known as the "dumb ox" to his peers, he studied at Monte
Cassino, Naples, Paris, and then Cologne under his fellow Dominican St Albert the Great. He died at Fossanova in southern Italy in
1274 on his way to the Second Council of Lyon.

He is the greatest theologian of the second millennium and provides a fascinating contrast with St Augustine, the best of the first
millennium: a European aristocrat and a mixed-race North African
separated by more than eight hundred years; a member of the new
Order of Preachers and the bishop of a small African town; a system-
atizer and a pioneer.

The author of the first Western autobiography, a convert with a
partner for many years and a son, fascinated by himself, but with
a greater love and fascination of the good God, the ancient ever-new
Beauty, a Platonist after years of following the bizarre teaching of the
Manichees. This is Augustine.

An enterprising Spanish bishop had commissioned a Latin translation of Aristotle's writings, which had re-emerged in the West,
and Aquinas baptised Aristotle, building a new and comprehensive
system, e.g., the *Summa Theologica*, ordered and impersonal, which
dominated Catholic life for centuries, was repudiated by the Protestants, and given new life by Pope Leo XIII late in the nineteenth
century. As a change agent, Aquinas was controversial, with the archbishop of Paris ordering his books to be burnt publicly.

At Corpus Christi seminary in Werribee, Victoria (1960–1963),
we followed three years of philosophy, from Latin Scholastic manu-
als, with no primary text prescribed from the masters. While a group

of us got together to go through Plato's *Republic*, I lament that I did not spend more time on Aquinas' writing, although under the guidance of Archbishop Eric D'Arcy, who lectured in philosophy at Melbourne University for twenty years, I later did a lot of work in Aquinas' moral philosophy and theology, planting myself firmly in his tradition of moral realism.

A dose of metaphysics is also very useful for a priest. I remember a New Zealand bishop lamenting that his seminarians, because they had studied little philosophy, found it difficult to distinguish an official from a functionary, an office from a succession of functions, with unfortunate consequences for the concept of ministerial priesthood. A minimum of two years of philosophy is, and should be, mandatory for all Catholic seminarians and should contain a good introduction to Thomistic metaphysics and moral theory. This study of philosophy helps explain the formidable contribution of priests over the centuries. It is always useful to be able to say what you mean and vital to mean what you say.

Today I received my quota of about twenty letters and a couple of large envelopes from Tim O'Leary with copies of articles on various theological and cultural topics. One article by Fr Raymond de Souza, the Canadian writer, in London's *Catholic Herald* was accurate, just, and depressing. Entitled "We Used to Believe Bishops Told the Truth. What Happened?", it recounts the falsehoods told about the veneration of Pachamama[7] in the Vatican Gardens, the Vatican finances, and the Zanchetta case,[8] and especially Donald Cardinal Wuerl's protestations of ignorance about the misconduct of ex-Cardinal Theodore McCarrick.

I cooperated usefully with Cardinal Wuerl on a number of issues, admired his competence and clarity of mind, and know that he is better than this terrible lapse to the public, his people, and his priests.

---

[7] Pachamama is revered in the Andes as a fertility goddess and a protector of crops. Some thought that her image was being venerated in the Vatican Gardens prior to the Amazon Synod, while others maintained that the statue was only an indigenous representation of Our Lady.

[8] In 2015, sexual misconduct charges were made against Gustavo Oscar Zanchetta, bishop of Orán, Argentina. Bishop Zanchetta said he was innocent of the charges, and in 2017 the pope allowed him to resign from his see for health reasons and become the assessor of the Administration of the Patrimony of the Apostolic See. He was suspended from this role in 2019, when the Vatican announced that he was the subject of a canonical investigation. In April 2021, Bishop Zanchetta returned to Argentina to face the charges against him.

The report on the McCarrick story is soon to be published and won't provide easy reading.

The day was warm and uneventful, at least for me. I had a second unexplained blood test in ten days and was interrupted by the transitions officer, who wanted to know how I had settled into Acacia and the date of my appeal to the High Court. We discussed what might happen if the appeal were successful, and I explained I would not need to go to Centrelink[9] for help. We also discussed the options that followed an unsuccessful appeal.

I believe that the Church in the United States is facing up to the challenges of secularism and post-modernity as well as any church in the Western world. Besides spectacular lapses, we have dynamism and fidelity, so that this crisis of credibility, the decline or withdrawal of donations, must not be allowed to cripple the growth, to smear all or most of the Church in America with the same tar brush.

No quick solution is available. The bishops will have to continue to work hard, pray and serve, and tell the truth. And most of the examples de Souza gives are not in the US.

You must not abandon the ship in a storm because you cannot control the winds. . . . What you cannot turn to good, you must at least make as little bad as you can.[10]

Wednesday, 29 January 2020

One of the pluses, the small blessings of ten months in jail, was to be introduced to the sermons of Sr Mary McGlone by our chaplain, Sr Mary O'Shannassy. I am not suggesting that McGlone is another Augustine, but every week she faithfully presents the Gospel teaching, illuminates the message, and relates it to our thought world and daily living. It is not written from the grime of parish life, but the message is learned and wise.

For the Second Sunday of Ordinary Time, she begins with a saying from Thomas Merton. "If you want to identify me, ask me not

---

[9] The government social welfare office.
[10] From *Utopia* (1516), by Thomas More.

where I live or what I like to eat or how I comb my hair, but ask me what I am living for."[11]

In my improved situation at the maximum security prison in Barwon, with a regular daily routine, plenty of books and articles, time to write and watch some cricket and tennis, Merton's question is a useful one for me to consider.

Living in jail and on prison food does not provide reason for boasting. A couple of days ago, I had my first steak since February last year, and I am pleased I did not have to pay for it. That said, I have no reason to complain about the food, which is better than I received at Propaganda Fide seminary in Rome in the sixties and in my few years of boarding at St Pat's College, Ballarat, in the fifties. And my hair needs to be cut.

I remain faithful to my daily round of prayer, although I am only saying one rosary each day rather than two. Otherwise, the daily program is the same. Neither am I experiencing anything like a dark night of the soul, mainly, I believe, because of the prayers of thousands of people for me. I am on an even keel, more or less, spiritually and psychologically. I thank God for all this. But I don't "feel" as religious, as spiritually focused, as I was when my situation was more difficult. It is just another example of how easy it is to let God slip away a bit when we are busy or distracted and happy enough.

I am not living for my early release, although an unsuccessful appeal would be a mighty blow. I do hope to live long enough to speak at the pre-conclave meetings before the election of the next pope, to have at least some years of working retirement, to spend some time with my family and many loyal friends.

If I am doing this well and prayerfully, then I am preparing for life with the Lord, in heaven (God willing). I don't know how regularly I will get to the Book of Revelation to meditate on what is to come. Today, for the second time, I watched part of an unusual SBS program about a large boat travelling the waterways of Norway, being greeted by groups of young and old along the river, with plenty of silence, no dialogue, but regular music at intervals. I was surprised I

[11] Mary M. McGlone, "Second Sunday in Ordinary Time: Questions to Set Us on Fire", *National Catholic Reporter*, 18 January 2020, https://www.ncronline.org/news/spirituality/scripture-life/second-sunday-ordinary-time-questions-set-us-fire.

enjoyed it so much and returned to it, so peaceful and idyllic. And I concluded that this in a small way was a foretaste of heaven.

If better times come again, I must ensure that the good Lord remains at the centre of my life.

Warm weather is returning, and I was outside until midday, when Kartya arrived with some Roman bank documents for me to sign and an updated visitors' schedule. We went through the list of Friel's articles, and I highlighted what I wanted her to read. I spoke to David, who was spending a couple of hours at work, and also with Margaret for the first time in three days. Desley Walsh was with her, having driven up from Melbourne. She has been a good friend to Margaret for years. I spent my morning outside, once I had moved through my prayers, in reading the articles Tim O'Leary had sent me. Another bunch of twenty-plus letters arrived.

Today's second reading in the breviary was from St Bernard's commentary on the Song of Songs. Bernard is boasting that what he lacks himself he confidently takes from the Lord's compassionate heart. He then continues.

But the nail that pierced became for me the key that opened the door so that I might see the will of the Lord. How should I not see through that opening? The nail cries out, the wound opens its mouth to cry that truly God is in Christ reconciling the world to himself.

Thursday, 30 January 2020

Today's second reading is from the Book of Deuteronomy, where Moses is urging the path of virtue on his followers, God's Chosen People, and pointing out the dire consequences for them if they disobey. The law is not in the heavens or across the seas, but is "in [their] mouth and in [their] heart for [their] observance".

He gives them the alternatives of life and prosperity or death and disaster, and we read again those famous words: "I set before you life or death, blessing or curse. Choose life, then, so that you and your descendants may live, in the love of the Lord your God, obeying his voice."

Did Jesus abolish the wages of sin? The Jews were well aware that bad things happen to good people and believed that the ancestors of these unfortunates must have sinned. When the tower at Siloam[12] collapsed, Jesus explained that the victims were not at fault and were not the cause. Some violence and misfortune are random, and we and many sinners seem to do well in this life, although the actual number of successes is probably lower than it appears.

But the wages of sin continue to be real in the Christian dispensation, often in this life and always in eternity, where the scales of justice balance out truly.

In the physical order, we understand much more clearly than in the past the costs we pay when we violate the laws of nature, whether it be erosion in Australia through over-clearing, the poisoned rivers and pitted buildings of Communist Europe, the choking smog in China through industrial pollution, and the more frequent flooding in Bangladesh caused by upstream deforestation. We now know open sewers spread disease.

Similar damage occurs in the moral order when natural norms are violated. Our ancient wisdom reminds us of these truths. The touch of Midas tells of the consequences of greed; the shepherd who cried "wolf" tells us about lying, and we know those who live by the sword die by the sword. At a broader and grosser level, we have the Nazi Holocaust, the elimination of six million Jews; the Soviet Gulags and the famine in Ukraine; Mao's famine in the Great Leap Forward in China with forty-two million deaths and then the Cultural Revolution; and the one or two million deaths under Pol Pot in tiny Cambodia.

Every generation is offered life or death, blessing or curse, and many migrate to English-speaking countries, not just because we are prosperous, but because our predecessors struggled toward justice and peace rather than tyranny and violence. Watching others helps us stay on course and strengthen our efforts to maintain social capital. However, millions of abortions and now euthanasia are not options for life.

Just before Christmas, *Crisis* magazine posted an article on the October meeting in Salzburg of the Order of St George, a European Order of the House of Habsburg-Lorraine. They began with a panel discussion on the question "Quo Vadis, Europa?" (Where are you going, Europe?), the question St Peter asked the Lord, who appeared to him as he began to flee Rome.

---

[12] Luke 13:4.

The Order supports the notion of a strong Europe, opposed to blind nationalism, but proud of its Christian roots and traditions. The Order's procurator lamented that more and more of what held society together is being softened and weakened and that the family, the foundation of community, is being undermined. He also lamented the lack of public leaders who stand for values, have courage and the wisdom to identify what is central. For the Order, the soul of Europe is Christian.

Australian society is a British transplant, different from continental Europe in significant ways, not least in its approach to immigration and in the percentage of Muslims already present (lower in Australia).

One paragraph in the article is unusually blunt and perceptive. It reads:

> The soul-less body that Europe seems to be becoming is dominated by what is essentially a paradoxically Marxist-consumerist elite—hollowed-out men who appear to be marking time until the day when demographics allow Islamist fundamentalism to swallow them whole. In reaction to their fecklessness, it seems inevitable that the sort of nationalist extremists they routinely denounce will unseat them if, as, and when Europeans grow fearful enough—and that, as the Old Continent experienced before, may well come with its own price.[13]

I am intrigued by the secularists' carelessness or enthusiasm for Islamic migration in such large numbers. I suppose workers are needed, and that will continue even with the arrival of increasing automation; and alternative workers are not available in big numbers. Many secularists before September 11 were tempted to think that all religions were spent forces and that the Muslims over a few generations would lapse into neo-paganism as they had. Muslims are also anti-Christian, and this was another plus.

Many Muslim migrants are colonists, not immigrants, who want to recreate their home society in their new workplaces, not adapt to their new situation.

It is not surprising that the formerly Communist countries are more alive to this threat than many in the West, because they have lived

---

[13] Charles Coulombe, "Quo Vadis, Europa?", *Crisis*, 18 December 2019, https://www.crisismagazine.com/2019/quo-vadis-europa.

under forty-five years of anti-Christian governments after their brief Nazi experiences. The Communist governments were totalitarian, not tolerant, not committed to the principle of "live and let live". Neither is Islam. Islam recognizes no equivalent to the separation of church and state, and even once-secular Turkey, under Erdogan,[14] is coming closer to their traditional patterns.

Boris Johnson isn't a Christian enthusiast, but he knows history and should realise the contribution Christians continue to make in maintaining what is good.

It was hot today, so it was my task to water the young plants before the heat arrived. My back continues to trouble me, so I received some Panadol, deep heat, and the promise that I will see the physio at the end of February. Hearing that news, I replied that I could be dead by then, and the nurse hoped this would not be the case.

To my considerable disappointment, Ash Barty, the Australian favourite, lost in the semi-final of the Australian Open. The qualities that make her such a pleasant personality also inhibit her tennis. With her departure, I am even more enthusiastic about the return of the Big Bash cricket tomorrow night.

God our Father, we pray for all the societies which belong to the Western tradition and especially for their Christian communities. Give these Christians wisdom, courage, and perseverance to remain as the leaven in the dough, to inspire and encourage more and more persons, especially among the young, to choose life rather than death, blessings, not a curse, human flourishing, not a childless dystopia, the love of the Lord, not the lies and hate of the Evil One.

Friday, 31 January 2020

It was hot this morning, hotter than yesterday morning, and the temperature passed 40°C [104°F]. I faithfully watered our young plants.

---

[14]Recep Tayyip Erdogan (b. 1954) became president of Turkey in 2014 after having been prime minister for eleven years. He has promoted a more traditional Islam than that tolerated by the previous secular governments and turned the Church of Hagia Sophia into a mosque, which it had been from the Ottoman conquest of Constantinople in 1453 to 1935, when the Turkish Republic made it museum.

Later in the morning, it was windy, with unpleasant winds, but the commentator at the tennis mid-afternoon announced that the change had already arrived in Ballarat, where the temperature had fallen to 27°C [81°F].

I had a small incident when I was trying to get out of bed this morning. The bed is low, one foot was on a raised blanket rolled out next to the bed, my back was twinging, so my bent knees didn't arrive to a stand-up position, and I toppled over to the right, landing on my sleep apnea machine. I wasn't hurt, and my first concern was that I had damaged the machine; but it has a sturdy frame and was safe and sound.

Because of my back, I had to ask for help to get on my feet. The warder distributing breakfast needed to call for assistance, so two or three extra warders arrived with two nurses. They confirmed I was OK, with no pain, as I had fallen or rather rolled to one side from a low point. My blood pressure was up, but it was back to a healthy level by mid-morning.

I received a huge tube of a type of Voltaren and learnt my visit to the physio has been advanced to Monday week, ten days away, rather than at the end of February. This is progress. I haven't fallen in three years, although my balance is not perfect, and from now on I shall rise from my low chaste couch with considerable caution.

Archbishop Barry Hickey, the emeritus archbishop of Perth, arrived to see me at 11:00 am for a 12:30 meeting. He had received a lift to the jail from Fr Jim Clarke, who is now in charge of St Mary's Church in Geelong. At eighty-three years of age, Barry remains fit and alert, still regularly playing tennis. He is an excellent player and an excellent bishop.

I caught up on the news from the Perth Archdiocese, led by Archbishop Tim Costelloe. I was especially pleased to hear of Fr Christian Irdi, who had studied with us at the seminary in Sydney before studying in Rome, where our paths crossed again. Barry felt my reputation for financial integrity in Rome was widely recognized, although he, too, was dismayed by the general situation and aware the Vatican was losing money each year.

The number of letters is diminishing, as I only received four or five yesterday and again today. I received my first letter of support from Russia, from a seminarian in Moscow. A woman from Lancaster in northern England spoke of the benefits she had received from my books. A young father from Slovakia whose son has been taken from him said he, too, realised what it was to be alone at Christmas and requested me "to offer a bit of your suffering for us poor sinners". Which I do readily.

Sr Mary always passes on to me the Sunday sermon of Fr Brian Gleeson, and he recently pointed out that in the famous painting of William Holman Hunt *The Light of the World*, where Jesus, crowned with thorns and carrying a lantern, is knocking on a closed door, the door has no handle. The artist explained that this was no mistake; the only handle was inside, because only we can open the door to let in the light.

Another letter was quite different, coming from a devout parishioner in Kensington, NSW, who had been blessed previously when God had answered his prayers. He prayed hard for me and "was expecting a miracle".

He still prays for me after the unsuccessful appeal, but he had been mightily disappointed. He continued, "I was so disappointed and angry that He had all the power in the universe and would not intervene to help you overcome your burden." He acknowledges God works in mysterious ways and prays that the final outcome of my case "will in a strange way contribute to His glory". He realises that his reactions were mistaken. So he now prays "asking for His forgiveness in doubting Him and apologising for my remarks about redeeming Himself over your case.... My anger got the better of me."

I have some formidable allies, and I feel constrained to put in a word to the good God for my intemperate friend by praying from Psalm 34.

> *O Lord, you have seen, do not be silent,*
> *do not stand afar off!*
> *Awake, stir to my defence,*
> *to my cause, O God!*

> *Let there be joy for those who love my cause.*
> *Let them say without end:*
> *"Great is the Lord who delights*
> *in the peace of his servant."*

Saturday, 1 February 2020

As I begin to write this entry, I can hear the rain falling outside; a cool change has arrived after yesterday's heat. The rain and the cool are good, and it is also good to be able to see the rain and hear it fall.

Anne and Tim McFarlane visited for an hour today, and as I explained the advantage of Barwon jail over MAP, Anne remarked how we can come to appreciate basic facts, blessings we normally take for granted.

Tim is the driving force for the annual Red Mass[15] to open the legal year in Melbourne and was well pleased with the numbers, despite a hostile article in *The Australian*. He reported proudly that Archbishop Comensoli did well by speaking with the twenty-five or so protestors before Mass and then, when he had finished preaching, saying a few words to a noisy protestor who interjected during his sermon. Melbourne continues to be a more contentious city than Sydney, more secular, without the Sydney Anglicans, with more mutual hostility. Unfortunately, the Catholic chaplaincies at the Melbourne universities are not too lively despite many fine young priests.

In the wider world, it appears that the Republican votes in the US Senate are holding firm and that the failed impeachment of President Trump will be concluded next week.

The most important event in the Anglosphere yesterday was that Britain officially left the European Union at 11:00 pm. Nigel Farage[16] and his supporters celebrated outside the Houses of Parliament, with Farage proudly announcing "the victory of ordinary people against the Establishment".

Boris Johnson, the British prime minister, the author of a first-rate biography of Winston Churchill, is a highly sophisticated European. Steeped in the Greek and Roman classics and a splendid writer (a better writer than a public speaker), he rose to the occasion, proclaiming that Brexit was not an end but a beginning. "This is the moment the dawn breaks and the curtain goes up on a new act."

---

[15] The Red Mass, so called for the colour of the vestments at this Mass of the Holy Spirit, is held in many major cities around the world to open the legal year, with judges and lawyers in attendance.

[16] Nigel Farage (b. 1964) was the leader of the Brexit Party from 2019 to 2021.

Like Disraeli, he is a "one-nation Tory",[17] who is also keen to retain his newly won Northern seats and spoke of the "dawn of a new era in which we no longer accept that your life chances ... should depend on which part of the country you grew up in. This is the moment when we begin to unite and level up." And he very prudently gave most workers a £104 bonus, as a kick-start to the "Brexit bounce".

The London *Spectator* promised that Britain would be Europe's best ally, and Ursula von der Leyen, the new European Commission president, explained they were about to build an alliance, not just dismantle one. The German attitude was one of regret, not hostility, while President Emmanuel Macron in France was characteristically ungracious, which is understandable given the level of anti–European Union sentiment in France.

Naturally writers were seeking historical precedents. At the Synod of Whitby in 664, England moved in the opposite direction, electing to follow the Roman method for dating Easter and abandoning Irish practices. Today the two countries, neighbours, England and Ireland, are still on different sides of the fence. History cannot be rewritten, especially centuries of injustice and mistrust, but the countries are natural allies as the enormous number of English-Irish marriages have demonstrated for decades in Australia, now disguised by both sides simply calling themselves "Australian". In the Ballarat of my youth, while many of us carried English names, we were educated as small-"i" Irish Australians, but no one ever asked me about my heritage until my Italian Rector Msgr Felice Cenci at Propaganda Fide college in Rome enquired. I told him I was Australian. He replied that he knew that, but where did my parents come from? When I went to work in a North Baltimore parish in the US in the northern summer of 1967, I was regularly quizzed in a friendly way about my ancestors.

It has been clear to me that the closest historical parallel for Brexit is Henry VIII's break with Rome. Given my instinctive sympathy for Brexit, although I have lived happily in Italy for two periods of four years, forty-five years apart, I wondered where my instincts, as distinct from my head and theology, might have been in the first half

---

[17] A term for a certain form of conservatism coined by the nineteenth-century British prime minister Benjamin Disraeli.

of the sixteenth century. The papacy then fluctuated between world-liness and corruption, and More and Fisher both died for that papacy, for what they saw as Christ's will for his Church, even when it was implemented imperfectly.

Henry VIII was an obnoxious tyrant, but a religious conservative who wanted to stabilise his dynasty with a male heir. He had to put down numerous armed rebellions, after he tricked the Pilgrimage of Grace[18] into dispersing.

I might have fallen into the new scheme of things out of fear, but while the popes were worldlings, and occasionally incompetents like Clement VII, whose double-dealing helped provoke the Sack of Rome by German troops in 1527, they were not the equivalent of the interfering, fussy enforcers we find in the European Commission. Henry and his allies, to whom he assigned part of the loot, were much less interested in people's taxes than in the wealth of the suppressed monasteries.

Henry imposed English law and local government on Wales and in 1547 became King of Ireland. He, and more particularly Elizabeth I, set the United Kingdom (then minus Scotland) on a new path, which included a relentless and persistent persecution of Catholics for nearly 250 years, which was heroically resisted by the martyrs and by an indomitable minority at home and in the English colleges abroad.

Henry was not a religious reformer like Luther or Calvin or Knox, who were driven by ideals of gospel purity (imperfect ideals imperfectly executed). His appeal was to nationalism, not religion.

If the Christendom of Catholic Europe was an inspiration to Henry's opposition, no one would have been tempted to vote "remain" in the European Union for religious reasons. A majority of practising Christians in Britain supported Brexit, and all the sympathies and prejudices of my mixed Australian heritage impel me to believe that the worst "perfidious Albion"[19] might do in a religious sense is better than the worst their European secularist comrades would inflict.

My back may have improved this afternoon, but it might simply have been a result of the Panadol.

---

[18] A popular Catholic uprising in Northern England against Henry VIII in 1536.
[19] "Perfidious Albion" was coined by the French to refer to their British enemy.

This morning, Kartya brought me a copy of the prosecution document which was delivered to the High Court yesterday. Today's *Australian* ran an article headed "Pell's Team Ignores Evidence, Says DPP",[20] outlining some of the content of the submission, without any analysis. I wasn't impressed by the respondent's submissions, while Kartya and Ruth were not surprised, except perhaps by the omissions, e.g., no reference at all to the rehearsals.[21] More on this topic later.

St Thomas More was caught up in the violence and turmoil provoked by Henry VIII. While he was in the Tower of London in 1534 before his execution, he wrote the following prayer, and we conclude with his famous words on the scaffold.

Bear no malice or evil will to any man living. For either the man is good or wicked. If he is good and I hate him, then I am wicked. If he is wicked, either he will amend and die good and go to God, or live wickedly and die wickedly and go to the devil.... [Then] I may well think myself a deadly cruel wretch if I would not now rather pity his pain than malign his person.

On the scaffold on July 6, 1535.

I die the King's good servant, but God's first.

---

[20] Director of Public Prosecutions (DPP).

[21] The rehearsals attended by choir members immediately after Mass.

WEEK 50

Currents for Good and Ill

2 February–8 February 2020

Sunday, 2 February 2020

Today is Candlemas day, the feast of the Presentation of the Lord in the Temple, which is rarely celebrated on a Sunday.

I am sure that this ceremony when a Jewish child is claimed for God was a regularly happy occasion, like a baptism is for many of us. Over the years, I have inclined to overemphasise Simeon's prophecy to Our Lady that Jesus would be contentious and divisive and that a sword would enter her own heart. This certainly would have been a dampener, but Simeon was delighted to have met the light and salvation promised for centuries and to be present when Jesus was solemnly acknowledged as a member of his own Chosen People.

I woke up just after 6:00 am and heard Fr John Corrigan from Ballarat Diocese conclude his sermon. He is the best preacher on the panel of regular Mass celebrants and spoke of light coming into the darkness, of the candles which breathe and are consumed as they give out light and heat. They remind us of living and dying and are a good symbol of Christian living and especially of priestly service.

Today is much cooler, and I needed my second long-sleeved cardinal-coloured tracksuit top to keep warm while I was outside for breakfast. The dew was heavy on the grass, the plants are coming on, and Paolo told me he pulled out one of the tiny spring onions and ate it. Its taste was good.

Joseph Prince preached on the Emmaus incident in what seemed to me to be a different and smaller hall. Joseph's hair was not slicked down; he wore only two rings, no tie, with a dark jacket, which had an ornament and chain from his top pocket, and dark jeans. The sermon was well prepared and thorough, but he was shouting a bit.

On the way to Emmaus, Jesus was explaining how the Scriptures referred to him, and Joseph explained that the two men had a mistaken concept of Messiah. We receive our blessings, we don't take them, just as we receive Communion, he added.

The first scriptural references to bread and wine are not favourable as, after original sin, bread has to be earned by the sweat of the brow; while Noah's drunkenness is the first reference to wine. The New Agers were rebuked as eating Jesus raw without consuming the blood which remits sins.

Joel Osteen praised Naomi and Ruth and urged us to kiss disappointment goodbye, because God is still in control. We should be at peace with our past, be it good, bad, or indifferent; kiss the chip on our shoulder goodbye. We should avoid those who are peace-stealers or dream-killers, and should disappoint people rather than God. But once again, Joel promises to deliver redress in this life.

Both the *Compass* program on the Christian Brothers College in the Fremantle initiation program on becoming an adult and *Songs of Praise* were repeats.

I spent most of the day preparing ten pages of notes on the prosecution's latest contribution, and now I shall watch at least some of the Australian Open men's tennis final. The old guard prevailed, and Novak Djokovic, the Serbian, defeated the young Austrian Dominic Thiem to win his eighth Australian title, a record. He is a magnificent player, not a crowd favourite, but I am sympathetic toward him, not least because he is open about his Christianity—Serbian Orthodox.

God our Father, we thank you for the blessing of international sport. May we never take it too seriously, but be grateful for what we have.

Monday, 3 February 2020

By prison standards, today was busy, but not because we celebrated the feast of St Blaise, who was a fourth-century bishop in Armenia, the first kingdom in the world to declare itself Christian, in the early fourth century. Constantine did not declare religious toleration for

Christians in the Roman Empire until the Edict of Milan in 313; only later did Christianity become the official religion.

We in the Roman rite in the Western world know very little about the history of Christianity outside the borders of the Roman Empire. There were highly developed and missionary churches to the east of the Roman Empire, where Edessa was a theological centre to rival Antioch and Alexandria. A large amount of Syriac theology remains untranslated into English, even today, perhaps a task for some of our young Australian priests from Middle Eastern families.

The kingdom of Ethiopia, which then included most of the area south and east of Egypt, also became Christian sometime before 341, when the coins of Emperor Ezana began to carry the sign of the Cross. The first bishop was St Frumentius, who had been captured in Palestine and brought to the Ethiopian court as a slave. Who would have predicted all this at the height of Roman persecutions under Diocletian around A.D. 300? Nor do we know the future today! None of the experts predicted Trump's election, much less that he would attend and speak at the recent March for Life in Washington, the first president to do so.

However, this does not explain my devotion to St Blaise. When I was young, I was frequently sick with throat trouble, regularly hospitalised for some years with a growth. Mum knew from somewhere that St Blaise was the patron saint of those with bad throats, so we regularly invoked his support. I was completely cured.

My doctor, whom my mother trusted completely, was John Greening, locally born and educated at St Pat's as I was, who had been one of the first Catholic doctors in Protestant Ballarat. He had assisted at my birth, and it was my privilege to preside at his funeral and commit his soul into the hands of our good God.

This morning was cold, uncomfortably cold, so I enquired about the regulation jacket I was entitled to have and finished up with a couple: a lighter and a heavier one, which both fitted me.

I was called midmorning to visit Dr Said, the medical officer. I told him about my sore back, and he told me to keep exercising and that he would refer me to the physiotherapist. I didn't enquire when the appointment might be.

Katrina Lee came down from Sydney, and the jail gave us a couple of hours, which we used well and pleasantly, discussing the recent document of the prosecution, our next response, and what I might say and do if and when my appeal is successful. I repeated that I would be living in Sydney, after visiting Margaret and David in Bendigo, and seeing some of my friends in Melbourne. She has been somewhat unwell, but looked good. Completely loyal and highly competent, she will continue to deal with the media for me.

Thirty letters arrived after a quiet weekend, while the property department sent three paperback books: the biography of Mother Teresa I had requested, along with Fr Brendan Purcell's gift of Andy Roberts' biography of Churchill and Diarmaid MacCulloch's biography of Thomas Cromwell—both of which received excellent reviews, although Hilary Mantel's high praise for the Cromwell book made me wary. Mary Eberstadt's *Primal Screams* did not arrive, presumably because it has a hard cover! However, I am well above my official limit of six books.

Particularly in the world of affairs, but also in the Church, we often cannot identify where the powerful currents for good and ill are running below the surface. The recently canonised St John Henry Newman recognized this:

Such is the rule of our warfare. We advance by yielding; we rise by falling; we conquer by suffering; we persuade by silence; we become rich by bountifulness; we inherit the earth through meekness; we gain comfort through mourning; we earn glory by penitence and prayer.

Tuesday, 4 February 2020

The weather was beautiful today, at least for my purposes. It wasn't perfect for the beach, as we still had some dew on the grass at 8:00 am, but the air was crisp and clear, almost like a Victorian autumn, which is the best season of the year here in the southeast, away from the northern humidity and before the winter cold. For the first time, I sat out for an hour in my exercise area (after I had returned from the lawn) and started to move through the biography of Mother Teresa, now St Teresa of Calcutta, based on her spiritual journals.

I was surprised and many were shocked to learn that from the time of the mystical experience which prompted her to found the Missionaries of Charity to work with the poorest of the poor, she had lived in interior darkness, feeling as though God had left her. She maintained her cheerfulness, emphasising that it was important to know how to suffer and to laugh at the same time. I had purchased this work in 2009, after its 2007 publication, but had only read sections. For me, she and St John Paul the Great were the Catholic luminaries of the late twentieth-century world, so I concluded that jail was a good setting to complete reading what I had started and should have finished years ago.

This reminds me that my only regular correspondent from Singapore informed me that around Christmas a group from the Melbourne Vietnamese Catholic community walked around MAP saying the rosary, mindful of the fact that Cardinal Van Thuan had spent nine years in the harshest of solitary confinements. I might have heard of their presence, but certainly did not know these details.

My major task was to fax my ten pages of notes on the prosecution document to Kartya. After speaking with her just after midday, I learnt that everything had arrived except page four, so then I arranged for that to be sent also.

The prosecution document is more of the same and of indifferent quality. It does not set out the facts clearly, muddies the waters, makes claims which are not justified by the evidence or their notes, proposes lengthy distractions, e.g., on the non-calling of Fr Egan,[1] and misrepresents Justice Weinberg's views on the parting of the alb[2] by an incomplete and misleading reference. The complainant was unable to produce any corroborating evidence, so the jury and the majority judges appeal to his credibility. Therefore, it is necessary in my view to demonstrate clearly the many changes in the complainant's story and the impossibility of his being in two places at the same time. The prosecution has opted differently from the majority about when the "hiatus" occurred, the six-plus minutes necessary for the alleged activities and gross crimes in the sacristy. Did this occur before the servers arrived or after they arrived and mysteriously left

[1] A priest who had concelebrated Mass with Cardinal Pell on the same day as the assault was claimed to have happened but who had never been summoned by police for an interview.

[2] The accuser said Cardinal Pell parted his robes, but they were seamless and could not be parted.

the sacristy for six minutes to do who knows what in the work area or the corridor? Even the chronology proposed by the complainant for the offences, i.e., in the same choral year of '96, about a month apart, cannot be squared with the fact that the archbishop only celebrated two Sunday Masses at the cathedral, on 15 and 22 December, in 1996. And so on. Ruth and Kartya are hard at work going through the document sentence by sentence.

About a dozen letters arrived today along with the January–February issue of *Quadrant*, crammed with interest. I am not short of reading material.

Michael Portillo's first instalment of his *Great Australian Railway Journeys* was shown on SBS, while Channel 9 had a long interview with Thomas Markle, the father of the Duchess of Sussex. A sad story, which is unlikely to get better. He was probably correct when he said the ex-royals are like "lost children". I particularly fear for Harry.

A grandfather from Toowoomba wrote to me asking for prayers for two of his grandchildren (one of whom is sick) and promising me his continuing prayer. He sent me a poem by Sr Mary Ada (like him, I do not know who she is or where she is from) which tells of the Old Testament people waiting in Limbo for the crucified and risen Christ to liberate them. He compared this to my situation. Would David lead a song or the three children from the fire sing the canticle of praise? Then Jesus appeared "splendid as the morning sun and fair" . . .

> *No Canticle at all was sung,*
> *None toned a psalm, or raised a greeting song.*
> *A silent man alone*
> *Of all that throng*
> *Found tongue—*
> *Not any other.*

> *Close to His heart*
> *When the embrace was done,*
> *Old Joseph said,*
> *"How is Your Mother,*
> *how is Your Mother, Son?"*

Wednesday, 5 February 2020

I spent some hours in the middle of the day going through the mail of the last three days. Fr John Andersen, the only Sydney missionary priest and a regular correspondent, wrote for Christmas to tell me of the sudden death of his fifty-six-year-old bishop, Miguel Olaortúa Laspra, OSA. In any diocese, this would be a shock but especially in a small missionary diocese—in the Amazon region of northeast Peru. The bishop had felt unwell at the Amazon Synod in Rome and had returned for tests. He was to travel to Lima for further tests, "but Sister Death came first." Fr John continued, "Cardinal George, the circumstances of Bishop Miguel's passing have had a big effect on me, and much passes through my mind and heart. In the end, we are all in the hands of the Lord." Indeed we are, and we never know what time remains. *Carpe diem,*[3] as they used to say. The bishop's last and recent ordination to the priesthood of Fr Juan Andersen Perez Ramirez, obviously from Fr John's parish, is a wonderful sign of the blessings he has brought through decades of missionary service. *Ad multos annos*[4] for the new priest and the Aussie who baptised him.

Another letter was different in a different way: anonymous and signed "some nondescriptive agnostic sandgroper living in Queensland". He was outraged that I had "been shipped off to a maximum security prison" and interpreted this as an attempt to break me, similar to an incident he had read about an Orthodox priest in Romania being tortured by the Communists. "Ten years ago, I thought this Slavic exuberance. And in this country never."

The reason for my transfer remains a mystery. How could the authorities have known the drone was trying to photograph me when I was only outside in the garden for a couple of hours twice a week? However, my living conditions and daily routine are clearly better here in Barwon.

Another letter actually came from a small Greek Catholic prayer group from Bucharest in Romania who were praying for me, as were "many Orthodox Christians" and groups in Poland, the US, and Argentina.

---

[3] "Seize the day"—grab the opportunity when it's there.
[4] "Unto many years"—many happy returns.

They continued, "We do recognize the same pattern in the current-day, anti-Christian persecutions. Indeed, there is a striking similarity between the way the courts used to function here in the 1950s and the way they worked in your case!"

The Romanian group sent me a photo of an icon of the seven Romanian Greek Catholic bishop martyrs who were beatified on 2 June 2019, explaining that they were praying to them to intercede for me and other Catholic bishops.

One of the signatories was Dr Anca-Maria Cernea, who had been at the 2015 second Synod on the Family, in Rome, where I also was a member. She enclosed a copy of her synodal speech. As a medical doctor, she insisted that the causes of the crisis in the family were not material poverty or consumerism or income disparity or climate change. For her, "the primary cause of the sexual and cultural revolution is ideological." Evil comes from sin. The primary cause is cultural Marxism, and she traces the development from Lenin's sex revolution through Gramsci[5] and then the Frankfurt School[6] to the current gay rights and gender ideology.

A number of Australian writers, e.g., Kevin Donnelly, are making similar claims about the cultural Marxism dominating many of the humanities faculties in our Australian universities. Another similarity with the political and violent classical Marxism before 1989 is the ruthless way they deal with dissent, trying to bully and exclude people into silence.

As Dr Cernea was addressing the synod, she concluded by quoting some Orthodox faithful (making a point Anglican archbishops have made to me): "If the Catholic Church gives in to the spirit of this world, it is going to be very difficult for all the other Christians to resist it."

The day was overcast, not as pleasant as yesterday, but it improved as it went. I had a brief but relaxed visit with the Uniting Church chaplain, the Rev Tevita, who came from Tonga in the 1980s. I managed to speak with Margaret and with Bernadette Tobin, who has just returned from Rome and New York, with some time in London.

---

[5] Antonio Gramsci (1891–1937) was a founding member of the Communist Party in Italy and one of the most important Marxist thinkers of the twentieth century.

[6] The Frankfurt School refers to the scholarship and the intellectuals associated with the Institute for Social Research founded in 1923 at Goethe University, Frankfurt. It was the first Marxist research center at a German university.

Of the orders of nuns today, I feel closest to the Michigan Mercies [Religious Sisters of Mercy] and the Nashville Dominicans, both of them having reformed their original charism, whom I invited to the Sydney Archdiocese. The Ganmain Dominicans have also been very loyal, with someone writing nearly every week.

This week's letter from them quoted from "The Tears of God", by Fr Gerald Vann, OP.[7]

Evil produces its ineluctable consequences, and the world is drenched in pain, but at every point in time and space where pain has its kingdom, there are also the tears of God, and sooner or later through the tears the soul of the world is renewed.

Thursday, 6 February 2020

We celebrate today the feast of St Paul Miki and the other Japanese martyrs, twelve laymen and four boys, who were executed in 1597 in Nagasaki by spear thrusts. Originally, the Jesuit missionaries were able to teach freely, and I have read claims that one-third of the population of Japan was Catholic earlier in the sixteenth century, because when the head man converted, the clan followed. Others have responded that this is a serious overestimate. Tradition has it that when a proud Spanish sea captain showed on a map how much of the world the Spaniards then ruled, this confirmed Japanese fears that missionaries were a prelude to conquest. Ruthless persecution started and lasted until Japan opened to the world again in the nineteenth century. The great Japanese writer Shusaku Endo,[8] the Japanese Graham Greene, in novels such as *Silence* has taken us into this merciless struggle, spelling out the daily consequences of heroism and weakness.

In 1997, I represented the Australian Catholic Church at the fourth-centenary celebrations in Nagasaki, where the papal legate was the American cardinal Ted McCarrick, who, the locals told me, had

---

[7] Fr Gerald Vann, OP, *The Pain of Christ and the Sorrow of God* (New York: Alba House, 1994), p. 97.

[8] Shusaku Endo (1923–1996) was a Japanese writer who examined the relationship between Eastern and Western culture from a Catholic perspective. While primarily known for his numerous novels, he also wrote short stories, plays, essays, and a biography.

a better Japanese pronunciation than Pope John Paul II. McCarrick was reduced to the lay ranks when his double life was revealed, causing immense damage to the Church leadership in the US.

The Catholic Church in Japan is in trouble, with few vocations and a thoroughly liberal and quasi-Protestant agenda, and is probably in numerical decline. Symptomatic of their approach and of their weakness is the fact that the Japanese Bishops' Conference has prevented the Neocatechumenal Way from continuing their work in Japan and expelled their seminary.

Two incidents from my own experience are compatible with this sad story. I knew an Australian missionary priest when he was a seminarian and met him again in Japan. A good and pleasant man, he performed no evangelical activity whatsoever, although he prayed, and, I presume, he celebrated Mass. I am not suggesting his pastoral approach was typical, as the Masses at the Sophia University church were well attended with a spirit of faith and reverence.

My second example is even less reassuring, but less open to the charge that the example is misleading and doesn't give an accurate picture of this minority Church. I once attended a wonderful seminar on science and religion at Stanford University in California. One of the small number of participants was a Japanese astronomer, with a Buddhist background, who told us he loved the universe. He explained that in every country he had visited, the Catholic Church worked with the poor, except in his own country. He asked me why this was so. I couldn't answer and didn't know enough to dispute his claims.

Japan is prosperous, although the economy has been sluggish for some decades, sophisticated, and technologically advanced. It is also the first and most spectacular example of population decline, now that Putin claims that Russia no longer disputes for the infertility crown. Ettore Gotti Tedeschi was head of the IOR bank at the Vatican, one of the reformers who was cast out, quite unjustly, before my time. He is a learned man and an unusual thinker, who argues at length and cogently for a connection between a declining population from a low birthrate and economic stagnation, an inability to stimulate economic growth. Japan is also hostile to immigration. I haven't studied the issue but would not be surprised if there were causality, not merely concurrence.

About a dozen letters arrived today, which was overcast when I was outside. Aileen, the Catholic chaplain, brought me Communion, and I was able to give her a copy of *Magnificat*[9] for February as Eugene and my Singapore correspondent had each sent me a copy.

I spoke with my lawyers, who had received a request yesterday from the High Court about Case M on whether appellate courts should be required to view replays of trials as well as studying the transcripts. Neither the request nor any ruling on this point would seem to be significant for my appeal.

A doctor from Bronxville, New York, informed me I had been enrolled at the National Shrine of St Jude, who is the patron of hope in difficulties. This is better than describing him as the patron of hopeless cases. I conclude with this prayer to St Jude.

> *Most holy apostle, St Jude, faithful servant and friend of*
> *   Jesus ...*
> *Please intercede on my behalf.*
> *Make use of that particular privilege given to you to bring*
> *   hope, comfort,*
> *and help where they are needed most. . . .*
> *Bless me with faith and hope that come from a heart that is*
> *   open to you*
> *and to all God offers, in love and gratitude. Amen.*

Friday, 7 February 2020

Not much in jail is unexpected and unusual, once you have settled into the routine and recognized your place. Today, however, we had a couple of unusual occurrences.

Tim O'Leary drove down from Melbourne to see me as anticipated at 12:30 pm, but after about fifty minutes, the guards told us that there was an "aqua alert", which meant the prison was locked down and I had to return to my cell, and that this could continue for twenty minutes or two hours or? At 6:00 pm I am still not sure whether it is all over, although we did receive our midafternoon meal. This meant of course that Tim left to return to work.

[9] A monthly magazine that includes texts from the Liturgy of the Hours, the lives of the saints, and the daily prayers and readings for Mass.

He brought me news that Linda, Dr John H. Weigel's wife in Port Republic, Maryland, had died from cancer. May she rest in peace. I had been told that she was sick, but her death was unexpected for me, a possibility which had passed me by. John, who is George's younger brother, had been a good friend since I worked in the new cathedral parish of Mary Our Queen in Baltimore, Maryland, in 1967.

My brother, David, had passed on to me the news that one of my oldest friends from Ballarat, Les Dickinson, was seriously ill in hospital in Melbourne. We had been in the same year at school in Ballarat, and I had been a guest in his home at regular intervals for nearly fifty years. He is a loyal supporter with Trudie—a great wife and mother. If we live long enough, these items of news become more frequent.

I have celebrated many funerals over fifty years of priesthood, and the grief of the family, friends, and congregation differs radically depending on the presence or absence of belief in life after death. This is true whether the death is tragic or timely; of young or old; a speedy release or after protracted suffering. Christian hope is a powerful human support, based on the belief that our God, the only God, is good. In the days of faith when the dead had lived a sinful life, their loved ones prayed that there had been a last-minute repentance, that God would repeat his kindness on the Cross to the good thief. Those who do not believe in an afterlife or have rejected the notion of a God who judges hope that death means extinction. These alternatives are expressed by the mourners. The funeral of a believing Catholic who has led a productive life and is not leaving before his time is often a magnificent celebration.

Tim also had a garbled report from George Weigel that a nuncio from somewhere had commented that when I was cleared I might go to Switzerland. As the visit was cut short, I was unable to ask him to get more information on this. I will phone through the request tomorrow. Every aspect is intriguing, and I have no hypotheses.

During the lockdown at about 3:30 pm, four warders came to the cell door and said that the jail governor had given me five minutes to speak to my lawyer. I concluded that the missing page four, which had not arrived to Kartya at lunchtime, was not the reason.

In her phone call, Kartya informed me that the missing page four had just arrived. I think she said "by email".

A cyclone was moving down the country near Port Hedland in Western Australia, and massive amounts of rain, sometimes over 200mm [8 inches], had fallen over most of Queensland and into northern and central New South Wales. The biggest news in the outside world was the spread of the coronavirus. Although only fifteen cases are reported in Australia, Monash University has delayed its opening and Chinese students are being denied entry here. The Wuhan doctor who discovered the virus and was reprimanded by the authorities has died, and international health authorities are complaining about the lack of reliable information from China.

At the other end of the spectrum of importance, one arm of my spectacles has fallen off. Some days ago, they fell to the ground, and while I was still sitting in my chair, I put my big left foot on them. The left glass fell out, which I replaced, but when the glasses were on my nose, the right lens drooped spectacularly. My repeated low-level attempts to bend the frame back to normality then resulted in the detached right arm. However, the two lenses are now almost level. The authorities have been alerted to my predicament, and when the optometrist next visits the jail (who knows when?), he will effect repairs.

Prison life was very different when I had only my breviary to read and no books and would be different again if I could not read, if I were without glasses. Otherwise I am on an even keel, able to pray and meditate, although becoming a little "toey" as the High Court date approaches. I am looking forward to examining the draft of our final presentation, while Paul and Kartya are also heartened by the evidence of High Court activity on my appeal.

A Jewish lady and her husband who writes in *Quadrant* have written to me on a number of occasions assuring me of love, admiration, and reverence from outside the Catholic community. She was pleased to hear I was writing and sent me a quotation of Ralph Waldo Emerson:

I am not solitary whilst I read and write, though nobody is with me.

Saturday, 8 February 2020

A nondescript day today, overcast and slightly humid in the morning, so I did not need my overjacket for my half-hour walk. I have started to walk on the narrow concrete border of the lawn to try to improve my balance. Plenty of room for improvement, but I discovered that if I angle my feet outward I do better, covering about ten metres [11 yards] on one occasion before I over-balanced. The sun came out during the day with some heavy winds, and I sat outside in my exercise pen on return from the lawn to read the *Weekend Australian*—a boon and a blessing.

Greg Sheridan had a splendid article on Trump, saying that Trump was the only person who could prevent his own re-election after the acquittal. His sacking of the two officials who gave evidence against him is pretty appalling and one example of what is possible. Boris Johnson disappointed me by coming out to acknowledge the cloud of carbon dioxide enveloping us, foreshadowing electric cars and announcing a claim to leadership for Britain in this climate-change era. He has captured the "zeitgeist" for the moment, but I hope he doesn't believe the pseudo-science behind it. It is ironic that a man like Trump is closer to the truth on this issue than the highly educated Boris. I hope he doesn't get too many more of the big issues wrong, and it would be more dangerous if he accepted the theorising of the alarmist (whatever the level of study he devoted to the problem) than if he were merely espousing a popular cause. 2035 is a long time away from today, especially for any prime minister, when a week is a long time in politics.

Made some of my weekend phone calls and asked Anne McFarlane to inform Teresa Pietraviva, who I suspect was involved in writing *The Australian*'s editorial on no-competitive, no-scoring team sport for young boys and girls, that it is important for young people to learn how to lose with dignity and without whingeing. Many intoned this piously. But it is equally important for youngsters to be encouraged to strive and to win, especially poor kids. I particularly remember the wife of a successful lawyer (she and her husband were serious, believing Catholics) telling me she did not believe in competitive sport, while I knew that her husband was in those days organizing competitive examinations for the law graduates who wished to work in his firm. Boorishness, "unsporting" behaviour is a serious problem in youth sport, not just between the competitors, but between supporters and parents. But the answer is not to deny the competitive instinct, but to channel and control it so that small victories can be celebrated with restraint and defeat is not regarded as the end of the world or a reason for a tantrum.

Mussolini in Italy supported competitive team sport and believed it helped explain British achievements. For the politically correct who espouse the "wussification" of sport, my quoting this Fascist leader in opposition to their position would be manna from heaven, regarded as a confirmation of their argument. However, on this point and not too many others, I suspect Benito was on to something (and he did make the Italian trains run on time). It is another infrequently acknowledged fact that the notoriously undisciplined English schools in the nineteenth century were transformed for the better by the introduction of competitive sport.

I urged Michael Casey to continue his efforts to develop the argument in my court case on compounding improbabilities, either verbally or mathematically, so that it can be stated clearly and comprehensively for "deplorables" like me. He was also able to throw some light on the proposal that I go to Switzerland. Apparently the suggestion was made months ago, not by a nuncio, but by someone from an order of knights. This is still mysterious but marginally less bizarre.

More than twenty years ago, when I was archbishop of Melbourne, I met a South American Divine Word priest, who had been in Australia a year or so and was working as a chaplain in a Catholic boys' secondary school in the prosperous eastern suburbs, who told me that the boys' religion was not Catholicism, but sport. I was quite affronted, because in my day sport and being a confident, prayerful Catholic were not alternatives for the great majority of us at my Christian Brothers College in Ballarat. The faith was strong and pervasive.

Times have certainly changed in seventy years. Many of the migrant children are not into sport as much as the Anglos, but the faith has slipped more, and it is not surprising that sport has moved into the vacuum. Boys enjoy belonging to a tribe, especially with goals and ideals and the occasional "war". Sport is like money, which is a useful servant but an unsatisfactory master, while being less destructive than money. I thank God often that I didn't devote my life to sport, although I still enjoy following it.

William Cowper's "Exhortation to Prayer" gives us perspective.

> *Prayer makes the darken'd cloud withdraw,*
> *Prayer climbs the ladder Jacob saw,*
> *Gives exercise to faith and love,*
> *Brings every blessing from above. . . .*
>
> *Were half the breath thus vainly spent*
> *To heaven in supplication sent,*
> *Your cheerful song would oftener be*
> *"Hear what the LORD has done for me."*

WEEK 51

Optimism but No Certainty

9 February–15 February 2020

Sunday, 9 February 2020

One of my correspondents surmised that I would be "redoubling" my prayers for a successful appeal as the date for the hearing came closer and closer. I'm not doing this, but I'm certainly continuing my daily rhythm of prayer. Our Lord warned us against multiplying our prayers as the pagans do, because he already well knows our needs. But, on occasion, he prayed all through the night.

There are many other more important issues than my release, although I want to be freed very much, and for the Church's sake more than my own. As Gilbert wrote, the "punishment should fit the crime",[1] and there is no crime to pin on me or the Church in this instance.

The coronavirus is still spreading, with 811 deaths (although only 3 percent of those infected become seriously ill, according to one report); one mad and bad soldier has killed twenty-six people in central Thailand. And I heard the tragic story of an Asian fellow in a Victoria jail, psychotic, damaged by ice, who is threatened with deportation because he infected with HIV his wife in an arranged marriage, another wife, and a couple of teenage girls also. Now he is full of rage and self-pity and has already been in a jail fight, punching and biting, which drew blood. To round out the story, if he returns home, his family will seek to kill him because of the shame he has brought upon them. May the good God help his victims, may he be

---

[1] From Gilbert and Sullivan's operetta *The Mikado*.

prevented from further infecting others, and may he see some light in his hate and rage, in his blindness.

God has no hands but ours, and some good people are trying to help this wretch; but the prospects for improvement are slim—to put it optimistically. These tragedies help me put my own troubles in perspective when I am tempted to feel sorry for myself. So I keep up my prayers, which are not all prayers of petition, and I share my petitions around, especially for those near and dear to me and for those in trouble much worse than my own.

I woke in time for 6:00 am *Mass for You at Home*, again celebrated by Fr John Corrigan. For some reason, as the program started, I thought how terrible it would be if my jail term were to be prolonged and I were unable to celebrate Mass for nearly four years. One year is bad enough, although I had originally and optimistically estimated my stay would be for three or four months. Optimism brings its advantages, even when it proves unjustified.

The sermon was on Christ as the salt of the earth and the light of the world. John pointed out the various uses for salt in Jesus' time, as a preservative, a weapon of war, e.g., in Carthage, a commodity for food, and even as a currency, arguing that Jesus' teaching was often ambiguous, leaving us to draw our conclusions.

In Australia, it is a compliment to describe someone as the salt of the earth. Thinking of those he himself described in these terms, John conceded they were very different, but all loved God and encouraged others. The sermon amply satisfied the high ranking I gave him last Sunday.

Joseph Prince was soberly dressed in a dark jacket and jeans, with a T-shirt, following his recent practice. He spoke on being as a virgin, on being married or as a mother. He used the Hebrew alphabet and language to speak about man and woman, saying that "husband" and "wife" are English terms. Women are noted for their intuition and prudence, and if a man treats his wife badly, he will not prosper. "Go back to your wife, go back to your husband and say, 'Woman, you're my woman'.... And lady, say what? 'You're my man.' And all the ladies who are single say what? 'Amen.' Just one, okay?" Certainly Joseph does not espouse gender fluidity.

Joel Osteen told each of us to be satisfied with what we have, because each of us is a masterpiece in God's image. We should not envy others, because we don't need what they have. We only need God's approval, not the approval of others. Moreover, God will always have what we need within reach. God steps in when we come to the end of our ability. We need to set the tone for God's glorious day. Within this, his invariable scenario, I don't know how he would explain Jesus' suffering and death on the Cross.

Songs of Praise highlighted the semi-finals of the young choir competition in Britain. The hymns were well sung, and I presume it wasn't a repeat of what I saw ten or eleven months ago.

The weather was pleasant when I went out at 8:00 am, becoming warmer and blowy after lunchtime. Torrential rain continued in Queensland and New South Wales.

God our Father, we know that your love sustains all creation, which is mysterious and beautiful, but sometimes evil and tragic. We still turn to you in Christian hope, quite different from human optimism, certain that you are with us in the darkness and that you have promised us another life of light, love, and peaceful justice.

Monday, 10 February 2020

It is about 8:30 in the evening as I sit down to write today's journal, and I can hear a group of birds chirping breezily nearby. It is reassuring and very pleasant after ten months when I could hear next to nothing from outside my cell, except the New Year fireworks.

I am still basking in the improvement on MAP, but my companions have passed beyond the novelty stage. Paolo has spent two years in this section, is keen to go out on parole, and laments the limited grassy exercise area, where our small plants are growing, although a couple of pots have yellow leaves. I presume this is a sign of disease.

The youngest fellow doesn't even go outside and sleeps through the morning. He regularly comes to my small cell window for a few words, so I suggested he might take a bit of exercise. He ducked the issue and explained that the psychologist is going to help him ask for a transfer. He telephones at the top of his voice and gets cross every once in a while with his callers.

Derek was told he was to be in court in Melbourne at 10:30 am, so his family and the press were there waiting. Some time after 9:00 am, he was informed of the afternoon starting time. These unexpected events happen in jails.

I believe his claims that he was framed on a murder charge and has spent nineteen years wrongly in jail. I heard that Ron Iddles[2] investigated his case, found that he had been set up, and wrote a report to that effect, which a senior police officer just set aside.

Another issue. While I haven't seen the article myself, it was reported that the chief prosecutor has publicly criticized the police for their failure to cooperate fully with the Royal Commission on Lawyer X.[3]

These two facts confirm my belief in the existence of a vein of corruption in Victorian public life. The only questions concern its length, breadth, and depth, how far it rises, and where it runs.

The highlight of the day was a visit from my nephew Nicholas. They gave us nearly one and three-quarter hours together, and we spent most of the time discussing my case, which Nick has followed closely, and on social media.

He brought me the good news that Les Dickinson had an operation but is already out of hospital, organizing the district, and likely to return at regular intervals for follow-up treatment in Melbourne.

My sister, Margaret, is back in hospital with some inflammation in her legs. Please God it will be quickly brought under control.

Strangest of all, Nick brought a message that the higher authorities in Rome had halted Frs Robbie and McCulloch, who were clearing out my Roman apartment to send my contents to Australia. Heaven only knows what is behind this, but it is not quite as bizarre as going to Switzerland!

Nick looked better than I had seen him in the last three years and ascribed the improvement to his no longer doing a daily routine with the weights after a hard day's physical work.

I had expected a visit to the physiotherapist today but discovered that I had an unexpected appointment with the podiatrist. This was

---

[2] Dubbed "Australia's greatest detective", Ronald Iddles (b. 1955) was a police investigator for forty-three years.

[3] The commission investigating the police's employment of a lawyer to inform on her clients.

a relief, as I had anticipated a new struggle to set up a local arrangement to look after my feet. However, it was the same woman who had looked after me at MAP, who followed her nominated schedule and did her usual excellent work. While my toenails had grown at quite different rates, there was no ingrowth, and at no stage has she cut my toes inadvertently; which is rare in my experience. The medical care has been good in both my jails, if a bit slow and sometimes overzealous.

I had my third blood test since I arrived here to ensure my blood is not too thick, i.e., to ascertain the effectiveness of the Warfarin. I suggested that one test a month would be sufficient.

As I was coming back from the podiatrist, while walking along the edge of a large exercise area, a group of workers in the factory one hundred metres [110 yards] away recognized me and called out my name. Fortunately, I couldn't make out what they were saying, but while it didn't sound vicious, I don't think it was high praise. My isolation is for my protection and peace of mind.

During my life, I have often prayed the rosary, but not every day, until the last few years. With Mother Teresa, it was different. I am moving through the book on her journals and thoroughly enjoying it. At this stage, she has just started work with her new companions in the slums of Calcutta in late 1948, after the war, a famine when two million died in Bengal in 1942–1943, and then the Hindu-Muslim riots. She and her followers always "recited the Mother's praises" before starting work in "the streets and dark holes of the slums". Mother Teresa instructed:

Cling to the rosary as a creeper clings to the tree, for without Our Lady, we cannot stand.

Tuesday, 11 February 2020

Today marks one month before the start of my High Court appeal, which I will not be able to follow live. I am not sure how I will fare during these weeks, but I have coped with previous run-ups to significant trials, and I am sure that one essential is to keep up my daily routine and focus on each day. This appeal is different in two ways.

It is my last chance for exoneration, and I have sounder reasons for optimism—but no certainty whatsoever. As I wrote to one of the young Sydney priests today, I am in God's hands through the hands of the judges.

Apparently Friel keeps turning out articles that are "ad rem", for the case, and the Council of Trent[4] is forwarding them to our lawyers. Strangely, I have not been able to speak with them this week. Today, I repeated my two requests, but only to the telephonist to be put to Bret and Ruth today during their meeting in Sydney. How do they propose to deal with the issue of compounding improbability? Did the accuser make any significant mistakes in not recognizing changes made to the cupboard areas in the sacristy after 1996? I have asked to be shown the final draft while there is still time for changes to be made. Terry Tobin has reported that Greg Smith has done some good work on the compounding improbability issue in tracing down precedents, etc.

On the local front, Derek is in court for the second of the three foreshadowed days, and Paolo heard that the officer who reviewed his parole situation last December still had not provided her recommendations. He was very upset, so I urged him not to make any mistakes which they could use to delay his release further. He must not let this setback break him. I don't know what he thought of my advice.

Each day we are given a request sheet which we hand in at the beginning of the day. I requested information on my physiotherapist appointment which had been promised for yesterday, when I had received an unexpected visit from the podiatrist (as I reported). Both words begin with P. They thought the physio was coming today, but nothing eventuated for me. Perhaps she didn't get through all her appointments. I will repeat my request for information tomorrow and at some stage will explain that I don't like being strung along by ineffective half promises. It is impossible to know whether you are confronting ignorance or incompetence or a small dose of bastardry. And in my case, it is no big deal!

I watched Question Time in the House of Representatives, and it was neither entertaining, informative, nor impressive. None of the speakers seemed very sincere, except for the speaker, who came

___
[4] Council of Trent is a group of friends in Melbourne who meet regularly.

through as a formidable chairman. Otherwise, it resembled a bad school play—plenty of overacting.

The news told us that already a thousand people have died from the coronavirus, most of them in China, and thirty-two thousand persons are infected. Only fifteen Australians have contracted the disease. Xi Jinping visited Beijing's hospital, and two senior officials were dismissed as criticism mounts in China over the government's response.

Last night I watched a program on a small British expedition into immense forests in central Borneo, largely untouched by human activity with an area half the size of Belgium. Ancient wall paintings were discovered in two caves: those in a dark brownish colour allegedly 20,000 years old, and those in red, 40,000 years old, which they claimed as the oldest in the world, made during the last ice age, which ended around 12,000 years ago. Ice has covered planet Earth for most of its history with comparatively brief warm intervals of 10,000 to 15,000 years. By some standards, the next ice age is a bit overdue, although one study claimed that we should be safe and warm for about 30,000 years due to specific conditions. Most of the Borneo paintings were hand outlines; one portrayed a type of ox or bullock. If they are genuine, this would increase the chances of UNESCO banning agriculture there.

I am deeply suspicious and will reserve judgement until further studies are done. I smell a repeat of the hoax diaries of Hitler's last days.[5] Time might be able to tell.

What is true in any event is that we are dealing with tens of thousands of years of history. How old is the human story? How far back do we go to Adam and Eve? God is immensely patient and has chosen to work in particular through a small, unusual group of tribes, the Jewish people; in the middle of the great ancient empires of Egypt, Assyria, Babylon, and the Persians, and then with the Greeks and Romans. The kingdom of China, the Indian subcontinent, and the civilisations of the Americas are extraneous to this, apart from some later Christian missionary activity. Good and evil are everywhere, but God's special activities have followed a strange path: tortuous, slow, and often late on the scene.

---

[5] In 1983, diaries attributed to Hitler received international publicity but were later exposed as forgeries made by Konrad Kujau.

I don't know whether the unimaginable immensity of the universe is a greater mystery than the slow-moving story of human development, because we know of no other intelligent beings with free will in the universe. Leaving aside the angels in their own different world, humanity is the peak of God's achievement.

But in space, God has left himself plenty of room to move. If the new heavens and the new earth, which will accompany the resurrection of the body in the end time, after the Last Day of judgement, are somehow related to our plane of existence, heaven would not be crowded even if most humans arrived there. And we hope and pray that hell is not crowded, although Jesus told us the road to perdition is broad indeed. One Jesuit friend of mine, and a good Jesuit, claims that the Catholic decline in the Western world since the 1960s is heavily influenced by the diminished or abolished fear of hell.

We find many references to this theme in the Gospels. Here is one from Luke 13:23–24. Someone asked him, "Lord, are only a few people going to be saved?" He said to them,

Make every effort to enter through the narrow door, because many, I tell you, will try to enter and will not be able to.

Wednesday, 12 February 2020

My routine was disturbed today as the jail held a management lockout training day, which meant everyone was confined to his cell while the jail "locked down" between 11:30 and 2:00 pm, the period I usually spend in the large common room, kitchen area. Paolo generously volunteered to remain in his cell, so I managed more than an hour inside (able to phone and access the refrigerator) before spending an hour or so outside. Derek was again in court.

There were showers during the night, so the lawn was wet when I went outside, although the day was slightly humid. A mild humidity by Sydney standards, but nothing at all by Queensland levels.

The jail governor visited and saw my glasses with only one arm. I stressed that I could still see. Later in the day, I was asked to fill in the form for the optometrist, but no word whatsoever on when an appointment with the physiotherapist might occur.

Last night, I finished reading Grantlee Kieza's biography of Lachlan Macquarie, the fifth governor of the British colony of New South Wales, after Governor William Bligh had been ousted by a local rebellion. Appointed in 1809, Macquarie remained in charge until 1821, and the colony grew spectacularly under his leadership from a small penal colony of 11,590 people to a prosperous settlement of nearly 39,000, caring for 100,000 cattle and 290,000 sheep and with 12,000 hectares of land under cultivation, a fourfold increase.

I read a section every night when I went to bed, often continuing longer than is prudent. I'm not sure many topics deserve more than 250 pages, but I happily concluded 570 pages on Macquarie, which is a tribute to Macquarie and the author. While I abandoned Hobbes' *Leviathan*, this story did not tax my powers of endurance.

I would like to visit the mausoleum in Scotland where the governor is buried with his second wife, Elizabeth, and two children, with the inscription "The Father of Australia". The title is deserved. He was our first great champion, a visionary, and an optimist who defied his persistent local opposition and the critics at home in England, who were disturbed by the expenses he was incurring and especially by his willingness to enroll emancipated convicts in the leadership of the colony as, e.g., magistrates and officials. Australia is still defined by social mobility, and the challenge will always be to achieve this in successive generations as well as Macquarie did.

Macquarie was no saint, but he was an experienced soldier in the British Army who had served in North America, the West Indies, and for twenty years in British India. His was a career of solid, not spectacular, military achievement, but he was also an effective "networker", socially acceptable because of his bluff, shrewd personality and the fact that he came from a family of Scottish aristocrats, even if they were far from prosperous. He contracted a touch of syphilis in his early years and was caught out exploiting the system by enrolling young relatives as part-time officers (with a salary), far before they were old enough for military service.

A tough, decent man, he fostered Anglicanism, family life, public decency, and law and order, and he prevented the successors to the Rum Corps[6] from dominating the colony. He worked hard to help

---

[6] A corrupt group of officers in the early years of the colony of New South Wales.

the Aborigines but authorised one brutal punitive expedition after settler casualties. It is to his credit that he was an opponent of the Rev Samuel Marsden, a hard and bitter man, hostile to emancipists. He expelled Fr Jeremiah O'Flynn, an Irish Catholic priest who had arrived without permission in the colony, but then welcomed Fr John Therry, a difficult man who worked heroically in and around Sydney. The governor laid the foundation stone for St Mary's Cathedral.

One of my proud moments as archbishop of Sydney was to preach at the Mass in the Basilica of St Paul Outside the Walls in Rome for the seven to eight thousand Australian pilgrims who were present for the canonisation of St Mary MacKillop in 2010. St Paul's had a long connection with the English-speaking world, as before the Reformation, the King of England was an honorary canon there, and in the latter half of the nineteenth century, Bishop Salvado of New Norcia in Western Australia brought two young Aborigines to St Paul's to begin training as Benedictine monks. Their health collapsed, both dying young, one of them in Italy.

Although I had worked hard to prepare a sermon that was religiously adequate for such an important occasion, I was surprised at how well it was received. One point I made was that Macquarie opened up Australian society so that capable people could get ahead and make a contribution, even if they had earlier made big mistakes or came from poor and less educated families. And I added that it was the likes of St Mary MacKillop and her Josephite Sisters who enabled the children from these families to benefit from the human advantages which accompany faithful Catholic lives and exploit the openings in Australian life which Macquarie and like-minded leaders had opened up. Catholic schools provide similar opportunities for the children of today's migrants. The pilgrims were overwhelmingly devout, people who gave primacy to the nuns' religious contribution, but they also realised how important was the human development that the Sisters fostered in the schools. My Australian congregation, far from home, was there to celebrate St Mary of the Cross, but was also grateful for the traditions which Macquarie created. Until Macquarie, Mass could not be celebrated publicly in the colony (except for a brief period under Governor Philip King).

The number of letters has diminished, with about sixty arriving in the last week. One unhappy piece of news was that a law group in Rhode Island in the United States has filed a class lawsuit against the bishops for fraudulent promotion of Peter's Pence.[7] Please God, it won't gain too much support, not least because the US bishops made no decisions on expenditure for Peter's Pence. However, this is another example of the wages of sin, paid, in this case, by someone else.

On a happier note, one writer remembered my speaking in the Camberwell Town Hall in 1996 when I became archbishop of Melbourne and quoting from Campion's *Brag*, the magnificent pamphlet the Jesuit martyr St Edmund Campion published in Elizabethan England when the practice of the faith was forbidden:

My charge is, of free cost to preach the Gospel, to minister the Sacraments, to instruct the simple, to reform sinners, to confute errors—in brief, to cry alarm spiritual against foul vice and proud ignorance, wherewith many my dear countrymen are abused.

Thursday, 13 February 2020

Early in the afternoon, the younger Muslim prisoner came to my door to tell me Pope Francis was maintaining the discipline of celibacy for priests. He supported this, as he believed each religion should retain its own traditions. My first reaction was surprise and relief, although a moment's reflection brought the realisation that the most likely outcome was a reaffirmation of the Latin rite practice across the world, while allowing an exception in the Amazonian area. I will try to get accurate information on the news tonight.

A letter from Mark Withoos, which I received today, foreshadowed a document authorising a change of discipline for the Amazon. More on this later with better information.

The morning was overcast, quite grey and slightly humid, although the sky cleared and it warmed up around midday.

Aileen the chaplain called and brought me Holy Communion. Sr Mary is recovering and has left hospital for rehabilitation. I also had a

---

[7] The Peter's Pence collection is a donation made by the faithful directly to the Holy See to finance corporal works of mercy.

brief meeting with the Sentence Management Branch, a body within Corrections Victoria that supervises placements, and explained that I had no complaints. They, too, were enquiring about what the procedure would be if my appeal were successful, and I explained that I did not know when my release might occur, i.e., on March 12 or later.

Another letter has arrived from Oran Park in New South Wales, from my earlier correspondent who has been predicting that I will be freed. Not only does he make predictions, but he claims they are regularly, indeed always, correct.

He does not have anything on the precise timing but thinks March is the most likely. He believes my case will be seen as similar to that of Lindy Chamberlain, will have a great and positive impact for the Church, and will serve as "an important lesson for the world about hate and vilification". The emerging lynch mob mentality needs to be brought into check, he added.

I feel uneasy again about even mentioning his predictions, because his self-understanding and certitude are powerful countersigns. He gives every appearance of sincerity and is obviously an intelligent person who reads events well and has a generally sound estimate of what will happen. It is reassuring when the estimates of shrewd observers are favourable and run in parallel to one's own. And it is certainly easier to read predictions that tell of good times ahead (however poorly based they might be) than to have Jeremiahs predicting doom.

The letters continue to arrive from many different parts. The director of an Italian jail near Padua wrote to express his support for me and dismay about the legal proceedings. Lorena, who was now on the governing council of the Fraternas[8] in Peru and who had worked in Sydney with their pioneer group, which did outstanding apostolic work, wrote to promise continuing prayers. A younger friend from Sunbury here in Victoria felt embattled. "The wind is really blowing hard against us now, our backs are to the wall, reminds me of the *Narnia* and *Lord of the Rings* end battle scene with our last and only hope coming from above. Do you think it's possible that we have reached the final battle or are close to it?"

As a matter of fact, I don't believe we are in or even near the final battle. But we are in for harder times, and we were spoilt by having

---

[8] A Catholic group of consecrated laypeople founded in 1991.

a pope like St John Paul the Great to lead us for so many years. My correspondent then went on to complain about mixed signals.

The father of a family of seven daughters from Calgary in Canada wrote to reassure me that I continue to serve the Church while in jail and that during the last conclave, as part of an online initiative, one of his daughters had drawn me as the particular cardinal she was to pray for during those days.

Another gentleman from Toronto, Canada, believes that I will be God's instrument to help "bring back many to Christ and his Church". He wrote that he had never been to jail, but had been accused and ostracised because he would not "become a useful idiot for ... immoral purposes".

The evening news confirmed that my young Muslim companion was correct: Pope Francis had ruled out making an exception for Amazonia on priestly celibacy. I was delighted. I believe it is the correct decision. The alternative would have been destabilising and divisive. This still leaves unchanged the religious decline in the West, but the decision is a useful example of the exercise of papal authority against those who would push the Church toward a federalism model of continental or national churches and reminds me of Paul VI's reaffirmation of the ban on artificial contraception. *Deo gratias.*

Elizabeth Lev is an art historian who lives and works in Rome as a specialist guide. She became convinced of the malice of my accusers when I was indicted on the feast of Saints Peter and Paul in 2017. She wrote to tell me about Anne de Montmorency, born in 1493, who became Grand Master of France and a champion of the Catholic cause against the Protestants. He was male and received his strange name because at his baptism he was held by Queen Anne of Brittany.[9] He grew up with the future King Francis I but fell afoul of Henry II and Catherine de' Medici and was exiled for a period, before remerging at the age of seventy-seven to defend Paris against the Protestant insurgents. While in exile, he often prayed in his chapel this prayer dedicated to St Christopher.

St Christopher, Precious Master of God, I pray you ... that before God and his holy Mother you might be merciful to me your servant and

---

[9] His godmother.

a sinner, in order that, through your pious intervention, you may cause me to overcome all those who have thought evil toward me; and by that light burden, which is Christ, whom you happily merited to carry across the river on your shoulders, deign to relieve my present anguish. . . . So that my life enduring and my honour safe, I may be able to rejoice with you until all ages. Amen.

Friday, 14 February 2020

When I went outside this morning, it was misty and overcast, clearing later to reveal light clouds. We had nearly an hour of heavy rain, Sydney rain, after lunch, so that the broken-down pipe in my exercise area spewed out torrents of water. Nearly two-thirds of the lawn area was covered by a giant puddle. We would have received more than an inch of rain.

I wrote back to Fr Mark Withoos and then answered the letters from three prisoners. Terry and Bernadette Tobin arrived a little before 12:30 pm after a small scare. During the morning, I mentioned to the warder that I was expecting visitors today. She replied she had nothing on her list. Having messed up arrangements a couple of times already, I now retain the documents when I change the list of ten authorised visitors and when particular visits are approved. I retrieved the documentation and reluctantly passed them over as she went off to clarify the situation. I was confident enough all would be well and would have been really upset if they had travelled from New South Wales and could not come in.

The Tobins, with the help of their daughter Caitie, Michael Casey, and Margaret O'Reilly, are arranging for the journal volumes to be typed up. Caitie was amused to read that after one of their visits I claimed that they did not have much news. They had plenty of news today.

Cardinal Barbarin has been completely exonerated, and I requested that they ask Jean-Baptiste de Franssu to pass on my congratulations to him. Unfortunately, Christoph Cardinal Schönborn from Vienna has been very sick, but is now much improved.

They brought a little more clarification on the Amazon Synod document as the Holy Father dealt with the issue of the possible ordination of *viri probati*[10] by saying nothing on the topic at all. This throws another light on the situation, but the Holy Father is not likely to give his approval for a change in the near future. I suspect we might have seen a different result without the combined intervention of Pope Benedict and Cardinal Sarah. But this might gravely understate the commitment of Pope Francis to priestly celibacy.

Bernadette recounted a couple of messages from Sir Michael Hintze in London, who says that across the ideological spectrum in the UK they realised that I have been "stitched" up. He also sent a message that the whole of the Curia is up in arms, furiously resisting the pope's decision that all investments are to be made through the IOR. Terry was surprised by this hostility and inclined to dismiss it, but I explained that this proposal is ground zero, one of the most basic issues, because it removes the possibilities for patronage and corruption which have been built up over the decades (I don't know how many decades) and exploited so profitably by criminals. The forces of corruption have been badly weakened, but they will fight tenaciously, if not fanatically, with their customary ingenuity and guile and by trying to besmirch the reputation of the reformers. Pope Francis will need his adamantine will and capacity to persevere for this initiative to succeed and will be handicapped by the lack of competent senior personnel to implement the changes, although these might be available through the board of the IOR. Please God on this occasion he will keep his hand on the plough.

The consequences which are at stake are enormous. The Vatican is not paying its way and has alienated donors, especially in the United States. One element in a successful turnaround must be to obtain sound returns, financially and ethically, on their investments. A small organization like the Vatican cannot afford to lose €400–500 million [$500–600 million] every forty or fifty years.

The Holy Father, or one of his successors, will have to face up to the fact that the Vatican cannot afford to retain staffing at present levels. The only just way to achieve a remedy is to offer generous retirement packages, hoping that close to the required number would be taken up voluntarily. This would be expensive in the short term.

---

[10] "Approved men", i.e., approved married men.

The property portfolios also need to be reworked and managed efficiently. Any building which has a commercial value which cannot be realised, must be renovated so that it can return an appropriate revenue or be sold and the revenue used to make other properties marketable. The honest application of basic principles is the first requirement. No sophisticated rocket science is needed to effect an improvement.

After so many blows and disappointments, this furore over investments is the best news for some years. The battle is on, but the field is not yet won.

Our small world in Unit 3 at Barwon is returning to its normal routine as Derek is present again after his days in court and well pleased with the proceedings. The younger fellow was in court today for sentencing and also seems happy enough. He was not looking forward to the judge's summing-up because he is ashamed of what he did under the influence of drugs. Paolo was away this afternoon, so I don't know whether there is any improvement in his situation.

Because of my visitors, I missed out on my time in the interior common room. Derek volunteered to remain outside so I could have forty minutes there. A kind and appreciated gesture. Derek was educated in Catholic schools, but I am not sure he would know of, or remember, the kindness of the good thief on the cross, or his reward.

Saturday, 15 February 2020

The highlight of the day was the visit of Archbishop Peter Comensoli of Melbourne, seeing me for the second time. I particularly appreciated this because he was publicly criticized for his earlier visit. I was able to commend him for speaking with the protestors at the Red Mass. His people were proud of him. He is feeling more settled, more in charge of the situation, especially with his new staff in place. The financial pressures on the archdiocese are also being reduced. I encouraged him by explaining that the archdiocesan deficits were not as bad as the Vatican's.

He has read Pope Francis' post-synodal document on Amazonia with its silent refusal to authorise a change on priestly celibacy. The Holy Father also did not authorise the diaconate for women, saying that he did not wish to encourage a clericalising of the laity. Peter highly praised the letter, saying some of it was beautifully written as it called us to concentrate on the work of evangelisation.

Sr Mary is still in rehabilitation but had been seriously ill with complications unrelated to her successful knee operation. I put in a request that her twenty-five years' chaplaincy work be recognized by a papal award and was delighted that not only was this process already in hand, but the archbishop is seeking Australian government recognition, too.[11] I mentioned also that one of her admirers among the prisoners, who has been a guest for about three decades, is sending her a get-well card. He admired her immensely and was a little scared of her. She comes from good Western District[12] Irish-Australian stock!

The *Weekend Australian* arrived for only the second time, and I saved it until I had finished the bulk of my praying. Much experience has taught me that any alternative to early prayer can so easily lead to many, many more alternatives and then a frantic effort to meet minimum requirements late in the day or even in the night.

A couple of good articles on the Chinese and the spread of their power and influence, not just through Asia, but in Papua New Guinea and the Pacific Islands.

Fifteen hundred people have now died from the coronavirus, including a number of doctors and nurses, and sixty-six thousand persons are infected, most in China. The entire eleven million population of Wuhan are quarantined and confined to their houses. It was in Wuhan that Bishop Galvin[13] of Hanyang founded the missionary society of Columban priests, and in 1989, a few months after the Tiananmen Square massacre in Beijing, I met in Hanyang a couple of Chinese nuns who were living in retirement near the cathedral. They had been expelled from their convent when the Communists took power and compelled to work in factories for forty years. When the general situation eased, they resumed their daily round of

---

[11] I have since learnt that she was awarded an Order of Australia Medal in 2017.

[12] An area in western Victoria.

[13] Bishop Edward Galvin (1882–1956) was born in County Cork, Ireland. Ordained to the priesthood in 1909, he became a missionary to China in 1912. He founded the St Columban's Foreign Missionary Society in 1916 in order to recruit more priests to help him. After Communists took over China, he was placed under house arrest for three years. In 1952 he was tried and expelled from the country.

prayers and duties as de facto nuns, one inspiring example of fidelity among many. Now it seems that the hard times of hostile pressure on Catholics are returning and that the recent agreement the Vatican has concluded with the Chinese government has achieved no improvement for them whatsoever. My dream of a Chinese Constantine is suffering a severe setback.

In the last issue of *Annals* in December 2019, I reviewed William H. Overholt's book *China's Crisis of Success*. My dear friend Fr Paul Stenhouse, the editor, willed himself to live long enough to publish it. The article was too long, and in one section which was omitted, Overholt had pointed out that no ruler in China's history had decided, as [President] Xi Jinping has decided, to oppose simultaneously so many hostile forces in so many areas, internally and externally. Overholt's point is that it is unprecedented: no other leader has done this. Unlike our young TV journalists talking about climate change, Overholt would understand what the word "unprecedented" means and is claiming that in more than two thousand years of history there is no precedent.

In such a fraught situation, the coronavirus could have totally unforeseen consequences unless it can be brought under control quickly. We are already suffering here in Australia with many of our hundred thousand Chinese tertiary students unable to enter Australia and a ban on Chinese tourists. China needs 5 to 6 percent annual economic growth to continue the progress of absorption of the three hundred million Chinese who are outside their economy. No other economy in history has enjoyed such a long, unbroken run of economic growth. The stakes are high, also in unrecognized areas.

Moving in a completely different direction, the magazine of the *Weekend Australian* had an article recounting how the only hundred mature Wollemi pines (in four small groves a couple of hundred kilometres [125 miles] from central Sydney in the Blue Mountains) had been saved from the recent bushfires. The pines, which constitute a whole species, have existed on earth for around two hundred million years and are unchanged for a hundred million years. They disappeared everywhere else millions of years ago. The story of the planning and execution of their rescue, by planes and helicopters, by dropping fire retardants and water bombs, by the installation of basic but effective pumps, and by human bravery, is inspiring.

Ultimately Steve Cathcart, an area manager with the National Parks, was winched down into the smoke and ash, amid fallen trees and spot fires, to re-activate the pumps, kick hot coals away from the trunks, and move burning branches from the pines. He and the whole operation were successful. It is a wonderful story.

While there are now tens of thousands of Wollemi pines planted around the world, with a couple in the Sydney Botanic Gardens which I sought out years ago, it is a continuing marvel that yet again they have survived our bushfires in their original habitat.

The psalms often sing of the glories of God's creation as we hear in Psalm 18:

> *The heavens proclaim the glory of God*
> *and the firmament shows forth the work of his hands.*
> *Day unto day takes up the story*
> *and night unto night makes known the message. . . .*
>
> *At the end of the sky is the rising of the sun;*
> *to the furthest end of the sky is its course.*
> *There is nothing concealed from its burning heat.*

WEEK 52

A Devastating Argument

16 February–22 February 2020

Sunday, 16 February 2020

There must be a nest outside, not far from my cell, because every evening and regularly early in the morning I can hear birds chirping. I realise that it is unusual for me to be banging on about the birds once again, but deprivation makes you more aware and more grateful when these small blessings return. Birds were rare at MAP, even in the garden, where you heard the sparrows more frequently than you saw them, whereas here in the countryside I regularly hear and see the magpies, the crows sometimes; and one of my local prison correspondents, who regularly looks after wounded young sparrows, tells me stories of marauding hawks and the occasional eagle. Apparently, cormorants also fly around. He sent me a photograph when I explained that I didn't know what they looked like. Having received the photo, I am not sure I have spied any, so I have asked him to tell me their size. This long-term prisoner is a Francis of Assisi with injured birds, which he cares for regularly, and I am told it is not unusual for prisoners to care for birds and even mice in similar ways.

In Melbourne, I noted that I heard almost no blasphemy among prisoners or warders, and the same vacuum exists here. Aileen the chaplain explained that her experience was similar, although I have overheard plenty of arguments, some serious, often stupid, while many are only semi-serious hyperventilations. Generally, the abuse is crude and repetitive, with references to rats and dogs, etc., and a boring overuse of one adjective—and it is not "bloody".

Paolo arranged for a bucket of hot water and a mop to be left at my cell door so I could mop the floor (which I did) and told me to leave the bucket outside my door, because it would be too much for my back to empty it myself! He would organize Abdullah, the younger fellow, to empty it.

On the face of it, Paolo's situation is unfortunate. He was due for bail last September, and his parents flew in from Europe to see him. He is still here and was expecting to learn the date of his release sometime soon. Instead, he was told that he had to undergo a three-to-six-month course about violence before that could occur. Naturally, he took it badly. I don't know the nature of his offences or whether he has misbehaved in jail, but one is entitled to suspect a level of caprice or vindictiveness in their saying nothing about this course since September. He probably could have completed it before Christmas. My high profile certainly brings me a level of protection with the authorities. Whether you are a senior executive or literally powerless, the same survival skills are needed, but they have to be exercised very differently.

Judicial activism is a concern among English-speaking conservatives, who believe Parliament should make our laws. The advantage of this is that the people can vote out the legislators if a majority strongly disapprove. The United States Supreme Court decision to find a right to abortion in the right to privacy is the most egregious example of this activism.

The chief justice of the Supreme Court of Victoria, one of the majority who refused my appeal, has been active in a different way, writing recently to her fellow judges urging them to consider their options carefully before attending the Catholic-sponsored Red Mass and suggesting that they not wear their gowns if they did attend. It is also a classic example of identity politics. The other religious ceremonies for the new law year commencement did not merit similar comment or concern.

I woke in time for *Mass for You at Home* celebrated by Bishop Mark Edwards, who preached a brief, mysterious sermon. He started off by expressing his conviction that many Pharisees were good people and wondering what Jesus was condemning in them, then went on to tell of a woman who was unable to visit a badly sick friend until she was inspired by the Holy Spirit to do so. I must have missed something.

Joseph Prince was conservatively dressed, following his recent pattern, and preached on our tripod, the three bases of our religious life:

Jesus Christ, Israel, and the local church. He stated explicitly that there is no such thing as the universal Church. I wonder which local church had St Peter for its foundation, for its rock-man.

Recently Joel Osteen has been preaching week after week around the same theme. He makes no concession to a liturgical cycle, or rather a cycle of feasts or commemorations, because he has no liturgy. We were urged to "believe big" so we could "receive big". His theme was, "It's Only a Matter of Time". When we pray to God for something, God begins acting immediately below the surface, although we might not perceive any change. We should not keep repeating our prayers of petition to God when our prayers appear to be unanswered, but rather thank God we are healed.

Compass has a repeat program on the Polish priests and nuns in the Highlands and the Sepik area of Papua New Guinea, noting their "quaint" missionary work of evangelisation alongside their humanitarian contribution. Everyday heroes.

Songs of Praise had the second semi-final for the secondary school choirs. Impressive as ever, with a Northern Ireland choir giving a beautiful rendition of "Be Still My Soul".

In his commentary on the *Diatessaron*, St Ephrem had some good things to say. I am not sure what Joel's response would be:

The thirsty man rejoices when he drinks, and he is not downcast because he cannot empty the fountain.

Be grateful for what you have received, and do not grumble about the abundance left behind. . . . And do not abandon out of laziness what you may only consume little by little.

Monday, 17 February 2020

Karl Morris' visit was nearly shipwrecked. Due at 12:30 pm. When no one had called me by 12:40 pm, I phoned the centre to ask whether any visitor had arrived for me. "No" was the answer. About ten minutes later, a couple of warders came to say a visitor had arrived, but had been sent away because he was not on my list. I objected emphatically and said that I would demonstrate everything was in order by bringing the evidence from my cell. I now carefully retain all evidence, as Tim O'Leary and Fr Victor Martinez have each been sent away twice, although I myself erred on a couple of these occasions. Karl's name was on the list, and I had a signed form approving the visit today. Once again, I reluctantly passed the evidence to the warder to take off to the visitors' office.

A ten- to fifteen-minute pause followed, during which I phoned Kartya (my lawyer), who had already been contacted by Karl, to tell her that the paperwork was in order. I was hopping mad because Karl had flown down from Brisbane, and I hoped he was still in the car park. He was, after being strongly counselled to stay by Louise, his wife, whom he had telephoned (as I discovered later). The warders returned to tell me the visit was approved and then melted away. Another ten minutes plus went by before a different warder emerged through the barriers. I could come through. What was the hold-up for this last delay? I asked. They had been occupied in another prisoner transfer.

Well aware of my own irritation, I hoped that Karl was not upset and had not expressed his feelings too enthusiastically. This was an entirely misplaced suspicion, sprung from my own frustration, as Karl was relaxed and smiling when we met through the glass, and he explained that the office had been very polite and helpful.

When confronted with the evidence, the warder at my end explained it was due to human error. As this was the second hiccup in a row, I am unsure about the cause, but I will be certain to take extra precautions to ensure we avoid further confusion with future visits.

Karl brought greetings and news from his family and from good friends like James Power in Brisbane. He had spent a day with John Howard,[1] who sent his best wishes. I continue to be grateful for John's public support. Karl informed me that Australian officials are concerned that the official Chinese statistics might be concealing a wider spread of the coronavirus, although Australian Catholic University, where Karl is now a senator, has few overseas Chinese students, unlike the University of Sydney, which has ten thousand. Both the University of New South Wales and Monash University in Melbourne have similar if not greater numbers.

---

[1] John Howard was the prime minister of Australia from 1996 to 2007. He was a member of the Liberal Party.

The Australian Catholic University is looking to purchase a new Roman campus as the property on the Janiculum which they were leasing is not for sale to them, and the Vatican has decided it will be used or sold to an order of nuns. I repeated to Karl my enthusiasm that the purchase would be completed while Greg Craven was still vice-chancellor and suggested that Fr Robert McCulloch, the procurator of the Columban Fathers in Rome, would be a useful contact for the university.

Karl had been a valued member of the Finance Council of the Archdiocese of Sydney, which served the archdiocese well in my time. I had assured them I would never act financially against their majority advice. John Phillips, the former deputy governor of the Reserve Bank (of Australia) was another key member, while Danny Casey was finance officer. It was a formidable operation, which oversaw the Sydney World Youth Day in 2008, the establishment of Domus Australia[2] in Rome, and the Benedict XVI Centre in the countryside at Grose Vale.

At one stage, I was dissatisfied with the return on the Sydney portfolio of investments, and the half-serious idea was floated that Karl and I would take control of half the patrimony for investment. To my surprise, John Phillips did not veto the idea immediately, but I did not go ahead. As a diversion, Karl donated $50,000 to the Priests' Retirement Fund, and together we decided how it would be invested. The shares that were most successful were chosen by Karl, as my selections were cautious blue-chips. The idea was to see how it would go over the years in comparison with the diocesan funds. This must have occurred about ten years ago, and while I followed it for some years, our gains did outpace the diocese, whose money continued to be well-placed. Today Karl informed me that "our" fund was still going very well and that it had at least doubled in value.

Two thoughts. Sometimes I feared that I enjoyed my finance work too much. It was fascinating and beguiling. And the good order in Melbourne and Sydney helps to explain my dismay and disappointment at the shambolic condition of many Vatican investments. Some, of course, were indeed sound, as either Pope Pius XI or someone in his Curia[3] knew how to make investments for the long term. The

---

[2] An Australian guesthouse and pilgrim centre in central Rome.
[3] Bernardino Nogara was director of the Holy See finances (1929–1954).

"voices" also claim that Francis Cardinal Spellman of New York was an indispensable help to Pope Pius XII in resetting the finances after the Second World War.

The summer has been unusual, not least because of the combination of bushfires and floods; neither unprecedented. February so far has been so cool, unlike the "normal" hot February days when the children go back to school. This morning was magnificent, cool and fresh, with some light cloud. Much warmer, but not hot in the afternoon.

Today's excerpt from the Book of Proverbs has some good advice for those working with money:

> *Happy is the man who finds wisdom,*
> *and the man who gets understanding,*
> *for the gain from it is better than gain from silver*
> *and its profit better than gold.*

Tuesday, 18 February 2020

One of the characteristics of my period in jail has been that life is quiet and uneventful, apart from my disastrous Court of Appeal verdict and my successful application to be heard in the High Court. I started off in jail by taking my shower around 5:00 pm, as a high point for the afternoon before the news. Prayers dominated and gave focus to the morning. Life is still quiet. But not today.

The first surprise came as I was completing my thirty minutes' exercise around the lawn when a warder came to say that she had good news as I was going outside for a trip to a medical specialist. My reply was that I knew nothing about this, despite being with the doctor yesterday and as the draft of my High Court submission was being brought down today by Kartya, I would prefer to receive that than go to the doctor for some unknown reason. The mind races in a bizarre direction. Had yesterday's lung test thrown up evidence of cancer? I gave permission for the warder to ask the reason for the visit, and the reply was that my heart pacemaker needed to be checked. So I decided to do this, knowing that Kartya would leave the document.

I thought we would be travelling to St Vincent's Hospital in Melbourne, so I brought my breviary, as I anticipated waiting for my appointment. Instead, we went to St John's ward in the hospital at Port Phillip Prison near Deer Park, only forty-five minutes away. I walked immediately in for the test, which showed the machine was functioning well, with capacity for another eleven years (which might see me out), and my heart condition was unchanged.

I travelled in a modern three-seater paddy wagon and was handcuffed by the wrists for the two journeys. On this occasion, my ankles were not cuffed. All in all, I had to endure three body searches, when you are stripped naked. The most irritating was the last, conducted by a younger officer who, among other things, asked me to lift my higher and lower lips, presumably in case something was hidden there. I commended him as "very thorough". To this his companion replied that these searches were the worst thing they had to do. I had to change out of my red cardinalatial colours and put on the usual green prison uniform of tracksuit pants and T-shirt for the journey. For me and many others, the cuffs and body searches serve no practical purpose beyond ritual humiliation. But I must confess most of the rest of jail life is almost comfortable.

I managed to phone my sister just before 1:00 pm, when I was due to speak with Chris Meney and Archbishop Anthony Fisher. This was easily achieved, and all went well initially. I asked the archbishop whether he took credit for the Holy Father's decision to maintain priestly celibacy and not endorse the diaconate for women. He demurred, but insisted he had clearly expressed his views on these issues to many people.

I spent the afternoon studying the two draft documents to go to the High Court. They are outstanding, and my capacity to contribute further is limited. I have thought of a comparison. In Aussie Rules football, home and away games are played at a level of skill and intensity. In the finals, these levels are higher, and in the grand final, special skills are required, so that those who can get a few kicks in the home and away games might scarcely get a touch in the grand final. That is my situation. I made my contribution earlier.

About twenty letters arrived yesterday and today. I will conclude with one quotation from yesterday's batch. Tom and Clare were a young couple of strong faith who had a baby boy at the Mercy

Hospital, Melbourne, in 1990. They had come under fierce pressure for Clare to have an abortion, as their child had massive cerebral abnormalities, which meant he had no chance of survival even in the shorter term. They persevered, the baby was born, and I visited the three of them in hospital before the child died. A tragedy. They now have four other healthy children. Tom concluded a beautiful letter of support with these words:

We, Clare and I and family, are all praying for you, and I'm tipping my deceased son, Thomas Walter Ryan, whom you visited, who will be praying for you also.

Wednesday, 19 February 2020

The time is slipping by, and I am neither agitated nor any more impatient than my customary niggle.

Both yesterday's and today's weather were punctuated by rain showers; yesterday they were heavy, but light this morning and clearing by the evening. It was still unseasonably cool. At 10:00 am, I was called for an unexpected meeting with the lawyers by video-link. I was anticipating that the meeting would be held tomorrow as the document has to be lodged by Friday 21st. Ruth Shann, the junior barrister who had written the draft, was accompanied by the solicitor who was working with her, Kartya Gracer, and Paul Galbally.

Ruth spoke briefly by way of introduction, and I then proceeded to make the points I had prepared for the pages of notes I was proposing to write out this morning to be faxed or emailed to the office. This earlier meeting saved me a couple of hours of writing.

I began by thanking Ruth and Kartya for the first-rate quality of the document. It was written in High Court language, but the judges are those who have to be convinced.

Naturally, I could only follow from a distance the arguments about the correct appeals to precedents, and in a couple of cases I asked to know the basic facts so I could better understand the arguments.

The document began boldly by claiming that the prosecution's submission did not answer our arguments but, in fact, extended the errors of the two majority judges on the crucial issue of the burden and standard of proof and then went on to prove these claims. A key plank was that "using a belief in the correctness of the complainant to evaluate the other evidence is impermissibly circular and contrary to the onus and standard of proof."

We discussed at some length the argument on compounding improbabilities, and I requested a more detailed argument in the text on this matter after it was asserted that the prosecution's claim on one point was "plainly no answer". I explained how such a phrase triggered a reaction in me, requiring stringent supporting evidence, as I knew the temptation of raising one's voice to support a weak argument when we preach. I repeated my claim that an argument on compounding improbability did not require each element to be improbable or completely independent from the other elements. The point still at issue for me is whether these variables and their interaction can be usefully described mathematically in terms of chances. This work still needs to be done (if it can be done), and Ruth explained that this can be explained in the oral presentations (and would be).

I judged that our argument is sound, that the prosecution could not rely on Portelli's argument on one point, e.g., where robing occurred on 15 and 22 December 1996, and then dismiss his claim that he was always with me as "unreliable". The arguments for alibis were well made.

On ground two, the timing of the hiatus, the prosecution and the majority judges chose different goals. The majority put the time of the offences as taking place before the servers arrived at the sacristy after Mass. Not even a credible witness can be in two places at the same time, i.e., travelling in procession (by his own claim) and being violated.

The prosecution chose the second alternative, that the incidents took place after the servers arrived at the sacristy and then retired mysteriously to wait in the workers' sacristy to allow time for the crimes to be committed. This is directly contrary to the evidence of the two senior servers, McGlone and Connor,[4] and the prosecutor had conceded this with the words "there is, of course, no evidence of that."

---

[4] Daniel McGlone and Jeffrey Connor, former altar servers at St Patrick's Cathedral, Melbourne, testified on behalf of Cardinal Pell.

The High Court has given permission for the two pages of the court transcript recounting Ruth's question and the prosecutor's damning reply to be appended to our submission. The draft has to be reduced, as it is over the limit by a little more than half a page.

Win, lose, or draw, this applicant's reply is well done; devastating, in fact. I have enjoyed contributing to these arguments and helping to polish the penultimate draft.

I spent the afternoon opening the forty to fifty letters which arrived in the last two days.

Today's excerpt from the Book of Proverbs reminds us to keep centred:

> *The fear of the Lord is the beginning of wisdom*
> *and the knowledge of the Holy One is insight.*

Thursday, 20 February 2020

Today was a good day for a couple of reasons but mainly because Aileen brought Fr John McCarthy, now eighty-two, to celebrate Mass for me. I covertly concelebrated.

For some time, I wondered why I "enjoyed" it much more than the two Masses at MAP, and obviously a good deal depends on one's "religious" mood: dry or more open to consolation, realising or sensing more easily the spiritual significance of what we were doing. All of this is relevant, but the main difference was that today we were in our isolated small room, surrounded by quiet, conducive to reverence. At MAP, Fr Jerome celebrated Mass in the middle of the common room, where the work of the three guards continued around us and the prisoners locked in their separate cells were only metres [yards] away, behind their doors.

Once again, as Mass was beginning, I thought how terrible it would be to be prevented from celebrating or attending Mass—for nearly one year is bad enough—or worse than that.

The ancient ritual whose central elements go back to Our Lord himself is worth more than a thousand sermons and absolutely essential as the core activity to be enhanced by the readings from the word of God. The Roman rite we celebrated is probably more than fifteen hundred years old, and I rejoice again in the fact that 80 percent of the prayers, which we laboured so hard to translate into an accurate and beautiful English, come from Latin prayers a thousand years old. As St Mary of the Cross liked to say, "Remember we are but travellers here."[5]

The Gospel reading was about forgiving our enemies and returning good for evil, and Aileen told us that it provoked lively discussion among the prisoners elsewhere earlier in the day, when it had been read to them.

Fr John had been rhetoricians' prefect when I began at Corpus Christi seminary in Werribee in 1960. The Jesuits who were in charge left us to organize our community life (there were about 120 of us across four years) under leaders the rector appointed, and John organized and to a large extent supervised our daily life together on the bottom floor of the new wing as first-year seminarians. He was always a gentleman, a man of faith and kindness, recognizably the same now, only better than sixty years ago. It is no surprise that at eighty-two he was continuing to celebrate Mass in the jails around Geelong.

We occasionally tried his patience in 1960, and he confessed we were a "handful" every now and again. I remember him once remonstrating to us as a group, urging us to remember "we're in a bloody seminary."

With me a prisoner, our authority roles as bishop and priest were reversed, and John remarked that it reminded him of our "rhetoric" days—the name for the first year when he was in charge. We discussed some of the men in his year, especially Fr Michael Shadbolt, a clever man, long-term parish priest, a missionary in South America for seven years, with a doctorate in psychology and still working as an exorcist. I once lectured him in early Church history at Catholic Theological College, and the essay he gave me was better than my lecture. I kept it to help me do better with my course in the following years.

Fr Des Panton was ahead of both of us in the seminary, quite a character, a priests' man who did a lot for the Corpus Christi priests' group and occasionally a "handful" (like us as rhetoricians) for his bishops. I was deeply touched when John told me Des was praying for me every night.

---

[5] From a letter in 1867.

On coming back to my cell, I told the senior warder accompanying me that the life in my pre–Vatican II Council seminary, with its silence and isolation, was a good preparation for jail. She didn't warm to the idea at all.

I had made this point to a number of people, and more recently to Daniel Hill, who had been coordinator of the university chaplaincies, when he visited. He sent me a quotation from Evelyn Waugh's *Decline and Fall*, which I read recently: "Anyone who has been to an English public school will always feel comparatively at home in prison. It is the people brought up in the gay intimacy of the slums, Paul learned, who find prison soul destroying."

The quotation comes from before the time when "gay" had been captured by any one group. An English public school is different from an Australian boarding school and different again from a seminary, but the lines partly explain why some priests-to-be found seminary life difficult before the reforms, although community loyalty is strong in both seminaries and Australian boarding schools. The English differ among themselves by region and class, but the Anglo-Irish in Australia have more in common now with life in Britain than with, e.g., the Irish. This was a surprise to me, but the gruff, sardonic outspokenness of the Aussie stereotype is not found often in Ireland, but more frequently in the north of England and the eastern part of London.

I sent off four or five pages of thoughts to Archbishop Anthony on the future possibilities for Domus Australia and Australian Catholic University.

I was talking briefly with Paolo, my Muslim fellow prisoner, whose parole has just been extended for six months. He has now settled down. We both agreed that the good God is looking after us, but, I added, God is sometimes slow moving.

The words of Psalm 45 today are a help.

> *Awake, O Lord, why do you sleep?*
> *Arise, do not reject us forever!*
> *Why do you hide your face from us*
> *and forget our oppression and misery? . . .*
>
> *Stand up and come to our help!*
> *Redeem us because of your love!*

Friday, 21 February 2020

The unseasonable weather continues. It was cold this morning when I was outside, and yesterday was showery. More deaths from the coronavirus in China were announced, although the authorities there are claiming that the number of new cases each day continues to fall. One or two sceptics wonder whether this is due to a changed classification system, where the number of cases of suspected infection continues to rise. Chinese students are still banned from entering Australia so that the economic consequences to Australian universities and tourism will be considerable.

Unexpectedly I was called to the dentist, although I had first reported an intermittent toothache in my upper right teeth months ago. Vigorous brushing with a liberal use of toothpaste had eliminated most of the twinges, although, more recently, a long-term broken tooth had started to ache. To my surprise, the dentist discovered there were no cavities and that nothing could be done for what remains of the broken tooth other than to remove it, while the upper right teeth were surrounded by bad gums and encrusted with plaque. He quickly removed the plaque, and all the teeth remained, perhaps to be removed at a future date. With no cavities and the plaque removed, there should be no increase of pain. I lamented the difficulty of efficiently cleaning my teeth with the small brush we have to use, but no larger version was permitted.

Bishop Peter Elliott, an emeritus auxiliary bishop in Melbourne and a friend of fifty years' standing, came to visit, and they gave us a couple of hours together. The son of an Anglican vicar, he was studying at St Stephen's College in Oxford (High Church) to become an Anglican priest when I met him. About these days fifty years ago, Fr Michael Hollings, the university chaplain, received him into the Catholic Church. He had "swum the Tiber", although for some time previously his Anglican friends had dubbed him "Naples" because he was so close to Rome. On the following day, I celebrated Mass for him in the Lady Chapel at Campion Hall, decorated by Charles Mahoney's paintings, financed by a donation from the profits of Evelyn Waugh's life of Edmund Campion, and some little time later, I was Peter's sponsor when he was confirmed. When I was bringing him back from Boars Hill (where the bishop was confirming) on the back of my small 50cc motorcycle, he managed to gash his leg on the bike. But he survived to fight on.

Ordained by James Cardinal Knox, he worked as secretary to Bishop John Kelly, then later he worked in Rome at the Council for the Family, before coming home to Melbourne as my vicar for religious education and editor of the new series of catechetical texts *To Know, Worship and Love*, which are still in use. He also headed up the Melbourne campus of the John Paul II Institute for the Family, which was wound up some years ago, allegedly for financial reasons.

He has been a loyal, dear friend, who spoke up publicly for me on television when I was convicted. He is an excellent writer, whose publications have been on doctrine, liturgy, and history. His portrait with his cat made it into the finals of the Archibald Prize, something I never managed to achieve. We discussed many of the problems of Australia and the Catholic world, although I don't think we solved too many of them. He is also a first-rate cartoonist, often recounting the foibles of our changing Church. I best remember one of a feisty, attractive young nun saying to a tired and worried middle-aged mother, "You prepare the children for First Communion, and I will take the sex instructions." Those were the days.

About twenty letters a day continue to arrive, and I received three large envelopes of photocopied articles from Tim O'Leary and Fr Brendan Purcell.

Three new articles on my case came in from *Quadrant* online, two of them by Keith Windschuttle, the editor, entitled "The Crown Prosecutor's Retraction" and then "The Crown Prosecutor's Bent Trump Card". They ran in parallel with our final submission to the High Court.

In their High Court response, the prosecution did not endorse the majority option for the crimes being committed during the five or six minutes after Sunday Mass, for the good reason that the complainant was in the procession for most of that time. Instead, they opted for a second hiatus, a second six-minute pause while the altar servers, after entering the sacristy, then retired somewhere to wait for the crimes to be committed. A number of problems remained, as there was no evidence for the second hiatus; it was contrary to the explicit evidence of two of the adult servers, and in the trial the prosecutor had conceded all this; only for this rejected hypothesis to be presented again in the High Court.

Windschuttle concluded his second article thus: "This was an audacious manipulation of the evidence but Gibson[6] managed to bring it off." Despite his retraction, he was able to convince a jury and then two judges to take "a warped view of the evidence". "Gibson", Windschuttle opined, "must have felt very lucky, and probably very surprised that he got away with it."

Christopher Akehurst also had a colourful article entitled "Cardinal George Pell, Australia's Dreyfus".

Today is the feast of Cardinal St Peter Damian (1007–1072), a formidable proponent of reform in Italy, helping to improve a situation where the papacy was more corrupt than it was to become at the time of the Renaissance. I have a copy of his book on hell, which I have dipped into, but not read thoroughly. He certainly did not line up with Origen by opting for a universal salvation. Famously he once had to rebuke a powerful archbishop of Milan for going hunting on Easter Sunday morning! This would imply that the hierarch wasn't even a "C and E Catholic" (Christmas and Easter).

Today's breviary reading has an excerpt from one of his letters.

My dearest brother, when you feel the lash, when you are chastised by the rod of heavenly discipline, do not let despair crush your spirit. Do not break into grumbling complaints or brood in gloom and sadness. Nor must you lose heart and give way to impatience. . . . God's way of working is admirable. He chastises his own in this world to save them from eternal punishment.

Saturday, 22 February 2020

Today is the feast of the Chair of St Peter the Apostle, although my breviary uses the title of the See of St Peter, a very similar notion.

In St Peter's in Rome, we have an ancient bronze statue of St Peter on his chair just before you enter the area of the altar under the dome, topped by Bernini's baldacchino, also in bronze, allegedly stripped from the pre-Christian Roman temple, the Pantheon, and representing the veil held over a Jewish couple at their wedding

---

[6] Mark Gibson, QC, was the prosecutor in the committal and trials.

ceremony. So, too, the Eucharist symbolises the marriage of Christ and his Church.

But back to St Peter. The solid chair with its back and arms represents the teaching chair of the ancient Greek philosophers, which would be set up so that their students could gather around them. No doubt in more hierarchical times, the faithful compared it to the throne of a king. The ruler and the successor of St Peter did rule the Papal States in central Italy for more than a thousand years. The bronze toes of the statue have been worn down by the kisses of pilgrims across the centuries.

The term "cathedral" comes from the Greek word "cathedra", for chair, and is the principal church of the local bishop, where he has his teaching chair to teach as Christ taught, to maintain the unity of his flock and the unity of all the churches around the successor of St Peter. Despite being built over the burial place of St Peter and near Nero's Circus, where he was executed, St Peter's is not Rome's cathedral. That title belongs to St John Lateran's church, which was built on the land of the Lateran family given to the Church by Constantine, the first Christian emperor, early in the fourth century.

Just as the pope has an authority to teach and rule which is not shared equally by the other bishops, so each local bishop has a role to preach and defend the apostolic tradition, to have the last word locally on what teaching is truly from Christ and the apostles, a power which is not shared equally by the priests, religious, or laity.

My friend and mentor Archbishop Eric D'Arcy of Hobart, who had lectured in philosophy for twenty years at Melbourne University, was a learned man, who sometimes sat easily with theological customs which he regarded as less important. Once, when he was bishop of Sale, he told me he was thinking of inviting his priests to preside from his chair in turn when they were celebrating Mass in the cathedral. I was scandalised and explained that this would be an inappropriate symbol, for the bishop is the first teacher, priest, and ruler—as well as servant—of his people and priests. I did not convince him of many things over the years, but he conceded that logic and tradition were on my side on this issue.

The pope as successor of St Peter does have the power of the keys, to bind and to loose, but that is not the emphasis of the feast.

The pope, either acting alone or with the College of Bishops he convokes and leads, is the supreme embodiment of the Magisterium, which exists to ensure that "the People of God abides in the truth that liberates" (*Catechism of the Catholic Church*, 890). The Chair of St Peter ensures that the universal Church "does not fail because it is founded upon a rock, from which St Peter received his name ... for the rock was Christ (1 Cor 10:4) and on this foundation was Peter himself also built" (St Augustine).

The Vatican, like every human institution, has a spotted history, where its treasures are always contained in earthen vessels. Popes come and go, each having different gifts, but for forty or fifty years, the Vatican and the pope's Roman Curia have been plagued with intermittent financial scandals.

In the last week or so, the office of Msgr Alberto Perlasca[7] in the Vatican was raided by the Vatican police, and documents, computers, etc., were seized. I remain surprised that he escaped attention for so long, as he led the financial operations in the Vatican's Secretariat of State (which bought the larger of the two London properties) and was a fanatical opponent of any type of external audit of the Secretariat of State's finances. I also received unofficial word (not yet confirmed) that the Sloane Avenue property in Chelsea, London, which they purchased, was home to a high-class international brothel. Naturally, I did not expect them to be so careless, but very little would surprise me because the partners they dealt with regularly over the decades were often tainted and more than likely to be unconcerned by the existence of a brothel in a property they could sell to the Church for above current values. The story will become even more interesting if Msgr Perlasca starts to talk.

Pope Francis, our successor of St Peter, needs our prayers, and so do his civil servants, the Roman Curia.

I shall conclude with a couple of verses from the hymn of today's morning prayer.

---

[7] On 18 February 2020, Vatican officials raided the home and the office of Msgr Alberto Perlasca, chief prosecutor of the Apostolic Signatura, the Church's highest ecclesiastical court. He was a former senior official at the Secretariat of State, which was being investigated for financial misconduct.

Jesus, sole Ruler in the Church, your kingdom,
Yours are the keys that open David's city!
Yet till your coming Peter is your viceroy,
Keys in his keeping!

Jesus, we thank you for the Church, your Body!
Keep us all one with you and with each other,
One with our bishop, one with your chief shepherd,
Peter's successor!

WEEK 53

Lent Again

23 February–29 February 2020

Sunday, 23 February 2020

Bishop Mark Edwards, OMI, again celebrated the 6:00 am *Mass for You at Home*, and I think it was his parents who acted as servers, bringing up the cruets. On this occasion, he preached a good sermon on forgiveness, returning good for evil, and loving our enemies and persecutors. This is a suitable theme for me to ponder as I am sometimes tempted to relapse and become resentful toward judges and prosecutors, even more than toward the complainant. As well as being less than Christian (to the extent I succumb), it is only partly reasonable. They surely should understand the law better than a jury (which leaves the position of the complainant untouched), but both judges and legal officers are in a situation not of their own making, which still does not excuse major errors.

The bishop pointed out the challenge the gospel presents, and in response to the question: "How do we do what Jesus asks?", he discussed Jesus in the garden of Gethsemane and Mary at the foot of the Cross. On the Cross, Jesus took in evil to give back good. So, too, we should respond and not just react and so give back what God gives out. We have to be like Christ and act like a transformer, which changes the frequency of the electric current passing through it.

Mother Teresa went even farther in this direction, as I read in her biography, in words that surprised and disconcerted me. She wrote, "At the Incarnation, Jesus became like us in all things except sin; but at the time of the Passion, He became sin. He took on our sins, and that was the greatest of all the sufferings that he had to endure and the thing he dreaded most in the agony of the Garden."

We are looking at the deepest of mysteries, and a mystic like St Teresa of Calcutta is so much better able to speak of such things than I am; but I still wouldn't write that Jesus became sin.[1]

Joseph Prince wasn't troubled on that score, and today, for no bizarre reason, we had a Christmas sermon, where Joseph's daughter wore reindeer's antlers and Joseph preached on Adam and Eve. Joseph had a new dark suit over a polo-necked jumper rather than a shirt, as he reminded us that we had free will. God did not create robots, but humans like Adam and Eve, who were forbidden to eat from the tree of the knowledge of good and evil.

Joel Osteen's sermon contained a lot of good advice for Christians struggling with feelings of guilt, whether it was a healthy, deserved guilt or scruples suffered by those who make mountains out of molehills or cannot believe God has forgiven them.

He started by claiming God always hears but doesn't always listen, especially when we are beating up ourselves. He told the story of the Prodigal Son, whose father forgave him and loved him so much that he didn't even listen to his protestations of guilt. God's mercy is bigger than my sins, so we should come boldly to the throne of grace.[2]

It is only the accuser, the devil, who keeps a back-up list of all our wrongdoing. Didn't Jesus pay for everything on the Cross? We should make good decisions and start heading to our Father's house, where we find no condemnation, no judgement, only mercy.

He told the story of the young boy who inadvertently killed his grandmother's duck with a slingshot. He buried the duck and told no one; but his sister had seen the dastardly deed and then pretended he had volunteered to do all her house chores. After a couple of days of this forced labour, he decided to come clean and tell his grandmother. "I had seen it all," she replied "and I was waiting to see how long you would allow your sister to bully you." Joel might have

---

[1] 2 Cor 5:21: "For our sake [God] made [Jesus] to be sin"—to be understood symbolically, for Christ was sinless, for which reason the next words are "who knew no sin". It is also possible to translate it: "for our sake He made Him to be a sin-offering."

[2] Heb 4:16.

underplayed the need to repent, but the gospel teaching on sin and especially forgiveness was clear.

Songs of Praise showed the finals for the junior and senior choirs: six splendid performances.

Fr Anthony Robbie, who had been my secretary in Rome, flew out from Rome for a week and came to see me today, as the original date of tomorrow is a day of "lockdown". He brought the welcome news that the Roman authorities had told him to stop packing up my Roman apartment belongings as I was welcome to return to stay in Rome. This reflected a policy decision from the highest level and was welcome news. He mentioned that everywhere he goes in Catholic circles, people make sympathetic enquiries about my well-being. The nunciature[3] in Madrid had received three thousand messages of support for me.

We discussed the latest outbreak of news on the Vatican-London finance scandal, while he informed me that a mutual friend and ally had spoken with the Vatican police for some hours, helping them put together the many different pieces of information they already possessed. We still have some distance to run on these matters, although the Holy Father is insisting they arrive at the bottom of things. We shall see.

I signed my monthly evaluation, which had an additional clause about preparing for a possible release. My only other comment was that I regret the prohibition of leaving out bread for the birds. The official line that the birds were soiling the yard was produced. I suspect quite a few prisoners would be like me and see the bird feeding as good therapy.

The weather became warm and clear, thoroughly pleasant, so I sat outside reading *The Australian* in my exercise pen. The *Weekend Australian* has given my week a good boost.

We conclude with a few more words from St Peter Damian.

God lays low in order to raise up. He cuts in order to heal. He casts down in order to exalt. So, dear friend, strengthen your spirit to be patient by means of these and other assurances from Scripture. Wait gladly for the joy that follows sadness.

---

[3] The office of the nuncio, the papal ambassador.

Monday, 24 February 2020

The sun came through sluggishly this morning as we had a mixture of fog and mist, plus a low-level total cloud cover. While it wasn't cold, it was neither typical of summer (which has been non-existent for weeks) nor one of those wonderful clear autumn days. As I write this in the evening, after watching a three-person British team climb the highest mountain in the Arctic for the first time, the rain is falling steadily with the noise enhanced by the fact that most of the drain's downpipe is missing. I suggested the missing part be replaced to conserve the building better.

The "lockdown day" meant that from 11:00 am until 1:30 pm every prisoner was locked in his cell, visits were cancelled, etc. I still had two and a half hours outside and forty-five minutes in the internal common area, which enabled me to make a few phone calls, e.g., to discuss our submission with Terry Tobin and to request Tim O'Leary to contact Chris Friel and ask what mathematical methodology he used on the compounding improbabilities of my case to claim that, using the most conservative criteria, "the combined event would seem to be in the region of 1000-1" and that "the many other strange features of this case ... would render the odds [astronomical]."

South Korea, with the highest number of victims outside China, Iran, and Italy, has taken strong measures against the spread of the coronavirus, as some voices claim that a pandemic of disease across many countries is possible, although China reports a diminishing number of new cases each day in China. Wuhan is still closed down, the streets deserted.

Tim O'Leary has sent me some closely argued articles on my case from Christopher Friel in Wales, with Tim also informing me today that Friel produced another three articles this weekend! Three essays, with their detailed, step-by-step examination of the evidence, do not make for easy reading; but they range over all the information methodically and with unusual insight.

It is difficult to accept that the author is not a lawyer, but I suspect Bernard Lonergan's theory of knowledge has helped shape his approach. Fr Lonergan was a Jesuit scholar and lecturer at Rome's Gregorian University, known for many writings but especially for his book *Insight*, which I dipped into very shallowly and briefly, and the more accessible *Method in Theology*. I have high regard for Friel's intervention from the other side of the world, for he is an author whose previous enthusiasm was to defend Jeremy Corbyn, the leftist leader of the British Labour Party against charges of anti-Semitism. I consider his wonderful contribution providential. In range, he has rivals on my case, but in quality, no other writings are better. A few are more succinct and accessible, but he never aimed for this.

While we do not have the full story, Friel has identified many elements in the development of the complainant's account, including its similarities with the Billy Doe fraud in Philadelphia, touching on the roles of [Vivian] Waller, his lawyer; the mysterious composite Farlow;[4] Milligan, the author; [Doug] Smith, the recently retired head of the "Sano" police operation; [Andrew] La Greca, and [Bernard] Barrett from the victims' group Broken Rites. The case evolved and changed progressively as it confronted reality, and in his evidence the complainant changed his story twenty-four times. Originally, there was no reference to a Sunday Mass or to a procession. Friel wonders explicitly whether there was some coaching along the way.

The prosecution has to argue from an account of the events, even when they are tempted to leave their options open or covered in confusion. The complainant said he was abused after Mass twice, in the cathedral, a month apart, in the same choral year of 1996. Unchallenged evidence demonstrated that the only Sunday Masses I celebrated at the cathedral in 1996 were on 15th and 22nd December.

The majority judges opted for the offences to have occurred in the five to six minutes after Mass, the first "hiatus". This is literally impossible because the complainant and his companion were in the procession during that time, and, I repeat, not even a credible witness can be in two places at once. Friel and Windschuttle and Bolt and the defence demonstrated this impossibility.

The prosecution in their response to the High Court opted for a second "hiatus", a second period after the servers and the concelebrants returned to the sacristy, for the period of the crimes. This was an invention of the prosecution, without any supporting evidence, contrary to the explicit statements of two of the adult altar servers,

---

[4] Lyndsay Farlow, a pseudonym of someone or some persons issuing regular tweets against Cardinal Pell.

and the prosecutor Gibson had been forced to withdraw this claim, originally made before Justice Kidd, in the Supreme Court trial. Friel brings this out splendidly, just as he effectively defends the alibi argument that I was on the steps at the front of the cathedral during this time with Portelli and Potter, where I met McGlone's mother and where McGlone and Connor, another server, give explicit evidence that the clean-up of the sanctuary began immediately after the entry to the sacristy and bowing to the cross. Friel was very insightful in pointing out that the hiatus referred to the sanctuary, never to the sacristy, and that the concelebrants remained in the sacristy after the procession's arrival.

Friel's section on the compounding improbabilities is the most developed that I have read, and he is particularly useful in detailing the lapses in the complainant's evidence about the sacristy.

Friel's contribution is like having another Queen's Counsel[5] on the job, another Terry Tobin. He demonstrates how the claims are changed and reinvented and wonders explicitly about conspiracy. I myself have come to the conclusion that only a Soviet-type bench of judges could reject the appeal. This is a big claim, but one I have considered carefully.

Some lines from St Augustine make an epilogue for these thoughts (on the First Letter of St John, homily 8).

Consider that God wants to fill you up with honey. But if you are already full of vinegar, where will you put the honey? What was in the vessel must be emptied out; the vessel itself must be washed out and made clean and scoured, hard work though it may be.... Let us say honey, or gold, or wine, whatever we say it cannot be named, and whatever we want to say is in fact called "God".

Tuesday, 25 February 2020

Today's reading in the breviary is from the famous chapter 3 of the Book of Ecclesiastes:

[5] In a Commonwealth country, a Queen's (or King's) Counsel is a lawyer who has been appointed by the British Crown to be "Her (or His) Majesty's Counsel learned in the law".

There is a season for everything, . . .
A time for giving birth,
a time for dying;
a time for planting,
a time for uprooting what has been planted.
A time for killing,
a time for healing.

I used an excerpt for the first reading at my mother's funeral, because despite the wrenching loss of her death, I realised it was time for her to go, just as my time is now much closer than it was twenty years ago. At the time of my mother's death, I asked Richard Morrish, who lectured in psychology at Aquinas College where I was working, whether the death of a mother or the death of a spouse was more painful for most people. I half expected him to dodge the question, but, with many caveats, he thought the death of the mother is more difficult in more cases. Unlike myself, he was married, and happily so.

I have often remarked that the Wisdom literature generally, and Ecclesiastes certainly, is the most "pagan" in the whole Bible and probably only just received enough divine inspiration to be included in the Old Testament list or canon.

For me, a pagan is someone who does not acknowledge the existence of the one true God, and on that score this chapter 3 is certainly not pagan, because God is handsomely acknowledged. Food, drink, and happiness are gifts from God. "What God does, he does consistently. To this nothing can be added, from this nothing taken away; yet God sees to it that men fear him." This is no longer true for a good number in the Western world; unbelievers are still a minority in most places, unlike, e.g., [the former] East Germany's majority's unbelief, but the number is still increasing for the moment. But many neo-pagans do finish up fearing something which is not too demanding on them personally. An atomic war has been replaced by the hypothesis of damaging climate change. It doesn't seem to matter that even if we did know cause and effect accurately in the climate world, we in Australia could do nothing to change any end result.

The author of Ecclesiastes is world-weary; man is a brute beast to his fellow man and the criminal is where the good should be. "Man has no advantage over the beast, for all is vanity." He is radically agnostic about life after death. "Who knows if the spirit of man mounts upward or if the spirit of the beast goes down to the earth?" Bleak, but beautiful.

On a happier note, today brought a total surprise. On December 2nd, I had ordered a radio and CD player and ten CDs, only to discover that you are restricted to one CD purchase a month. I heard no more about it after trying to order a CD of Pavarotti's favourite arias put together by SBS, although at one stage about $90 disappeared from my account. I queried this, heard nothing, and was transferred here on January 10th. I had enquired about obtaining some Christmas music, once again with no effect. Life moves slowly, but the end result is a bonus after nearly three months. The machine and recording arrived.

The recording is not of the highest quality (not from SBS), and so far I have not been able to raise either of the fine music radio stations, as I am out here in the countryside surrounded by large thick bricks. But it is a blessing, and it was wonderful to listen to Verdi, Puccini, and Donizetti.

I am obviously a special fan of Pavarotti, and I am pleased that Joan Sutherland helped his career along by singing with him when he was starting out. When I left for Italy to study as a seminarian in 1963, I took records of Joan Sutherland in *Lucia di Lammermoor* and Churchill's war speeches! I still love the melodies, the sweep of emotion, and the high drama of Italian opera, even if the framework stories for the music are implausible, if not a bit ridiculous. Verdi and Puccini are part of the Italy I love and part of Italian genius along with Dante, Michelangelo, da Vinci—and Machiavelli.

Solitary confinement for twelve months might have dulled my critical faculties and heightened my tendency to lapse into superlatives. But Damian Thompson's article on Beethoven was a "bottler", a term of the highest praise from my youth. It appeared in a January issue of the *Spectator* to commemorate the 250th anniversary of Beethoven's birth.

The *Spectator*'s stable of writers is among the best, and Thompson is among the best of the best, together with Bruce Anderson, who writes on wine every second week. I know next to nothing of European wines but read him without fail for the elegance of his language. Shades of Evelyn Waugh.

Thompson says he has been a Beethoven worshipper since he was eight years of age and ranks Bach and Mozart as his only possible equals. But to my mind, neither can match the range of Beethoven's musical achievement.

My musical tastes have changed and improved with the years. Some enthusiasms slipped down the list, e.g., for Mario Lanza, while I acquired new understanding for Mozart. But I loved Beethoven as a teenager and maintain that admiration today. I began with playing *Für Elise*, the extent of my prowess at the piano, moving through a love of the piano sonatas (e.g., the *Moonlight*), his only violin concerto, the Fifth and then the Ninth Symphony, and the *Emperor Concerto*. I still can't quite cope with some of the quartets.

Everyone knows of Beethoven's deafness, but for many years I did not know he was also an alcoholic. Thompson writes beautifully on this suffering in Beethoven's life, seeing him as "making musical recompense for his behaviour".

Beethoven prayed daily, had a strong faith, and was reconciled to the Catholic Church on his deathbed. Thompson does not believe he could have reached that "place of tranquility that lies beyond the imagination of any other composer" without his sufferings, without his deafness. I agree. Thompson also claims his music "slipped the bonds of earth to touch the face of God",[6] a splendid tribute from a disciple.

In his homily on Ecclesiastes, St Gregory of Nyssa wrote:

O that it may be granted to me to have a timely birth and an opportune death. No one can say that the Preacher shows this birth which is involuntary or this death that comes of its own accord as though there is therein the good action of a virtue.... No one can define as virtue or vice that which does not lie within our own power.

Ash Wednesday, 26 February 2020

Lent, the preparatory season for Easter, begins today, my second Lent in prison. Please God it will be my last. I was a bit down this morning for no good reason. I was disappointed that my breviary for Lent had

---

[6] A common phrase, joining the first and last lines, with small changes, of "High Flight", a 1941 poem by Canadian pilot John Gillespie Magee. "And touched the face of God" is the last line of the poem "The Blind Man Flies" by Cuthbert Hicks, printed in 1938.

not arrived, although I began my attempts to obtain it two or three weeks ago. Some dark thoughts were running through my mind about the High Court judges, especially after the recent split decision on Australian nationality.[7] This case is radically different from my own, and I realise full well that this pessimism of mine, these doubts, are more likely to be encouraged by the Evil One than by any other source. And they are to be resisted sensibly.

The McFarlanes had tracked down my Lenten breviary to their Torquay beach house, which I dubbed Hyannis Port after the Kennedys' beach house in Massachusetts. Their son Tim, now working in finance in San Francisco, is a fan of the Kennedy family, as I was and still am, despite all we know now of personal weaknesses. I am still pleased I met Bobby[8] on Capitol Hill in the summer of 1967 when I was working in North Baltimore. He was the epitome of Irish American charm, probably the best of them, and certainly the most religious of the males. It is a tragedy that the Democrats have become so antilife and antifamily.

Back to the breviary. After speaking by phone, I knew the McFarlanes were to drop off the breviary on their way back to Melbourne on Sunday, and I wrote an explanatory note for the authorities so that this could happen, although Anne and Tim were temporarily off my visitors' list. The warder declined to accept and transmit the letter, saying it was not necessary because they were obliged to accept such deposits, although I would need the governor's permission to swap it over. Nothing arrived.

I phoned Anne at lunchtime today and discovered their sorry story. When they came by on Sunday, the jail was already closed, so Anne drove down from Melbourne on Monday to deliver the breviary personally. The prison authorities refused to accept it, and when they learnt it was a religious book, they declared such books are prohibited.

Naturally, I was outraged that she had driven all that distance only to be rebuffed, so I penned a letter of protest about the property section and addressed it to the Barwon Prison general manager.

[7] February 11, the judges were split 4–3 over whether a person of indigenous extraction, born outside Australia, can be deported as an "alien".
[8] Robert Kennedy.

Whatever the written regulations (and my cell contains many religious books, some of which arrived by the censored mail), common sense should have prevailed and Anne's generosity been recognized. This is not the Soviet Gulag.

Actually, my complaint is a back-handed compliment to the jail, because if this is the worst of my grievances, life cannot be too bad. And it isn't.

Yesterday, I managed to obtain an appointment with the physiotherapist after a wait of three or four weeks. My lower back is much better, and he worked well there and at the top of my spine. When he promised to see me again in six to eight weeks, I replied that I had an appeal hearing in the High Court on March 11–12 and hoped not to be here.

I have probably only been seeking the repair of my glasses for a fortnight or so, but today the optometrist came for his monthly visit, tested my eyes, which had deteriorated slightly, and organized for a new pair to arrive. I insisted that I needed my misshapen one-armed glasses, as I need to be able to pray my breviary, read, and write. He understood. His name was Christopher, but I didn't ask where such a name came from.

My daily routine continues, almost unchanged, although I only do a couple of Sudokus a week, the very easy version from the *Herald Sun*. I succeeded today as I usually do, but conceded defeat on Monday, as I didn't have the moral courage or perseverance to track down my mistake.

Before concluding this, I will listen to Pavarotti once again.

For the third day in a row, the stock market fell as fear of a pandemic increases. The health minister in Iran has contracted the virus, and Iran, South Korea, and northern Italy are centres of concern.

All this is some distance from Lent, when we work to open our hearts a little wider to leave more space for God. Even in jail, it is not impossible to be taken up most of the time with other things. More than usually we remember in Lent that we are but dust and unto dust we shall return.

The *Magnificat* booklet was a useful means of meditating on Lent, since I did not have the proper breviary. Their intercessory prayers sought renewal for all those whose lives have grown dry with sin and refreshment for all those whose spirits are parched from lack of prayer.

I make my own this prayer from Psalm 89.

*Make us know the shortness of our life that we may gain wisdom
    of heart.
Lord, relent! Is your anger for ever? Show pity to your servants.*

Thursday, 27 February 2020

Today I complete one year in prison for crimes I did not commit.
This is no small thing from every point of view. In any system of
justice, decisions will be made which are not based in truth. This is
inevitable, but entirely regrettable. I have an even deeper sympathy
than previously for all those wrongly jailed, particularly when they
don't have the money or connections to battle their corner. My lawyers feel that my fellow prisoner Derek has spent nearly two decades
in prison for a murder he did not commit. And it appears he was
framed. This is a disgrace.

I don't know how many of those in jail who claim to be innocent
of the crimes which brought them here are in fact innocent. Even in
a law-abiding country like Australia, I suspect that some, too many,
are in this situation and believe that we should do what we can to
help them.

I spent yesterday evening writing up seven pages on my case, "The
Basis for a Narrative", to give to Kartya and my circle of advisers as
an *aide-memoire* when presenting my side of the story. I had arranged
for it to be faxed to the lawyers but discovered they are arriving this
afternoon, so I hope to hand it to them personally.

It was cold this morning when I was outside, colder than any day
for weeks, if not months, so I was pleased for a couple of reasons
when I was called to see Kevin, the assistant chaplain to Aileen,
who is away at a conference. It turned out that he is the husband of
Jenny Griffiths, who was a top student when I was at Aquinas and
went on to be a school principal in at least a couple of Catholic primary schools. I received Holy Communion and a copy of Fr Brian
Gleeson's sermon. Tim delivered a copy of the Lenten breviary to
the property office, receiving an unusually swift and positive reply
to his request.

Paul and Kartya arrived just after 2:30, as I was beginning to think they weren't coming today. Kartya brought my copy of the breviary, delivered to them by Tim McFarlane, and four *Spectators*. I also received the documents which had been consigned to the High Court, as we had been working on the penultimate drafts. The final version is better, although two-thirds to three-quarters is unchanged, because the section detailing the appeal to precedents is clearer, and the accusations and some claims are slightly nuanced (although the substance remains from the original) and not as confrontational. The substantial accusation that the prosecution had re-introduced an argument their barrister was forced to withdraw at the earlier trial remains strong, but not crystal clear unless you can go back to the cited documents, as I did.

Paul had been talking to Katrina about what I might say if I were cleared. My reply was that I would say what I had proposed before the disastrous Appeal Court result, with a new introductory point: that my trial was not a referendum on the Catholic Church in Australia. They were not to be worried that I might make a series of controversial interventions, because I have been out of public life for twelve months, and even more importantly, I will need to find a new equilibrium in freedom to follow the equilibrium I have achieved here, largely through the prayers and support of many people.

My three fellow prisoners continue to be kind to me as Abdul, the younger Muslim prisoner, showed that I could access many radio stations through my television and gave me the number of the ABC's fine music channel; and it works. With the Pavarotti CD and regular access to classical music, my Lenten prospects have improved. I will have to do some little penance to compensate for my good fortune.

Two breviaries have now arrived at the property section, but it remains to be seen when one or both are passed to me. In the MAP jail, when the unit commander realised the breviary was a daily prayer book, he organized a quick swap, and I did not miss the proper prayers for one day. No such luck here.

The second reading I used today was from the *First Instruction on the Faith* by the Irish missionary monk St Columban (540–615), who founded monasteries in France and in Northern Italy at Bobbio.

His subject is God, Father, Son, and Spirt, who is at hand, not afar off, but remains unutterable and inconceivable, unspeakable, undiscoverable, and unsearchable. The text is closely argued and theologically sophisticated, but as the Trinity is as unfathomable as the depths of the sea, Columban urges

Seek the supreme wisdom, not by verbal debate, but by the perfection of a good life, not with the tongue, but with faith ... for God must be believed invisible as he is, though he is partly seen by the pure heart.

The Supreme Wisdom is not "gathered from the guess of a learned irreligion".

Friday, 28 February 2020

Today we celebrate my brother David's birthday, and he and his wife, Judy, visited with my niece Sarah. They gave us more than two hours together, which was most appreciated, and the strip searches were not as intrusive. These are necessary before and after contact visits, not box visits, when you are separated from the visitor by a thick glass screen. Contact visits in my Acacia wing take place in a small private room, and I am not aware that they are bugged. In any event, we had a lovely couple of hours.

I had my blood tested today, particularly for viscosity and triglycerides. Given my daily dose of chocolate, apart from Friday, I will be interested to discover whether my sugar levels have risen.

The weather continues to be mild, not at all typical of summer, but it wasn't cold like yesterday.

This morning when I was called around 7:15 am, they did not pass me any food, as I was obliged to fast from midnight for my blood tests. I resolved to turn on the ABC's *Fine Music* program as background. To my delight, the first piece I heard was Beethoven's *Für Elise*, my ultimate party piece on the piano. As a young priest, when asked whether I could play the piano, I used to boast that I could manage *Für Elise* but did not have my music. A UK Air Force family at Crowley (I think) or Upper Heyford base, where I was celebrating a Sunday supply[9] Mass, then told me they had the music.

[9] To fill in for an absent priest.

My technical prowess was always limited, and without practice my progress through the piece was somewhat disastrous and certainly embarrassing. After this setback, I never again ran the line of not having my music. The pianist this morning played with a restrained and lyrical elegance which I never approached, although as a teenager I realised something of what I was not achieving.

I received about seventy letters this week, and the breviary from Geelong arrived this afternoon. The four *Spectators* and my own breviary, brought by my lawyers, are still being "processed" and are promised for Monday.

The letter writers often ask me for prayers and sometimes recount sad or tragic stories. I pray a Memorare each time I receive a specific request.

One writer from Atlanta, Georgia, was the mother of a clergy sex abuse victim who uses each Thursday as a day of fasting and reparation for priests. She assured me that thousands are praying for me, and she prays a daily Hail Mary for me and was elated that I am in good spirits.

Often the stories are similar, with good church-going parents seeing the world take their children in different directions, with the diversity compounded by marriage breakdown.

One mother quoted Our Lady's message to Fr Gobbi[10] from December 1984, where she speaks of many of the youth "inebriated with emptiness", surrounded with "so many frivolities". Young people of course can only live in the world their elders gave them.

The woman herself had suffered a broken marriage and had been a schoolteacher but feels "we, as teachers, failed to teach children our faith, our laws" in the Catholic schools. Her oldest child is about to be married after living with a partner for eight years, one has declared herself a pan-sexual, another is devout and works for the Church, while the youngest is brilliant with an addiction. I will certainly pray for her children as she requests, and, unfortunately, some variation of her family story is all too common. She is supporting me strongly.

---

[10] Stefano Gobbi (1930–2011) was an Italian priest. He founded the Marian Movement of Priests, which became a worldwide network of prayer groups for priests and laity. Many have believed that Fr Gobbi received messages from the Virgin Mary, but the Church has not officially declared them to be authentic.

One of my most regular and most stimulating correspondents is from Plano in Texas. She was delighted Trump attended the March for Life and gave a splendid speech, as he did in Central Europe, in Poland. She concedes he lacks decorum, has a vulgar mouth sometimes, and is "a bit of a blowhard", but he is fighting a street fight, and she believes he is "saving America from being robbed and strangled". He is certainly better than his first opponent, and the position of social conservatives and Christians is so embattled that we cannot afford to be censorious about allies who choose to fight the good fight for whatever reasons. Trump is unusual in many ways, not least because he keeps most of his promises.

My friend has accurately described a large portion of Western society in this way. "This culture is just too dehumanising, defeating and demoralising to try to stay on a good path without God's help. I feel so sorry for the kids growing up in it. I was probably the last generation to have grown up with two parents, married to each other, a moral code in social structures, a safe place to play and study, movies and television that had at least some restraint. Now, without God, the culture is guiding kids into things that steal away their humanity."

The big question is Lenin's question. "What is to be done"—in these changed circumstances—besides prayer?

We, too, are wandering in a dry, immoral desert, just as the Jewish people were in the wilderness for forty years on their way to the Promised Land. Psalm 78 refers to their infidelity.

> *Yet again they put God to the test*
> *and grieved the Holy One of Israel.*
> *They did not remember his deeds*
> *nor the day he saved them from the foe.*

Saturday, 29 February 2020

As I was being led to the visitors' box for the second time, one warder commented, "You are having a busy day today." "Yes," I replied, "I am run off my feet." It was good to have a couple of pleasant diversions.

The first was a professional visit from Patrick Santamaria, solicitor from Galbally and O'Bryan, who had worked to ensure one attempt to sue me was completely unsuccessful. He brought the signed papers confirming this and informed me about the second case which inferred I had authority over Br X when he was in Ballarat, calling him a priest, and should somehow have impeded his transfer to Melbourne decades later where he offended. Originally, the main target of the suit was the Archdiocese of Melbourne, but they are now seeking leave to redirect to the Christian Brothers, the proper authority. It will probably lapse as the case has been dealt with once, properly, and within the time limits. It probably cannot be opened up again, and in any case my alleged involvement, where I had no authority, becomes even more peripheral.

Naturally, we discussed my appeal and the general situation. The major domestic news is that Patrick's father is building a large aviary behind the house. Drawing on my extensive experience with Bishop O'Collins, I asked him to make sure the wire nets went deep into the ground so that the foxes would not be able to burrow in under the fences. He took note to remind himself to do so.

I was living with the retired bishop when the diocese sold the large area of land on the side of the house and going down to the lake. Both Nancy the housekeeper and I were delighted when the workmen came in confidently to demolish the aviary and were frustrated and dismayed to discover how well it was built and how many hours were needed for the task. Nancy didn't approve of the land sale (which made good sense) and used to change the pegs at night marking out the boundaries so we would retain a bit more land. I suppose they corrected them in the morning.

The second visit was from Tassilo Wanner from near Munich, formerly one of the "young guns" of McKinsey & Co., who had been seconded to us to work on the Vatican finances. Ralph Heck, a senior partner and a Catholic, had chosen the members of this group well. Most, but not all, were Catholics. Tassilo is blessed with a wife, a young son, and two daughters, the older of whom has just made her first confession. He flew out especially for the visit, which touched me greatly.

He is working for a German start-up company producing a small vertical-take-off electric aeroplane, with a range of 200 to 300 kilometres [125 to 185 miles], designed to fly people short distances, e.g., from a CBD [central business district] to the airport. It is some years off from distribution, and eventually it will be pilotless.

Naturally, we discussed the situation of the Church, the papacy, the Vatican, and the upcoming synodal process in Germany. It is not a synod, but a move designed to avoid the canonical restrictions on synods.

He was surprised and delighted that Pope Francis' post-Amazon letter had not endorsed a change in celibacy for priests. I felt able to ask him why the "orthodox", doctrinally conservative forces in Germany were much less visible and probably much smaller than in France. He acknowledged the Teutonic preference for discipline and order and thought that the French were also a Mediterranean people. The main reason was, he believed, that the neo-Protestant Catholic forces had billions of euros from the church tax, while the others were poor. He agreed with my interjection that it is a disgrace that a person who does not pay is excommunicated and cannot be married or baptised or buried in a church.

On the other hand, the Church in France receives no support from the government for ongoing day-to-day business and is often poor, while the traditional, "orthodox" wing is often backed by wealthy donors. This is even more the situation with the Society of St Pius X, but not the whole story, and perhaps not the main reason for the difference from Germany, partly a consequence as much as a cause.

I was scandalised to have it confirmed that Archbishop Heiner Koch, who is one of the spokesmen for the rebellion, was the Prelate Koch with whom we worked happily on World Youth Day, when he was vicar general with Joachim Cardinal Meisner in Cologne. Apparently the views of a number of the German bishops have matured in a disappointing fashion after promotion.

We were both surprised that Reinhard Cardinal Marx will not be a candidate to be the next president of the German Bishops' Conference. Perhaps this was a suggestion of Pope Francis. Tassilo also informed me that the huge Archdiocese of Munich has one seminarian, while the two seminaries with the largest number of Germans preparing for priesthood are outside Germany: at Heiligenkreuz Abbey in Austria and at the Community of Saint Martin seminary in France.

Tassilo also mentioned that an American group or website had publicised Friel's article on the "second hiatus", which he commended as a model of clarity. Apart from Friel's article in *Quadrant*, neither of us knew of any agency or paper who had used his material.

The *Weekend Australian* and the fine music radio stations are both welcome novelties in my routine.

Quite a number of my correspondents have been reading Cardinal Sarah's three books,[11] the last of which, *The Day Is Now Far Spent*, was sent to me recently.

His writing has taken on a prophetic urgency, as he wrote, "In my last book, I invited you to silence. However, I can no longer be silent. I must no longer remain silent. Christians are disoriented."[12]

He believes the mystery of Judas hangs over our times.

The evil of efficient activism has infiltrated everywhere. We seek to imitate the organization of big businesses. We forget that prayer alone is the blood that can course through the heart of the Church.... Someone who no longer prays has already betrayed. Already he is willing to make all sorts of compromises with the world. He is walking on the path of Judas.[13]

---

[11] The first two published in English by Ignatius Press are *God or Nothing: A Conversation on Faith* (2015) and *The Power of Silence: Against the Dictatorship of Noise* (2017).

[12] *The Day Is Now Far Spent* (San Francisco: Ignatius Press, 2019), p. 11.

[13] Ibid., p. 13.

WEEK 54

The Path of Forgiveness

1 March–7 March 2020

Sunday, 1 March 2020

Now that autumn has started, we had our warmest day for quite a while, after a sluggish cool start. After lunch, I sat out in my small exercise pen, open to the sky, and continued to open my letters.

The major news in the outside world was the spread of the coronavirus pandemic to more countries. In China, 85,000 have contracted the disease, and 2,900 have died, although only four new cases in China were reported a day or so ago. Travel bans have been imposed; arrivals from Iran to Australia are vetoed. Jane Meney, Chris' daughter, a music teacher at a Sydney high school, had organized a school music tour to Central Europe in a couple of months' time. It has been cancelled.

If the lockdown in Hubei province expanded widely in China, the economic consequences there could be terrifying for them and the world. Their levels of immense debt, 300 percent of GDP, and much of it dubious, are a backdrop concern, which will limit their capacity to respond. Already we hear talk of a travel ban to all Italy, not just to the northern region. This would have a drastic effect on the Vatican, where the finances are already parlous as they depend on the enormous (for them) income stream from visitors to the Vatican Museums.

Fr Michael Kalka celebrated *Mass for You at Home*, beginning with the Eastern rite Sign of the Cross, which goes first to the right shoulder.

He preached on the purposes of the Lenten season as a preparation for the feast of Easter, as we strive for behavioural changes, spiritual adjustments so we can be with God for eternity. We are to use prayer, fasting, and works of mercy, which activities should also be external and social. He gave a few good examples of what might be done in retirement homes or hospitals. The sermon was well-pitched, and the altar was without flowers but adorned with purple.

The lack of a calendar and the absence of feasts and of regular themes are a major deficit for the Evangelical preachers, such as Joseph Prince. I thought he had a new outfit, but the session was a repeat from 2009, introduced, I suspect, because he mentioned the flu virus and some of the congregation (in a smaller venue) were wearing masks. He was shouting a bit, even then, and his theme was the healing power of God's righteousness. He spoke of the woman with the issue of blood who was cured by touching Jesus, who reveals God's face, whereas in the Old Testament times, only God's back could be seen. Joseph told the story of the blue threads in the Jewish scarves. Apparently the formula for this blue was lost when Titus and Vespasian destroyed the Temple in A.D. 70 and had been rediscovered some little time before 2009.

Joel Osteen was insisting that good things will happen soon, as God is hastening to act. He is watching us and working out his plans. Once again, Joel had a good message for me as the appeal date is now nine days away. I never doubt God is looking after me and realise that my chances of acquittal are better than they have ever been, but I have become very cautious. So it was good to have Joel insisting that God will rush to my defence and is in a hurry to help. I, too, need faith.

He also pointed out usefully that we shouldn't keep pestering God, but keep on thanking him. That is also good advice.

Songs of Praise was based around the Royal Hospital for the Chelsea Pensioners, ex-servicemen in the UK, and the selection of hymns from churches around the country was traditional and delightful, ranging from Charles Wesley's "And Can It Be", the favourite hymn of the archbishop of Canterbury, Dr Welby, to "Dear Lord and Father of Mankind".

The news came through this evening of the first death from the coronavirus, of a man seventy-eight years of age from Western Australia, who had been on the liner *Ruby Princess*.

Psalm 3 has a message for me.

How many are my foes, O Lord!
How many are rising up against me!
How many are saying about me,
"There is no help for him in God."
But you, Lord, are a shield about me,
my glory, who lift up my head.

Monday, 2 March 2020

For the last two days I have been ahead of myself. Although I have been well aware that February has twenty-nine days this leap year, I had relied on my prison watch for the date, as I often do, being one of that ill-fated group who occasionally is not sure what day it is. The watch which provides a mass of information had not factored in the leap year, although it caused no disruption because I was quite sure about its being Saturday and Sunday! I merely had to change the last two digits in this journal.

I remember the hackneyed joke about the Scotsman who was asked about the Scottish summer. "It was terrific," he explained, "the best day of the year."

I had been expecting today to be hot, but I tried to come in from outside a half hour early because it was cold. Yesterday was the good day, where the temperature allegedly reached 30°C [86° F]. I doubt if we rose to these heights here.

Today I was called to the doctor to receive the results of my blood test. He sounded almost disappointed, informing me my results were perfect (after eight tablets a day). The most pleasing result was that my daily dose of chocolate, except on Fridays, had not damaged my sugar levels.

Peter and Fiona Tellefson called in, having taken a day off work, and remained at their beach house in Aireys Inlet, where the permissions have come in for their new house. Their ambition is for it to be ready for Christmas 2021. Time was limited to seventy-five minutes, presumably because other visitors were to follow. We shared our family news, and they were interested to hear how my case was proceeding.

Among the many letters, one was particularly interesting and consoling for me as a priest looking back on what I have attempted.

The writer, a retired, Australian-born, Melbourne-educated physicist, had sent me a beautiful photo, a science Christmas card, which
is still on the shelf near me in my larger new cell. It is a photo of
an infant in the Rotorua Redwoods Forest with the light shining
through trees. Like Graeme Putt, my correspondent, who wrote the
parable to accompany the photo, I also saw it as a symbol of the Trinity, with the child representing Christ, the light beams as the Holy
Spirit, and the Father the invisible photographer. The writer is a strong
supporter, judging the verdicts against me as preposterous and perverse,
reminding him of Arthur Miller's play *The Crucible*. He concedes that
my opponents see me as a warrior, "who takes no prisoners, always
on the attack, never defending", the biggest thing to hit Sydney since
Plugger Lockett,[1] but he is more positive about my role defending
God and the Church. For him, the big issue of the times is not global
warming but "the battle for retaining a moral ecology within mankind
based on a belief in God".

To my delight, he defined my "major ongoing strength" as being
a "spokesperson for belief in God". Leaving to one side the important question of how effectively I have managed to do this, it is gratifying to have a senior academic recognizing and endorsing what I
continue to attempt.

Yesterday when on the phone to Michael Casey, my former secretary, I recounted Graeme Putt's verdict on *God and Caesar*,[2] which
Michael edited for me, as a "classic piece of scholarship to which any
believer with a shaky conviction can anchor themselves. And I think
it will stand so, long after we have both departed the planet." Like
me, Michael was pleased to hear this.

There is no doubt that our opponents are working explicitly to
destroy and replace the Judaeo-Christian legal foundations of the
public view of the world, which has prevailed in the West for at least
1,500 years, from the time when Constantine's Edict of Tolerance
in A.D. 313 was developed into a more explicit Christian framework
under Emperor Justinian in A.D. 520. Social conservatives are well
aware of the assaults on the moral order, but fewer seem to be aware

---

[1] Tony Lockett, the highest goal-scorer in Australian Rules football.

[2] George Pell, *God and Caesar: Selected Essays on Religion, Politics, and Society*, ed. M. A.
Casey (Washington, DC: Catholic University of America Press, 2007).

of the underlying crisis of faith, of the need to keep God in the public debates and to remind the world of our unseemly claim that the good God will judge each of us at the end of our life to reward or punish us for the presence or absence of faith and love, expressed in daily living. For too long, in an attempt to find common grounds, we have followed our opponents by leaving God out of the discussion. And I found that I gain very little traction when I make this point about God to too many Christian activists.

The late-fourth-century Greek theologian St Gregory Nazianzen had a cast of mind different from ours but is a first-rate theologian (and was a controversial bishop), who wrote beautifully on God (Oration 14).

Who gave you the power to gaze on the beauty of the sky, the course of the sun, the circle of the moon and the multitude of the stars? Who gave you the power to discern the harmony and order that shines out like music in them all? . . .

Surely the answer to all these questions is quite simply God. . . . Although he is our God and our Lord, he is not ashamed to be called our Father.

Tuesday, 3 March 2020

A mildly eventful day, with a couple of pleasing developments, one unpleasant surprise (but not too bad), and an interesting discussion on SBS TV about voluntary assisted killing in Victoria, which was slanted toward the option quite explicitly but allowed a couple of pro-life speakers to argue cogently and compassionately that doctors should never intend to kill. The discussion was polite and respectful.

After coming in from outside, where I was constrained to hand in the chaplaincy breviary so I could receive my own (some hours later), it was announced that I had a visitor. My first thought was that the lawyers had come unexpectedly, but Sr Mary the chaplain had driven from Melbourne to see me. This was the first day on which she was permitted to drive after her right knee replacement. She gave me a short demonstration of her walking, on request, and it had improved.

While she looked healthy and fresh in the face, I was touched by her kindness in travelling the distance to encourage me.

The unpleasant news was that some mad person had phoned our lawyers, threatening physical violence against me, through a bashing or with a bomb. I replied to Kartya that being in solitary confinement at Barwon was as safe as you could be anywhere in Australia. The jail and the police were alerted, so it will be interesting to see if the police leak the news.

When I was living with retired Bishop O'Collins in the old Bishop's Palace in Ballarat in 1980–1983, an immense two-storey bluestone building, someone phoned threatening to explode a bomb in our basement. As we did not have a basement in the palace, this fact provided reassurance, and I explained to Nancy, the housekeeper, a dear friend and substantial lady, that "it would need a bloody powerful bomb to lift both of us." That settled her down, and she was reassured.

My brother sent me a copy of Chris Friel's 26th February post entitled "If the Wardrobe Does Not Fit the Jury Must Acquit" on the allegations against me. I think it is a fine article, although I would need a lawyer's opinion to be sure that the facts he presents warrant his conclusion. So I phoned Kartya, asking the team to read the piece and tell me what is wrong with it.

The article begins by pointing out that the breakaway choristers arrived at the sacristy either just before the servers did (despite the extra distance the complainant had to travel), or they arrived after the servers, when the sacristy became a hive of activity. These are the two impossible alternatives.

Friel made the effective debating point that as the complainant's dead companion had denied he was ever attacked, either he or the complainant must be lying.

His basic argument was that the complainant's evidence and what was claimed in court about the surrounds in the sacristy, the place of the wine and site of the attacks, vary from what was said in the police evidence in Rome. Originally the wine was immediately to the left of the door, and the choristers were in the middle of the room, but in the court they claimed the wine was kept in the alcove and that the attacks also took place in the same corner.

However, the sacristy had been renovated in 2003 or 2004, and in 1996 the area to the left of the door was used to hang albs, so that it could not have been the place where the wine was kept. Originally there were no sinks, and the wine was kept in the alcove corner. When the complainant described the scene, he mistakenly ascribed what we see now to what existed in 1996.

Friel's conclusions from the changes in story between the Rome interview and the courts are stark: "It's as if the matinée jacket of Azaria[3] had been staring at us all along."

The program on assisted killing (not "dying", as in the official description) reinforced my deepening convictions that we need to explain more about the Christian understanding of suffering in our catechesis and evangelisation and bring God's requirements into the discussion, not as the only basis for our position, but as an important consideration for the majority of Australians who do believe in God.

Psalm 2 points us in the correct direction.

> *Now, O kings, understand,*
> *take warning, rulers of the earth;*
> *serve the Lord with awe and trembling,*
> *pay your homage lest he be angry and you perish.*

Wednesday, 4 March 2020

While I was outside this morning, the sun shone for a while, so I thought we were in for a fine, clear autumn day. This was not to be, as the clouds soon reasserted themselves, and the day continued cool and overcast, with no rain. While I was talking to Terry Tobin in Sydney, he enquired whether we had received any rain, as it seemed Cyclone Esther was travelling southeast from Broome across the continent and might dump ten inches of rain on the Murray-Darling Basin, while spreading more widely. We shall see.

At lunchtime, I also spoke to my brother, David, about where I might live, if the appeal to the High Court was successful. To my surprise, he stated that the family would be pleased if I spent some time in Rome, with the implication that the public attitude would

---

[3] Lindy Chamberlain's baby daughter Azaria, a piece of whose clothing was found after six years in an area of dingo lairs.

have strongly hostile elements, especially in Victoria, and that a public endorsement of my return to Rome by the Holy Father would also help improve public opinion in Australia.

As I have received so many letters of support, my temptation is to underestimate the level of hostility, although I was under no illusions about the attitude of the Andrews government and the Victorian left-wing establishment.

A friend I have known for nearly two decades is now a prison chaplain and has written regularly. He mentioned that one of the hardest crosses for many prisoners was being forgotten and "aggressively forgotten". This is not my situation at all, and my friends and their prayers and donations are manifestations of God's providence.

He acknowledged that I had not been forgotten, and he ascribed this to "people knowing the content of your character". More to the point for our purposes, he then continued, "half this country is standing as character reference for you." That still leaves another 50 percent of the people, and while I don't believe half are hostile, and I am prepared to accept assurances that public opinion for me has improved since my High Court appeal was accepted and, e.g., through Andrew Bolt's efforts (and many other writers'), in Victoria, anger toward the Church and her officials and institutions is much stronger than at the turn of the millennium.

As I have been in Australia again for three years and my appointments in Rome have expired, I have been looking forward to settling down in Sydney, initially in the seminary. I was not attracted to the idea of a return for six or twelve months or longer to Rome. It could be a lonely life unless you made it otherwise.

I will see what the *alta autorità*[4] in the Vatican think and seek the opinion of the archbishops of Sydney and Melbourne. One possibility is to seek an appointment in Rome, not a full-time job, but, e.g., a return to the C9[5] (now reduced to C6) or an appointment to a Vatican congregation (any except the Congregation for Saints) to counter the argument that I am not wanted at home in Australia and barely tolerated in Rome. As I am well past the official retiring age of

[4] "The powers that be".
[5] The Council of Cardinals, the nine cardinals from around the world appointed by Pope Francis as his advisers.

seventy-five, this puts talk of a short-term appointment in a further light, as a remote possibility.

All of this presupposes that I win the appeal, and I repeat regularly that I have already been cruelly disappointed on more than two occasions, so I would be foolish to take anything for granted. So we go slowly, say a few prayers, talk to one or two more people, and then wait to see what develops. It is gratifying to learn that opinion in the Roman Curia uniformly recognizes my innocence. The ACCC[6] priests are holding a special prayer vigil on the night before the hearing, and quite a few, perhaps many, people have started novenas for a successful outcome.

The coronavirus is spreading more slowly in China according to their statistics, while the three other countries of greatest concern are Iran, conspicuous for its dearth of statistics; Japan, where a local doctor claimed there were thousands of unreported victims; and Italy, where the number of tourists has fallen in some places by 80 percent.

As a seminarian, I read Romano Guardini's book on Jesus entitled *The Lord*. It is a classic. The March issue of *Magnificat* quoted these words from him in the editorial:

[Jesus] does not vanquish by magic, nor by superior spiritual force, but simply by being what he is: invulnerable to the root, and vital through and through.

Thursday, 5 March 2020

It rained steadily through most of the night, so that the aftermath of Cyclone Esther has continued southwest, extending to Tasmania, with some drenching rains farther north in the Murray-Darling Basin and beyond. A welcome development, but a surprise, if not a disappointment to the climate prophets of doom.

Made arrangements for nephew Nicholas to visit on Monday, 16 March, just before St Patrick's Day, so that he can trim my hair. His father, David, claimed he is looking forward to the challenge.

A priest friend sent me the March number of the *Magnificat* magazine for the daily Masses, with the hope that this will be the

---

[6] The Australian Confraternity of Catholic Clergy.

last occasion when it is necessary. When the ACCC priests come together on next Tuesday night for Vespers, to pray for my cause, a member will preach on Pope Pius VII, who had been imprisoned by Napoleon and then gave refuge to Bonaparte's family in the Vatican when he was finally defeated at Waterloo in 1815.

Legend tells of the dialogue between the emperor, as he was to become, and an Italian prelate, when Pope Pius VI died in French captivity. "That is the end of the Church", boasted Napoleon. "Sir", said the bishop, "we clerics have been unable to destroy the Church in 1,800 years. You certainly won't be able to do so." And he was correct.

Pius VII was elected by the cardinals in the Monastery of San Giorgio in Venice, where I searched out the most likely seat of the Cardinal Duke of York, the last of the Stuarts, who was at the conclave, and sat there briefly. Pope Pius VII has been made the unofficial patron of prisoners (as he has not been canonised), and the preacher will say that Napoleon has had successors in this area, especially in Victoria.

Aileen, the chaplain, returned after her week's absence at the conference and brought John McCarthy once again to celebrate Mass, on this occasion offered for my release. We were given a small room closer to the central office, so at one stage the Mass was interrupted by a loud burst of good-natured profanity. As Jesus was born in a stable, he would have understood. After the Mass, I couldn't restrain myself from exclaiming that the Mass is so much better and deeper than a half-hour sermon. John responded to this by noting that I was as ecumenical as ever!

One of my ex-students from Aquinas, Susan, wrote me a fourteen-page letter. She had taught in both the Catholic and State education systems with considerable success, but no longer does so for health reasons.

She had many good suggestions for my lawyers, all except one of which they had already canvassed. I will pass on to them her observation that for those who knew me at Aquinas, it would be ridiculous to claim that I would have been outraged by young choristers drinking altar wine and then proceeded as alleged. She is quite right, because no sacrilege is alleged and from time immemorial servers have taken some wine to drink. It is a practice which certainly should not be permitted, but in no sense is it a hanging offence. This is another less important aspect of the implausibility of the accusations. After all, I grew up through my teenage years living in a hotel and working in the bar!

Unfortunately, Susan became a born-again Christian in 1990, to the consternation of her Italian parents, so that she has some harsh comments on Church sex abuse (which are justified) and on Church wealth, the number of properties, and the Church's capacity to pay damages to victims, which were misdirected and exaggerated in my view.

She and her friends strongly support my innocence. She prays for me every night, and once she believed the Holy Spirit said to her, "Don't worry, he's going to be declared free in the next court hearing." Divinely inspired or not, the news is encouraging.

She also conjectured that corrupt forces in the Vatican were involved in my troubles and that the complainant might have been induced to believe his story through hypnosis. She "smells a rat", thinks I was framed, and urges my lawyers to "follow the money". Susan believes I was kind to her when she was a student, so it was good to have her returning the kindness and more. But possibilities are not proof.

The coronavirus continues to spread. Visitors from South Korea are now banned from Australia, and those coming from Italy have to undergo a fourteen-day isolation. Pope Francis was unwell and unable to attend the Curia retreat, but they deny he is ill with the coronavirus.

Melbourne had one month's rain overnight.

Today's Gospel reading at Mass is from Matthew (7:9–11).

Is there a man among you who would hand his son a stone when he asked for bread? Or would hand him a snake when he asked for a fish? If you then who are evil know how to give your children what is good, how much more will your Father in heaven give good things to those who ask him!

Friday, 6 March 2020

I arose as usual when called about 7:15 am, although, unlike my usual practice, I had woken just after 4:00 am and did not return to sleep immediately. I did not have my rosary beads to help my rosary prayer, which nearly always sends me to sleep.

In the '60s, when I was once at the Oxford University Catholic chaplaincy, I met Auberon Waugh, then in his Catholic phase, one of the sons of Evelyn and also a good writer (but not in the same class as his father). He was a parliamentary reporter at that time, claiming he was radically unsuitable for this role, as whenever a politician rose to speak, his reaction was to go to sleep. This Pavlovian reflex had been established, he also claimed, by having to listen to so many Catholic sermons during his childhood and adolescence.

The day was cool, not cold, and the sun struggled out from behind the clouds now and again. The nurse brought me my new pair of glasses, urging me to delay signing for their receipt until I had taken them away for testing. This was not necessary, as I asked for a page of prescription, which I read quickly and saw the settings were perfect. The price was $245, which I presume I will have to pay by seeking cash from the amount with Kartya for my monthly allowance. I had chosen one of the frames available, of thin black metal, which probably makes my serene countenance appear a little more severe. I have not weighed myself for nearly two months, but I am not putting on weight and would remain 12–14 kg [26–31 lbs.] lighter than when I entered jail.

Professor Greg Craven, the vice chancellor of Australian Catholic University, visited me for the second time, and we had more than a couple of hours to catch up. He had pulled a hamstring muscle, because when he was at his country house at Wollombi, which has just received seven inches of rain, he stood on a brown snake as he was inspecting his aviary, turned quickly to flee, and did the damage. He said the snake followed him in a leisurely fashion as though he wasn't a worthy victim.

Greg agreed that my prison uniform was in cardinals' colours and was optimistic about my prospects of success in next week's appeal. I asked him a question I intend to put to my lawyers. Did he know of any cases in the High Court where discredited evidence, acknowledged as such by one of the parties, was presented again as valid?

He didn't think there would be many such lapses.

We discussed a possible relationship between Australian Catholic University (ACU) and Domus Australia in Rome, and he was open to the idea of a partnership. We also discussed, from a mutual ignorance, the real or imaginary financial pressures on the Archdioceses of Sydney and Melbourne and the real financial constraints on the smaller country dioceses with the flight of population and declining rates of practice.

He has worked consistently to strengthen the Catholicity of ACU through strategic senior appointments and reported proudly on the conversion to regular faith practice of one of his senior staff since coming to the university.

Unfortunately, the two video-link meetings with my lawyers proposed for this week have not taken place. I am sure they have been busy preparing documents for the court and answering unanticipated requests from the court. I have prepared a list of points for discussion.

The first of these will be an enquiry about whether they have been able to develop mathematically or linguistically the argument for the compounding improbability of the offences alleged. Do we have any photos of the "old" sacristy before the 2003–2004 renovations? Do they have any comments on my document, "The Basis for a Narrative", before it goes to Katrina and the team? I can convey these requests by phone on Monday if there is no contact during the weekend. Today Paul and Kartya were at a memorial service during the time when I could telephone. I spoke briefly to Margaret by phone, but she kept complaining she could not hear me.

It is a moot point how many extra prayers I should say as the appeal date approaches. The good God knows how much I want justice, and Jesus told us not to multiply our prayers like the pagans. But the Lord sometimes prayed all through the night! The good God also understands the benefits to the Church from a favourable decision. I must confess that I have asked a few people to continue their prayers to keep the pressure on God; so I hope he is tolerant and understanding.

Psalm 34 has some lines I can use.

> *O Lord, plead my cause against my foes;*
> *fight those who fight me.*
> *Take up your buckler and shield;*
> *arise to help me.*
> *O Lord, say to my soul,*
> *"I am your salvation."*

Saturday, 7 March 2020

Today is the feast of Sts Perpetua and Felicity, Carthaginian martyrs around A.D. 203 under the Roman emperor Septimius Severus. The reading for the morning prayer for the feast is taken from St Paul's Letter to the Romans and begins with these words: "Bless those who persecute you: never curse them, bless them. Never repay evil with evil but let everyone see that you are interested only in the highest ideals" (12:14–17). The Gospel is from Matthew: "I say this to you: Love your enemies and pray for those who persecute you; in this way you will be sons of your Father in heaven" (5:44–45).

On many occasions, usually in other contexts, I have remarked that no gains are complete and no gains permanent, and this is true of forgiveness. This was brought home to me when listening to a French member of the Emmanuel Community, who was returning regularly to Rwanda to work with the survivors of the Hutu-Tutsi pogrom, when hundreds of thousands were massacred. Clergy and religious were involved in the killings, with one religious famously declaring that forgiveness was a Western concept (not valid in Africa)!

It was not unusual for victims who had lost loved ones to make grace-filled decisions to forgive and then find later they had to contend with surges of hatred that threatened to triumph and had to be resisted and extinguished.

My difficulties are small in comparison with the aftermaths of these horrible mass murders, but I will be in a new situation when we receive a verdict from the High Court.

If the appeal is successful, I might be again tempted by surges of self-righteous indignation against some lawyers and judges and those who coaxed the complainant (if that is the case) to make these charges—much more than I am tempted to antagonism toward the complainant himself. And if my appeal is unsuccessful, then I will have at least four new judges to dislike and condemn.

In any eventuality, the Christian teaching is clear, not at all ambiguous. Enemies and opponents, real or imagined, malign or confused, are to be forgiven. The decision has been made, and it has to continue to be made, even when the emotions are rebellious. I forgive.

Some of the Irish are reputed to be great haters, and I have a large dose of Irish blood, mostly Catholic and some Protestant. And I have also seen how hatred can consume people, dry out their hearts, embitter, and destroy happiness. With God's grace and the help of many prayers, I will continue on the path of forgiveness. And actually, for nearly all of the time, the struggle has not been too difficult.

In today's *Weekend Australian*, John Ferguson had a long article: "High Stakes in Pell's Final Bid for Freedom". His leading points were that nobody is predicting how the High Court might act and that according to an article in the *Sydney Law Review*, "many independent voices suspect: Pell's convictions may be flawed." The arguments he cites are heavily in my favour, which is not surprising, considering there is no evidence for the complainant except his own. In a certain sense, an imbalance exists between Ferguson's conclusions and his argumentation, but this is as much as we could anticipate of any "impartial" writer who needed to keep open his channels to the wide-ranging prosecutorial party.

When speaking by phone today to the Tobins, I learnt a couple of pieces of news. Coronavirus has been discovered in a participant at the recent Academy for Life meeting in Rome attended by Archbishop Anthony Fisher and Bernadette, so it appears unlikely that Anthony will be able to come down from Sydney on Monday to visit me.

Terry also had news that my lawyers Paul and Kartya will come to see me tomorrow. They twice tried with the prison authorities to set up video-link meetings, only to be told that not sufficient staff were available to enable this; nor could they arrange a phone hook-up. Kartya has written off two letters of protest.

Original sin obviously exists among the warders, although I found less of it than I had anticipated before "doing time". The majority are very cooperative, all are correct and courteous, but there seem to be one or two more who are difficult in the section coordinating visits and contacts. Such is life.

Around the world, 100,000 cases of coronavirus have been reported in ninety countries. Most patients are in China, and, overall, 3,496 people have died.

During the Second Vatican Council (1962–1965), the Church was blessed with a large group of outstanding European theologians. The best known included the German Jesuit Karl Rahner; the French Dominicans Yves Congar and Marie-Dominique Chenu; Henri de

Lubac, another Jesuit from France; Hans Urs von Balthasar from Switzerland; and a younger German, Joseph Ratzinger. More controversial writers were Hans Küng, who recently announced he regarded euthanasia as an option, and the Dutch Dominican Edmund Schillebeeckx.

Bishop Bernard Stewart was bishop of Sandhurst in Victoria and a fierce conservative. I once said to him that a marvellous story was doing the rounds that he used to ask all his prospective seminarians to spell Schillebeeckx and then refused anyone who could. "That isn't a story," he retorted, "that's the truth."

Jean Cardinal Daniélou, a French Jesuit and a specialist in patrology, the early Church writers or Fathers, was one of this distinguished group and one of my favourites.

The *Magnificat* magazine had this quotation from his writing.

Going to Mass when we feel nothing for God is not at all a form of hypocrisy—it is faith.... To make the emotions the gauge of religion would end in many aberrations.... Loving God means knowing that we can count on God and that God can count on us in spite of our emotional complications.

WEEK 55

A Final Appeal

8 March–14 March 2020

Sunday, 8 March 2020

The day did not begin well, as I slept through until 6:35 am, by which time the 6:00 am *Mass for You at Home* was finished. My self-waking alarm was off duty today.

I scrambled to be ready to listen to Pastor Joseph Prince, taking my shower but not shaving. Joseph preached today on the theme "Believe Right and See Good", translated in biblical terms as the theme of salvation. Where sin abounds, grace is more abundant, because Jesus died for our sins, which were imputed to him.

Joseph insisted that sin should not be allowed to bully us by anger or lust. Even when we feel angry and lustful, with impure dreams, we are still righteous in God's eyes because we live by faith.

At the end of each weekly service of preaching, he urges the congregation and viewers to join him in a prayer, which I do, unless the words are theologically wrong or "iffy". I prayed most of his prayer with him today.

Fr John McCarthy, the Barwon Prison chaplain who celebrated Mass for me last week, tapes Joel Osteen's sermon every week, not so much for the theological content, but to see whether he can use in his sermon the funny story with which Joel begins each day.

Today his story about a pope and a lawyer going to heaven (the lawyer got the bigger house because a lawyer is so rare in heaven) was not too bad, but John's favourite told of a young girl asking her mother from where she, as daughter, was descended. The mother recounted the beautiful story of Adam and Eve and the succession of generations. The girl also asked her father, and he explained some of the basic links in evolution and how our predecessors were monkeys, baboons, or gorillas. Naturally, the daughter was confused, so she returned to her mother with the two different theories. The mother explained it all neatly: she was speaking of her side of the family, while the father was explaining his ancestors.

This has shades of the apocryphal exchange alleged of Bishop Samuel Wilberforce and Thomas Huxley at the Oxford Union in 1860, where later reports alleged the bishop of Oxford asked Huxley whether he was descended from the apes on his mother's or his father's side. Actually, Wilberforce had a good academic background in science and did well in the debate. His father was liberator of the slaves.[1]

Today, Joel spoke on the seasons of silence, those periods where God does not answer our prayers in the way requested. Then God is working on us, and he does his best work anonymously.

David had years of silent boredom as a shepherd before he was king, and the prophet Elijah spent three and a half years in the desert after rebuking King Ahab. These two Old Testament giants were then like Joel's leafless oaks in winter, quietly gaining strength for the summer. God doesn't create you to be you, but to become better and greater in God's eyes. His approval is what counts.

Songs of Praise had a variegated offering, ranging from US hymns by Fanny Crosby, which I did not know, to "Tell Out My Soul", that splendid version of Mary's Magnificat prayer.

Paul and Kartya, the solicitors, arrived at midday, when we met for an hour and a half. I went through my list of points to our mutual satisfaction, and I was pleased to hear that Ruth had read and mastered all Friel's material which was relevant. I commented again on the quality and immense amount of work in his more than seventy articles. The letters I had received and two volumes of my journal were at the main gate for Kartya to collect. Our legal preparation has been absolutely thorough, of the highest quality. We could not be better prepared. I should pray to Mary as Our Lady of Victories as I did at the conclave which elected Pope Benedict XVI.

---

[1] William Wilberforce (1759–1833) was a British politician who led the movement to abolish the slave trade.

The Holy Father, Pope Francis, has cancelled all his public gatherings in Rome to combat the coronavirus. He also has a cold.

The Epistle to the Hebrews spells out our duties to Jesus, our Redeemer:

You have come ... to Jesus, the mediator who brings a new covenant.... Make sure that you never refuse to listen when he speaks. The people who refused to listen to him on earth could not escape their punishment, then how shall we escape if we turn away from his voice that warns us from heaven?

Monday, 9 March 2020

The morning was so beautiful, a clear sky with a few clouds, the sun rising from the east as I sat out in the sun next to the lawn, that I stayed outside until about 11:40 am. I had been given leave to remain there until midday, but my visitor, Chris Meney, arrived more than an hour early. Although Archbishop Anthony Fisher has tested negative for the coronavirus, they had advised him to remain at home for another five days. So he sent his best wishes and apologies.

A news item from yesterday. Kartya protested by letter about the inability to establish video-links last week at her request of the prison staff. The answer was that the video is being used extensively, and more staff are required. She was happy to cooperate. This brought a happier slant to the problem than the one I had first envisaged.

As Paul was with me, I asked the question I had prepared for Bret. Did Paul think there would be many other examples before the High Court of the prosecution presenting to the highest bench in the land evidence that had been previously disallowed or disowned? To my surprise, Paul surmised that desperate prosecutions facing appeals against unjust verdicts might have used this tactic on other occasions. For us, it is certainly a *felix culpa*—a happy fault.

As Chris Meney has been with me at all the key moments of the past three years, we discussed what might be done if I am released. Katrina and the lawyers think I should go to a place with security, at least for one or two days, before going to the McFarlanes. I am not inclined to leave Melbourne immediately, but would like to stay a few days to meet with my close supporters before driving back to Sydney via Bendigo to see Margaret, David, Judy, and the family. Nobody is quite sure what form the ideological confrontation will take if I am released, but all to whom I have spoken expect the reactions on both sides to be lively.

Chris also brought another useful clarification. In Australia, a public Mass celebrant needs a card and a number, and they are generally not re-issued for some weeks or months after an acquittal. This brings another context to the question of what I might do in the months immediately after a "not guilty" verdict.

Six months or a year in Rome remains an option, which might or might not eventuate: the apartment is still available, the nuns are still there, and a Sydney priest might be doing a doctorate in Rome and could live with me.

Terry also informed me that Peter O'Callaghan, the founding director of the Melbourne Response[2] to sexual abuse, has died after some years of ill health. He did a fine job in a difficult area and was in many ways part of the pioneering operation. I prayed for him tonight. *Requiescat in pace.*[3]

God our Father, by whose Son's death and Resurrection we have been redeemed, you are the glory of your faithful, the life of your saints: have mercy on your servant, Peter, and as he professed his faith in the mystery of our resurrection, so may he gain possession of eternal joy.

Tuesday, 10 March 2020

As my High Court appeal is to be heard tomorrow, the temptation tonight might be to become too tense and serious. As an antidote to this, I will begin by quoting Mrs O'Brien from Kilanerin, County Wexford in Ireland, who began conventionally and a bit grimly by thanking me "for your defence of the family and the proper Synodal process" and even wondering whether "we are heading into rather

---

[2] The Melbourne Response was the policy the Archdiocese of Melbourne adopted at a public forum in October 1996 in response to the problem of sexual abuse.

[3] May he rest in peace.

apocalyptic times". Then she rallied with some good news: "On a lighter note, the local clergy here are all breathing a sigh of relief that they won't now have to get married."

One of the main surprises of my year in jail has been the number of letters I have received: now more than 3,500. They have provoked regular gratitude, but also thought and prayer. Some of them are very kind, sometimes too enthusiastic as they thank or praise me. Some I have mentioned at intervals in my daily journals, and I have pondered whether it was simply my vanity which "encouraged" me to do so. As someone who has been roughly treated by the mainline media and social media, it is nice to record many people who have coloured in the other side of the picture.

If I had not been in jail, I would never have heard so many "thank-yous" and commendations. Endorsements are always a consolation.

I have managed to do things over the decades, but I sometimes wondered how often I managed to produce some spiritual fruit. My letters provided reassurance to me on this point.

I know good priests wonder at times how much grace they channel or produce in our age, which is widely deaf and indifferent, and now increasingly hostile. If a spiritual mediocrity like me can provoke gratitude or faith by a small kindness or some words in a sermon or article, my example should remind priests that they, too, are regularly producing fruit when they do not see it and are not thanked for it. Thirty or forty years ago, an Irish-born priest serving in a small country parish in Victoria decided to leave the priesthood, and on his last Sunday in the parish, he preached to his people about his decision. He was overwhelmed with the number and depth of the thanks, prompting him to remark, as only an Irishman might, that if he had received these compliments earlier, he might not have left.

So it was good to receive news of a spiritual bouquet for me from a prayer group in Aurora, Ontario, Canada, which included 448 Masses and 482 rosaries, etc.

A letter from the mother of a homeschooled family in Michigan, US, told me she had used my *Issues of Faith and Morals*[4] with her teenagers, which helped to balance out the views of an Australian Jesuit writing in *La Croix International*.

---

[4] George Pell, *Issues of Faith and Morals* (London: Oxford University Press, 1996; San Francisco: Ignatius Press, 1997).

An Irishman now studying as a Conventual Franciscan at Black-friars, Oxford, consoles me by explaining that a sermon I preached on St Augustine at World Youth Day in Rio de Janiero in 2013 "had a profound effect on me in the midst of what had otherwise seemed to be a thankless and turbulent pilgrimage".

A number of letters tell of people's troubles, and I regret that I cannot offer Mass for them as I usually would in other circumstances. A prisoner who was lost and in darkness asked me to recommend a book. I suggested he start with John's First Epistle and then read Luke's Gospel.

One Melbourne writer told how his sister had just been diagnosed with a brain tumour, prompting him to meditate on Jesus' suffering (Jn 19:1–6), and concluded, "I love how God flips things around for the greater good and always wins, even if it is not in the way we would think or expect."

A number of people have organized novenas to conclude tonight, including Ed Pentin in Rome, a brave and capable writer on the Vatican, and the Melbourne Senatus of the Legion of Mary. The Catholic Women's League sent me the last two numbers of their magazine *Horizon*, asking my support for their drive to increase their younger membership.

Let me conclude by going to the matter at hand tomorrow, seeking the intercession of Our Lady of Victories and quoting Psalm 142.

> *Rescue me, Lord, from my enemies;*
> *I have fled to you for refuge.*
> *Teach me to do your will*
> *for you, O Lord, are my God.*
> *Let your good spirit guide me*
> *in ways that are level and smooth.*
> *For your name's sake, Lord, save my life;*
> *in your justice save my soul from distress.*

Wednesday, 11 March 2020

Last night I finished the evening unusually calm and slept through until 5:45 am. I had arranged to write up yesterday's journal after the SBS news and praying Vespers with the Melbourne priests. It concentrates the mind and stops it wandering uselessly. I also answered a few letters, mainly from prisoners, when I was having my chamomile tea and chocolate. The ABC had one of their regular programs for the 250th anniversary of Beethoven's birth, and I was able to listen to his first violin quartets, charming and heavily influenced by Haydn. The prayer and the music quietened my troubled spirit.

Yesterday, Terry Tobin had asked whether any plans were in place in case we received a decision tomorrow. I hadn't done anything, but on enquiry the team assured me the matter was in hand. Terry is prudent and cautious and would not have mentioned this possibility if it were farfetched.

As arranged, Kartya spoke to me from Canberra at 8:30 am, although I could not see her on the video-link. As anticipated, she had no breaking news, but recounted that Bret thought we might be over-prepared; I also found this consoling. The Melbourne *Herald Sun* had a broadly sympathetic article saying that I was optimistic and that much expert legal opinion supported this.

The morning eventually developed into a pleasant day, so I sat out for an hour in my own exercise area until the jail was locked down at 11:30 am. The permission I had organized to be outside in the common area between 1:00 and 2:00 pm was readily maintained, so I was able to receive an update from Terry on the morning's proceedings. He was satisfied with the progress, as was Bret at the morning break, and with the attentiveness and questions of the judges. Six of the seven had intervened.

Bret argued that a witness must prove to be reliable, as well as having a credible manner, and reliability is gauged in the light of the evidence. Some time was spent on the validity of watching videos of the evidence, as well as studying the script, and one basic theme was that there was no opportunity for the crime to have been committed. Danny Casey confirmed that Greg Smith, a former NSW attorney general and government prosecutor, felt the morning had gone well.

The ABC midday news was sympathetic enough, emphasising the absence of opportunity, while the evening news stressed that the complainant had no corroborating evidence. Outside the High Court, there were scuffles between my supporters, many from Sydney University and also some Vietnamese, with one man and a few allies who were condemning me to hell. As we prisoners are locked down at

3:30 pm, confined to our cells, I have to wait until 8:30 am tomorrow for an update from my team.

Tim O'Leary's three large envelopes of photocopies of a couple of articles on my case by Keith Windschuttle of *Quadrant* and another thirteen articles I had not read by Chris Friel from Wales (he has produced seventy-five articles to this point) kept me occupied throughout the afternoon and into the evening. Friel has become very blunt in his rejection of the prosecutors' activities, calling out their lack of principle, their attempt to have their hiatus and eat it. He suggests that "in the outworking of the case the Crown has no space left to hide—like a checked king moving from square to square before an inevitable and forced mate." The evolution of their case is for him a *reductio ad absurdum*.[5]

He has produced a second and sophisticated article on the mathematics of compounding probability. He accepts Robert Richter's list of ten things happening in a five-minute interval, and if each event is a 50-50 chance, then the odds are 1,000-to-1.

But for Portelli to lose Pell from the front steps, for the two choristers to break off from the procession unnoticed, for the sacristy to be empty for five minutes after Mass, each hypothesis increases the odds against this happening by 15 or 20 or 25 times or more. Such considerations on these three issues would lift the odds to more than 5 million-to-1. He sums up: "What Richter and Walker are indicating by their compound probability argument is that the scenario was utterly, mind-bogglingly, preposterous."

For four weeks I have been seeking space to write a few lines about Mother Teresa's biography based on her private writings, so I take this opportunity even though my daily quota of words is already full.

Most Catholics today know something about St Teresa of Calcutta's founding of the Missionaries of Charity to live as, and work with, the poorest of the poor, after she left the Loreto Sisters in 1948. By 1975, the Missionaries of Charity had one thousand nuns in eighty-five communities in fifteen countries. Malcolm Muggeridge first brought her work to the world; this proved a turning point for him, and he eventually became a Catholic, a writer, and a controversialist with few equals for Christ and the Church.

[5] "Reduction to absurdity".

Only now are we coming to learn of Mother Teresa's extraordinary personal journey of fifty years of darkness, a terrible emptiness, loneliness, no sense of God's presence, and icy-cold and blind faith. The motto of the Sisters "I thirst", repeating Christ's cry on the Cross, takes on a new significance, although she insists that she did not doubt. Just once is she recorded as saying, "Jesus is asking a bit too much."

Only St Paul of the Cross[6] is recorded as having a dark night of the soul of comparable length. She disconcerted me with her theory that Our Lord spent either his public life or many years in a similar anguish. I hope this wasn't the case, as I would want the Son of God to have been happy among us for a good period of time. He was certainly anguished in the garden on the Mount of Olives and in his last agony on the Cross, but to claim more is to go beyond the evidence.

Even the nuns closest to Mother never realised she was going through this trial, as she insisted that while it was important to know how to suffer, we must be able to laugh. Time and again she urged people to smile. "Suffering is the kiss of Jesus Crucified upon our soul."[7]

While I never met the saint, although I tried to do so once or twice, I did see her from a distance on a number of occasions, the last of which was her embracing St John Paul the Great in St Peter's Basilica. She did not appear cross or miserable, but serene, strong, and formidable. My boast is that I arranged for splendid portraits of each of them, by Paul Newton,[8] to be placed together in the beautiful chapel of Domus Australia, Rome, and to have a stained-glass image of her with St Mary MacKillop in the renovated chapel at Good Shepherd Seminary in Sydney. One or two murmured because none of these three had as yet been canonised, but that has now been corrected.

Saints come in all types and from all nations, and I am sure some are closer to God than others. Mother Teresa is certainly in the first division, not least for her courage in defending "incorrect" causes, such as her opposition to abortion.

---

[6] St Paul of the Cross (1694–1775) was the founder and superior general of the Congregation of the Passion (known as the Passionists), who combined devotion to Christ's Passion with preaching to the poor and rigorous penance.

[7] A quote used by Mother Teresa, taken from *The Virtue of Love* by Paul de Jaegher, S.J. (1955).

[8] Paul Newton (b. 1961) is a prize-winning Australian portrait artist.

I have visited her nuns in many countries, and everywhere I have been impressed by their faith and serenity, the simplicity of their living arrangements, and the beautiful gardens they always have, even around the most basic accommodation. I am consoled by their prayers for me.

St Teresa of Calcutta is quoted in today's meditation from the *Magnificat*.

Try ... to increase your knowledge of this mystery of redemption. This knowledge will lead you to love—and love will make you share through your sacrifices in the Passion of Christ. ... Without our sufferings, our work would just be social work, very good and helpful, but it would not be the work of Jesus Christ, not part of the redemption.

Thursday, 12 March 2020

The coronavirus has been accorded pandemic status; President Trump has cancelled personal travel to the US from Europe (except UK), but not trade, and yesterday all travel with Italy was banned. Their whole country is now isolated, and the financial consequences will be enormous as the economy is heavily dependent on tourism. It is also more unwelcome news for the Vatican, exacerbating its structural deficit, which is alleviated by the revenue from the Vatican Museum.

Once again I slept well, awaking a little after 6:00 am.

I was watching the Channel 7 news as I was writing and heard the shock news that the High Court was considering returning my case for another hearing with different judges in the Court of Appeal. Bret rose to his feet to proclaim that his party wanted the matter decided in "this court", the High Court. This is one outcome I had never envisaged.

At lunchtime, I spoke with Terry and Bernadette, who were driving back to Sydney for Bernadette's final meeting as chair of the Council of St John's College at Sydney University. Terry said the morning's proceedings could not have gone better, with the prosecutor putting in an unimpressive performance. There was much discussion of the time I spent on the front steps after Mass, and the judges seemed attentive to the points being made.

I wonder if anything happened during the proceedings this after-noon to cancel or diminish the progress which Terry welcomed in the morning.

This morning I spent a half hour at 8:30 am on video-link with Kartya, and she transmitted the barristers' views on the previous day. The judges were attentive, asking the correct questions, interested in the timing of the sequence of events and the hive of activity.

Paul counselled against expecting a verdict today and thought we would have a better estimate of where we are after the morning ses-sion. Bret promised that he would be in "hunt and kill" mode in his final summing up.

If all this was not excitement enough, someone from Brunswick has been arrested for threatening to kill me. Ironically I could not be any safer than where I am now in jail. What a circus!

I take a smidgen of consolation from the fact that the chief justice mentioned the impossibility of returning the case to the Victorian Supreme Court as she must have been aware of the stupefaction and outrage such a course would produce. A fifth trial!

I write this in the evening after watching an SBS show on MI6, the British Secret Service, which was interesting, but not telling me too much that I didn't know. The other news services made no reference to a referral back to the Victorian Supreme Court or to Bret's inter-vention. My first requisite is to find out exactly what was said and by whom at the conclusion of the sitting. Then we can conjecture. But it will be interesting to try to estimate the number of supporters we have among the judges, although our experience with Maxwell in the Victorian court exemplifies the difficulty inherent in any such exercise.

Where is God in all this? I don't even know the facts of the sit-uation, much less do I understand how God will use it. But God is there, and I hope I am not being called to nearly three more years in jail. God is patient. Look at the timescale for the universe since the beginning, whether it was the Big Bang or something else. Look at the millennial history of salvation with God working through the Jews, a small Chosen People, and then through the tiny, but slowly expanding, Christian minority (in terms of the world's population).

I am not naturally patient and will be happy to be better informed tomorrow through the *Herald Sun*, and then some phone calls and a 12:30 pm visit from Michael and Ruth Casey.

Robert Herrick[9] has written a well-known poem entitled "To Keep a True Lent":

> *It is to fast from strife*
> *And old debate,*
> *And hate;*
> *To circumcise thy life.*

> *To show a heart grief-rent;*
> *To starve thy sin,*
> *Not bin;*
> *And that's to keep thy Lent.*

Friday, 13 March 2020

While I slept through until 5:15 am, I had to work hard to stop worrying and wondering what had transpired in court yesterday afternoon and what consequences might follow for my time in prison.

My initial reaction was in response to a misleading Channel 7 report, which I might have misunderstood. Later I realised that I needed to have accurate information on what transpired in the court. The absence of news hostile to my cause in the evening's bulletins meant that no abrupt reversal of fortune had occurred.

I don't receive a newspaper on Friday, but soon after I commenced my walk around the lawn, Derek gestured to me to come to the door where it is easier to talk. There he told me all was well, pointing to the *Herald Sun* headline "Pell Tipped to Win".[10]

The crucial clarification for me was to learn that the reference to the Victorian Court of Appeal was not made by the chief justice, but by Kerri Judd, QC, the Victorian director of public prosecutions (DPP), who argued, according to the *Herald Sun*, that "if the court found an error in the Court of Appeal's judgement upholding the convictions ... it should revisit all the evidence itself or send the matter back to the Court of Appeal." Naturally, Bret Walker, my

---

[9] Robert Herrick (1591–1674) was an English lyric poet and Anglican clergyman.
[10] Shannon Deery, "Pell Tipped to Win", *Herald Sun*, 13 March 2020.

barrister, countered that this would be unjust, and he urged the court to "finalise the matter".

The judges gave the director of prosecutions a torrid time, and more than once she was contradicted and unable to produce evidence to support her own claims.

Bret Walker, SC, lived up to his promises in his final summing up, accusing the DPP of "prosecutorial improvisation" and of changing the parameters of the case on the run, changing the prosecution's stance on key evidence, such as the second "hiatus", a fanciful claim to a second pause of five to six minutes after the servers had arrived at the sacristy, which the prosecutor had been forced to abandon in the trial under Justice Kidd.

The *Herald Sun* described it as a "stunning attack". "It really won't do for the Crown to be cobbling together matters at this stage", Walker pointed out succinctly and accurately. Msgr Portelli's evidence was correctly seen as crucial, as were the timelines and the lack of opportunity.

I hope to be able to thank my team publicly for their determination to see justice done, to unveil the truth and throw light on the manufactured obscurity. I totally endorse Walker's criticism of the prosecution, who worked more and more as the trials progressed to obfuscate the situation, to spread and encourage confusion. The main Australian newspapers followed the same line as the Melbourne *Herald Sun*.

When I spoke briefly to Terry Tobin by phone just before the visit of Michael and Ruth Casey, Terry explained that the court had asked the defence view about how a decision on one set of charges relates to any second charge. I am not sure of the precise nature or consequences of the question, but we have already provided our advice, and the prosecutors have until Monday night for their contribution. Terry also reassured me that we had no reasons for concern on all this.

Michael and Ruth were in good form and last night had a meal with mutual friends Julien and Maryanne O'Connell. It was Ruth who informed me that the *Financial Review* thought a decision might be announced around Tuesday, and Terry was of a similar mind.

Michael was quite firm in his view that I should live in Sydney rather than Rome, which was music in my ears. At any rate, the coronavirus pandemic, which is guesstimated to last fourteen weeks, eliminates any possibility of travel to Italy during that period.

Ruth, like Michael, had read the final handwritten volume of my journal and was quite taken by it. Michael also informed me he has edited this first volume and that the request for a "synopsis" has come from Fr Alexander Sherbrooke in London and not from the publisher. This caused me to correct my first estimate that a request for a synopsis of a diary-journal is probably a polite way of saying "not interested". Michael's suggestion that we send a volume of edited text mirrors my own instincts.

Today I am now feeling a bit tired and lethargic because of the good news. On one or two other occasions, after long bursts of intense activity or periods of strain, I have felt like I do now, only more so. It is as though the body and soul need to pause, rest, and gather strength. Time heals, and after a quiet day, without any bad news, without any conflicts, I already feel somewhat better. So I pray, seeking the generosity of God our Father:

Deliver me from jealousy and self-pity when I see the good fortune of others, so that I rejoice in their happiness.

Let me see clearly the greater suffering of so many others, near and far, so that I might have a deeper compassion and wisdom to recognize Christ hidden in them all, whether they be beautiful or despised and rejected.

Saturday, 14 March 2020

The morning deteriorated from cool to cold during my time outside, and tonight, just after 11:00 pm as I am writing this, steady rain is falling. The coronavirus is still spreading, with Italy having the largest number of patients outside China. The US is denouncing China as the origin of the infection, while the Chinese counter with accusations of US germ warfare.

Kartya arrived around 10:30 am to give me news of the two days in the High Court in Canberra and to deliver the transcript of the proceedings. The first day of the proceedings is already available through live streaming, but the second day with Judd's inglorious display and the stunning rebuttal by Walker was sadly not available this morning.

I spent the day after lunch reading the transcripts, with the two submissions being as different from one another as the proverbial chalk and cheese in both content and style.

After reading the transcripts, I can well understand why our team was so pleased. Kerri Judd, the DPP, has a weak case, but she came across as underprepared with an imperfect control of her brief, willing to bluff clumsily and unable to produce proof when challenged. And, as Bob Santamaria once said about a notoriously long-winded South American cardinal, who was speaking to us in English, Ms Judd is no Demosthenes.

One retired judge thought that as well as being exasperated by her performance, the High Court seemed to be irritated by the fact the case had survived to come to them.

Bret's language and level of argumentation were pitched for learned judges, so I found it solid reading, packed with forensic logic, and on a number of occasions I left sections of text to come back to them. I breezed through the prosecution's material, interrupted only by my irritation. The best of lawyers will struggle with a bad brief, while Bret had four aces and a joker in hand, which he played brilliantly. But I suspect that another factor was in play, and that is incompetence; levels of learning and skill were insufficient for the occasions, both in the Victorian Court of Appeal and here. Another possibility is that they worked hard, like George W. Bush, to appear much slower than they are in fact. But this would add a level of infamy I am reluctant to accept. Maxwell's theory that the attacks occurred during the five or six minutes after Mass ended, while the complainant was still in the procession, by his own submission, is an enormous logical howler—for anyone, but particularly for the president of the Court of Appeal.

Judd rebuked prosecutor Gibson as over-generous for conceding there was no evidence the altar servers were waiting in the servers' room during the second hiatus and then was unable to produce any evidence to support her rebuke. I never felt I would feel a twinge of sympathy for Gibson.

Two other possibilities emerged from my reading of the transcript. At least a couple of judges seemed concerned the Victorian judges twice watched the claimant's evidence on video, enhancing the prospect of excessive influence from his demeanour (which I have never found convincing or credible!).

So, too, some judges were concerned that the police did not inter-view Fr Egan over the second allegation. If a ruling emerged that the police were obliged to seek out other evidence before proceeding on the bases of a complaint, this would be good for justice.

I was also pleased to note the judges drawing attention to some of the twenty-four changes of evidence made by the claimant. I have said on many occasions that not even a credible witness can be in two places at the same time. While any claim cannot be truer than true, the claim is doubly true of an incredible witness!

A magnificent meat pie with mashed potatoes and peas properly heated in the microwave and topped with tomato sauce brought back memories of the Saturday pie or pasty for lunch at MAP—but no spuds or peas then.

Edwin Muir has a splendid poem, "One Foot in Eden", on the web of good and evil, misfortune and happiness, which covers and infects us:

> *Time's handiworks by time are haunted,*
> *And nothing now can separate*
> *The corn and tares compactly grown.*
> *The armorial weed in stillness bound*
> *Above the stalk; these are our own.*
> *Evil and good stand thick around*
> *In the fields of charity and sin*
> *Where we shall lead our harvest in.*

WEEK 56

Awaiting the Decision

15 March–21 March 2020

Sunday, 15 March 2020

This morning when I woke up at 5:29 am, I decided to leave the night-light on, so I would not go back to sleep and would be ready for the 6:00 am *Mass for You at Home*. Turning on the television early, I caught something of the *Hour of Power*, an evangelical program from the US, with the young, pleasant pastor preaching on the wedding feast of Cana and reassuring us that God saves the best for last. A nice message for me in my situation.

I have often described Jesus' words from the Cross to Dismas, the good thief, "This very day you will be with me in Paradise" (Lk 23:43), as the most beautiful and reassuring lines in the Bible. For the ordinary punter, the miracle of the wine at the wedding feast of Cana is the second most reassuring New Testament text. Jesus did as his mother asked him, even if he might have been a little reluctant. Mothers are important, especially the Mother of Jesus.

Jesus was attending a wedding feast. He didn't answer the request for more wine by saying, "They have had enough to drink." And if one or two had imbibed generously, they would not have noticed an inferior type; but he gave them a top-quality wine. All this is an insight into the Godhead, the Father who shares Jesus' divine nature. And it is reassuring.

Fr Shabin Kaniampuram celebrated *Mass for You at Home*, preaching on the Gospel for the Third Sunday of Lent, John's account of Jesus' encounter with the Samaritan woman: quite a character. He concluded by praying that the Church would be like the woman at the well, open to truth.

Joseph Prince preached on the theme "Believe Right and See Your Youth Renewed". God does not lie, he promised, citing Abraham and Sarah, who waited twenty years for their son, Isaac, which means "laugh". Sarah became a mother at the age of ninety. The heart, belief, is central to what we do and become, to our quality of life. The moment Joshua believed, he stopped growing old. Fear is the devil's way of acting.

Joel Osteen was preaching the prosperity gospel at its most explicit with his theme of the overflow God. One of God's names is El Shaddai, meaning "more than enough". God knows how to increase you, so you have to get ready for the overflow. When the Jews were starving in the desert on the way to the Promised Land, one estimate had it that 105 million quails came into the Jewish camps on one day. Their huge numbers probably build on the Exodus claim that 600,000 men left Egypt. God is not limited by our small capacity to believe. In hard times, the God of the overflow is still with you. Don't believe the day is coming, because the day is here. 2020 will be an overflow year for you. I presume the sermon was preached before the coronavirus spread from China.

Songs of Praise came from Ireland, where the faith of many Irish pilgrims was shown at Croagh Patrick, with its barefoot pilgrimage to the top of the mountain and the shrine at Knock, which is visited by one-and-a-half million pilgrims a year. We also heard something about Grace O'Malley, the Christian pirate queen who controlled the seas before dying in 1603. The hymns were across a spectrum from the bouncy "All Things Bright and Beautiful" through "Be Still and Know That I Am God" to the seamen's "Eternal Father, Strong to Save". The faith of the Irish was strong, widespread, and impressive, much stronger than the chosen hymns.

The morning began with rain and remained cold to cool, although the skies cleared. We now have 298 coronavirus patients in Australia, and the SBS assured us there was considerable disquiet about the lower level of restrictions Boris Johnson's government is requiring in Britain.

At lunchtime, I had arranged to telephone Katrina Lee, who has looked after my PR during my troubles, at 12:30 pm, while she came in to visit Bernadette and Terry. In the light of previous failures, we are aware that our optimism needs to be validated by the judges'

decision. She agrees that I should make the statement we have prepared [when the time comes] at the boundary of the Barwon Prison,
and I was pleased to learn the prison authorities had consented to this.
We agreed on a text, and suitable accommodation has been arranged
for a couple of days.

Terry and I, and some of the warders, are inclined to think the
decision will be announced this week, while Katrina, with Ruth and
Kartya, believe it could be in the following week. Either timeline
is acceptable, provided the "correct" decision is made! We shall be
given twenty-four hours' notice of the announcement.

I conclude with another Edwin Muir excerpt:

> *But famished field and blackened tree*
> *Bear flowers in Eden never known.*
> *Blossoms of grief and charity*
> *Bloom in these darkened fields alone. . . .*
>
> *Strange blessings never in Paradise*
> *Fall from these beclouded skies.*

Monday, 16 March 2020

The first piece of good news for the day was Andrew Bolt's full article in the *Herald Sun* titled "Facts on Pell Just Don't Fit" (16 March
2020), once again a lucid defence of my innocence which demonstrated that Bolt was completely "over" the facts of the trial. As the
pendulum of public opinion swings, because accurate information is
available, support for my being "not guilty" is not as dangerous as it
once was. But Bolt is no "Johnny-come-lately" to my cause; he has
presented the truth bravely for years and suffered as a consequence. I
owe a debt of gratitude to many writers, both in Australia and overseas, but especially to Bolt and to Keith Windschuttle from *Quadrant*
magazine. The seventy-five articles (to my present knowledge) on
the Internet from Chris Friel in Wales represent another providential, and in this case totally unexpected, set of evidence, all closely
argued in extraordinary detail, foundational to my defence and for

anyone seeking an in-depth examination and analysis of the implausible allegations.

Bolt pointed out that "the headlines for Victoria's Director of Public Prosecutions after the court's seven judges had finished with her were terrible."

He had an interesting take on her performance. "No one should accuse Judd of incompetence. I suspect she's a conscientious lawyer who had to wrestle with an awkward reality", i.e., that I could not have committed these crimes.

Her approach differed from that of Boyce, the barrister who led for the prosecution at the Court of Appeal. At times he was reduced almost to incoherence by the evidence he could use to support his argument, but he did not bluff, did not introduce new theories unsupported by evidence, and did not reinsert evidence that had already been withdrawn. One cannot be sure of the cause or motivation of this last outrage, but outrage it is, meriting Bret Walker's scathing denunciation of "prosecutorial improvisation", a vehemence quite rare in his regular High Court appearances.

Bolt might have been closer to the mark, and this was a point made by some other lawyers, when he expressed his suspicion that "even Victoria's Director of Public Prosecutions believes Pell may not have committed the rapes at the time that was alleged. The facts don't fit."

In the trials, the prosecution left so much hostile and damaging evidence unchallenged, almost as though they were afraid of receiving rebuttals that were too convincing.

My nephew Nicholas was delayed at the jail entrance by a "black alert", which prevents all movement while it remains. "Black" signifies that someone is quite sick or hurt. We still managed more than an hour together, while he cut my hair with electric clippers, a comb I provided, and a large, grotty, silver-type mirror. It wasn't glass. He was stressed by the challenge, wondering whether he should proceed and fearful that he would make me appear less than respectable. I wasn't the slightest bit concerned on that score, and the end result was excellent. If I don't manage to appear respectable and presentable, at a possible release in the next week or ten days, it won't be because of the haircut.

I ran through with him what I am thinking of saying to the press (if things go well), and he was quite satisfied. He did not want me claiming to be a victim, much less appearing hostile or unforgiving.

At times I've been almost overwhelmed by articles and books, sent with the many letters and cards. One such book, which I finished a week or so ago, was the second book the American Jesuit Father Walter Ciszek had written about his priestly experience for twenty-three years in Russia, mainly in the notorious Lubianka prison in Moscow and then in the Siberian Gulag, where he was sent as an alleged Vatican spy for fifteen years. *He Leadeth Me: An Extraordinary Testament of Faith* wrestles with the problem of suffering, the strength from faith, and how he survived.

Walter came from Shenandoah in Pennsylvania, US, joined the Jesuits in 1928, and then answered Pope Pius XI's call for volunteer priests to work in Russia. His type was more common in Australian seminaries fifty or one hundred years ago than today, because he was tough, somewhat abrasive, and worked hard to conceal his pieties. He was a difficult son to his father and a difficult seminarian for his superiors, nearly expelled from the Jesuit seminary. He studied in Rome, learnt to celebrate Mass in the Byzantine rite, was ordained there, and sent to Albertyn in eastern Poland, which was captured by the Russians when the Second World War broke out.

The young Fr Ciszek volunteered to go to Russia with the Polish refugees, disguising his priestly identity. Many of the refugees were either Communist idealists or sympathisers, and his first shock was to find that no one would speak to him or his covert priest companion. They despised what he was.

The Russians soon discovered his priestly identity, and he spent the war years in Moscow's notorious Lubianka prison, in a small cell, with no other piece of furniture but a bed that he could only lie upon at night. Often the light was left on for twenty-four hours; he had no books, let alone a kettle or TV or breviary. Sometimes the interrogation sessions went on for twenty-four hours, with successive teams of persecutors. At one stage, he confessed to a set of crimes, so that he would be transferred to Siberia, but he rallied and refused to work as a Communist spy. He goes into harrowing detail about the isolation after the interrogations, of "how an hour can become an eternity" and every second of it can be filled "with a million thoughts and a million questions and a million fears". But above all, he said, he prayed, and he realised that he had "fallen" temporarily through relying too much on his formidable strengths and not enough on God.

In northern Siberia, the winter was extreme, food scarce, hours of work long, and the prison dominated by criminal prisoners rather than political prisoners. They were cruel and ruthless. He worked hard, which provoked a lot of discussion among his fellows. There were other priests, some very demoralised. He managed to celebrate Mass regularly around lunchtime or after work in the evening, after fasting from midnight and working all day! He organized many retreats for his fellow priests and had a circle of loyal faithful, mainly Poles or Lithuanians, Latvians, and Ukrainians. After fifteen years, he was unexpectedly released, having been told that this would never happen, and he was able to go to the southern Siberian city of Krasnoyarsk where he formed a small de facto parish, working happily and fruitfully. The secret police soon put a stop to this, expelled him, and sent him to another smaller city, Abakan, where he was forbidden to work as a priest and found a job as a mechanic, taking a room with a staunch Communist, who became a good friend.

Here he was able to get to know a number of Russians and talk with them. He was sympathetic to the idealism, the espousal of justice hidden in the Communist doctrine, although it was regularly abused by the authorities. He recounted the relentless Communist propaganda against Christians, the brutal repetition of the Church's failings, real and imagined. He was eventually freed as part of an exchange in 1963, to discover he had been listed as dead since 1947.

I shall conclude by letting him explain what he was about. Although he believed he was a "most stubborn pupil", he also knew that "God is a very patient teacher". He survived on the basis of his faith, the simple truths he learnt by trial and error, not by "some secret and mysterious formula".

Fr Ciszek wrote, "The terrible thing about all divine truth, indeed, is its simplicity" and "this very simplicity makes [it] so unacceptable to the wise and the proud and the sophisticated."

Much less elegantly he echoed the prayer "My Vocation" of St John Henry Newman that "God has a special purpose, a special love, a special providence for all those he has created."

No one is insignificant; God has a plan for each of us.

No one can know greater peace, no one can be more committed, no one can achieve a greater sense of fulfillment in his life than the man who believes in this truth of the faith and strives daily to put it into practice.[1]

Amen to that. He is quite correct.

St Patrick's Day, Tuesday, 17 March 2020

The sun came up for a wonderful mild morning for St Patrick's Day, with the good weather continuing. No one was wearing shamrocks in the prison, and the feast went completely unremarked. Phillip Adams in the *Weekend Australian* mentioned there were three million Australians with Irish blood, which I am tempted to believe an underestimate.

On this day, indeed, on each St Patrick's Day, Australian Catholics should acknowledge their debt to the Irish who planted the faith across the continent and particularly in Victoria. In New South Wales, we had two English Benedictine archbishops, English monks, some French Marist priests, Marist and De La Salle Brothers, but Victoria was almost entirely an Irish Catholic plantation, where the Irish Christian Brothers ran the majority of secondary boys' schools. The archbishops of Melbourne were all Irish-born until James Cardinal Knox, and the greatest was the legendary Archbishop Daniel Mannix, who ruled from 1917 to 1963.

Brothers and nuns, receiving no wages but only their keep and pocket money, educated at least three generations of boys and girls, causing a remarkable social mobility as they moved into the middle class. With no government money for Catholic schools until the 1960s, faith and practice remained high until then. This changed with the invention of the contraceptive pill and the permissive revolution. The Second Vatican Council brought many blessings, but the combined societal and religious changes provoked an exit from the priesthood and religious life, and vocations dropped dramatically. Most

---

[1] From the final paragraphs of *He Leadeth Me: An Extraordinary Testament of Faith* by Walter J. Ciszek with Daniel L. Flaherty (New York, N.Y.: Image, 2014).

religious orders are now passing into history; religious indifference and occasional hostility flourish among the Irish Australians, who are often indistinguishable in the tribe of "blue eyes", the Anglos, and too often tone-deaf to religion.

This is not the whole story, and one of the reasons for our surviving strengths, especially in Victoria, is the Italian Australian Bartolomeo (Bob) Santamaria, who after Archbishop Daniel Mannix is the most influential leader of the Irish Australians in the Catholic history of Victoria and more widely around many parts of Australia except Sydney.

Bob was born in Brunswick, Melbourne, was educated by the Christian Brothers, did a brilliant combined degree in law and arts at the University of Melbourne, and then went to work in the Melbourne Archdiocese in Catholic Action with Dr Mannix.

Mannix believed (correctly) that democracy offered new opportunities through the ballot box that were non-existent before the vote was widely available, and he and his protégé, B. A. Santamaria, tapped into the current of reform in public life sponsored by Pope Leo XIII in the 1890s and the earlier Irish traditions of Daniel O'Connell, the Liberator, who achieved Catholic Emancipation in the British Empire in 1829.

The Victorian Catholic Labor Party parliamentarian Bert Cremean asked Santamaria and his Movement to lead the fight against Communists, who were powerful in many unions, where they sabotaged the early years of the war effort in the Second World War, particularly in the ports. No other organization in Australia had access to men of principle, idealists in the working class, like the Catholics, and the Groupers or Movement, led by Santamaria, ousted the Communist union leadership.

One of Santamaria's sons recently sent me a paper he (Bob) had written in the 1990s on the historicity of the Gospels, criticizing a well-known Australian biblical writer, who paid B.A.S. the ultimate compliment of not replying to any one of the points of criticism. His son said that Bob was essentially, deep down, at his best as a teacher, but this is to underestimate him. He was a fine writer, a controversialist with no peer in Australia, but also a strategist, a political organizer, and an activist. He was a leader.

He himself, toward the end of his life, was pessimistic about his achievements (and excessively so), about the expulsion of the Groupers from the ALP, the Labor Party split, internal wrangles, and the decline of the Church, although he was a follower and admirer of Pope John Paul II. It wasn't a typical success story, and he remains a divisive figure.

Two further points (among many) might be made. Santamaria was heavily influenced by his Irish-Australian Christian Brother teachers, whom he admired, and his lieutenants and many of his foot soldiers were Irish Australian. In the multicultural Australia of 2020, this would be something, but in the Australia of the 1940s and 50s and much later, it was extraordinary and probably only possible in the Catholic community. My second point is that Santamaria's role in the rejuvenation of the Church in Australia, to the extent it has been achieved, often goes unnoticed. We owe much to his strategic vision, his recognition of the importance of ideas and, therefore, the universities and the monthly magazine *AD2000*, which for three decades explained the challenges and the futility of striving to be "liberal Protestant" and gave Catholics on the ground the information and the ideas necessary for action in the community. And the National Civic Council provided many wonderful men and women, effective agents of influence. The fight continues, and the slide is not always steep or ubiquitous. The increased hostility against the Church will help the Catholic community more than it will harm us. Suffering in faith is life-giving and causes some, perhaps many, to consider and decide what they want to stand for.

The recent protest meeting in Martin Place, Sydney, against abortion, organized by university students and attended by Archbishop Fisher and Anglican Archbishop Glenn Davies, shows the sparks are being fanned into flames.

If another Bob Santamaria were to arise to meet the new challenges (and please God he will emerge), he will suffer another disadvantage, because he won't have platoons of prayerful, faith-filled Irish Australians to be summoned into the struggle.

The coronavirus dominates the news with 182,000 cases around the world, 7,100 deaths, and increasing restrictions in many countries.

A few lines from a traditional Irish hymn will keep us on the narrow path to salvation.

I bind unto myself today . . .

The wisdom of my God to teach,
His hand to guide, his shield to ward,
The word of God to give me speech,
His heavenly host to be my guard.

Wednesday, 18 March 2020

An unusual morning today with the skies overcast, some wind, and somewhat humid. A bit more like Sydney's rather than Melbourne's autumn weather.

Late afternoon yesterday was spent rereading the transcript of the two-day High Court hearing. All the judges intervened, and no intervention was hostile to our cause. I will be surprised if we lose once again.

Felt a twinge of regret that we had no decision yesterday, although it was too early for the reasoning behind the judgements to be ready. If the court is to rule on the validity of an appeal court watching films of the proceedings and on any obligation of the police to obtain witnesses, then all this would need to be carefully worded. All in all, we can only conjecture when a verdict might be announced, and I am content with this.

I am always happy to acknowledge my debts to the Jesuits, in whose institutions I lived for nearly eight years, and especially to Fr Jim McInerney, my rector at Corpus Christi seminary in Werribee, and Fr Brian Murphy for introducing me to the English Catholic writers of the nineteenth and twentieth centuries. I had read widely, following a good English literature syllabus at secondary school, but was basically ignorant of Newman and Hopkins, Chesterton and Belloc, Greene and Waugh, Knox and Arnold Lunn. We all learnt, too, of the martyrs John Fisher and Thomas More and the Anglican writer T. S. Eliot. I cannot recall much enthusiasm for C. S. Lewis, and Tolkien came later, although I never became an enthusiast for his writings.

I was already a covert Anglophile. Later I was delighted to spend four years, 1967–1971, studying in Oxford and have returned on many occasions.

All this helps explain how pleased I was to receive a long essay from my friend Fr Alexander Sherbrooke to mark the tenth anniversary of the founding of the Anglican Ordinariate in the Church, on English Catholic life, weaving disparate themes around "Marian Devotion" and more particularly "Our Lady of Eton".

Eton College was founded in 1440 by King Henry VI to "make suitable honour to the same lady and our most holy Mother", linking the school to the Crown and to the universal Church. Henry was a pious man of faith, not a successful king or effective politician, who died in the Tower of London, probably murdered, according to St Thomas More, by the future Richard III.

Eamon Duffy's writings have demonstrated that Catholic life in England in the time of Henry VIII was not rotten and corrupt, not just a façade, but in fact responsible for all the welfare helps available in the whole nation. Enormous misery was caused by the closure of the monasteries, and many died. Decades of ruthlessly efficient persecution under Henry, then Edward VI and especially Elizabeth I, were needed to strangle the faith.

The story of how the pre-Reformation statue of Our Lady, high above the schoolyard at Eton, survives to this day gives one more example of Catholic resilience.

The statue of the Assumption in the tower, decorated with Madonna lilies, had only been placed there by Provost Roger Lupton some little time before More and Fisher were martyred. Lupton resigned in 1536.

Our Lady's shrine in the College Chapel had been demolished by Thomas Cromwell's thugs, and the painted story of Our Lady on the chapel walls whitewashed before Cromwell sent troops in the autumn of 1538 to demolish the statue. The masters were in hiding, but the students themselves, the king's scholars, refused to let the soldiers pass into the schoolyard. And they carried the day.

I heard of a similar story in Belarus, in Grodno, a large city I visited, where the Communists sent young troops to close the cathedral and take it over for secular purposes. The pious old ladies of the parish, the grandmothers, lay down in the square and the church, refusing to move, and the soldiers would not touch them.

Blessed Edward Powell, who was briefly headmaster at Eton, called Henry VIII "a common adulterer" to his face and was hanged, drawn, and quartered in 1540. Henry Cole, appointed provost by

Queen Mary, later died in Fleet Prison for the faith. The first of the martyrs to be trained in the English College in Rome, St Ralph Sherwin, was an old Etonian.

England, known popularly as Our Lady's Dowry, was consecrated to Mary by Edward the Confessor and reconsecrated by the tyrant King Richard II (1377–1399). Within a couple of weeks, on 29 March 2020, the Catholic community will rededicate England to Our Lady. I think Fr Alexander was correct when he wrote: "The motherhood and queenship of Mary held by generations of kings, nobles, and subjects were not empty mantras but expressions of how the world was seen, ordered, and to be governed."

I mentioned Msgr Ronald Knox, whose translation of the Bible we used at Werribee seminary and whose biography by Evelyn Waugh was an early seminary read for me.

Knox had been tutor in classics to Harold Macmillan, the future prime minister, dubbed "C" in Waugh's biography, who had also toyed with the idea of becoming a Catholic. They had been some years apart at Eton before the First World War.

Von Balthasar has written of the Marian dimension of the Church, and Knox explained this dimension after he became a Catholic, when he preached at Westminster Abbey on the feast of Edward the Confessor. Fr Alexander recounts that Knox asked who would one want to be on the day of judgement: an explorer, general, inventor, acclaimed statesman? Or "a political incompetent and failed politician like Edward, who was beloved by the poor, who nursed the sick, and gave succour to the destitute under the mantle of Our Lady?"

The tombs of Edward at Westminster Abbey and Henry VI at Chertsey and then Windsor were pilgrimage centres and the sites of miracles for hundreds of years until the Reformation.

Mater misericordiae, ora pro nobis.[2]

Thursday, 19 March 2020

Today is the feast of St Joseph, the husband of Mary and foster father of Jesus, described in the Gospels as *dikaios*, "a just man" who

---

[2] (Mary), "Mother of mercy, pray for us."

knew well and followed closely his Jewish religion. We owe him an enormous debt because he provided the male nurture, the model of manliness for his young foster child, just as surely as Mary, his wife, provided the human nature for Jesus, the incarnate Son of God. From the strength and compassion evident in Our Lord's adult life, we are entitled to conclude that Joseph did well. With so many divorces, non-permanent partnerships, absent fathers, and blended families, our society desperately needs many Josephs.

Fr John McCarthy came again to celebrate Mass for me on this feast. All was silent in our surrounds, and we had a beautiful low-key and prayerful celebration. I was very grateful. John told me "Robbo", Fr Peter Robinson, one of the seniors in John's year, a vocation from the Young Christian Workers movement, had died a couple of days ago. May he rest in peace.

The warders then invited me back to the video room. I said I was happy to wait for ten minutes and then call it a day if there was no action. They agreed; I entered the room, and about five minutes later Kartya and Ruth, my second barrister, appeared on the screen.

I always liked to discuss the case with Ruth, as I valued her opinions highly. She did most of the groundwork for the appeal. As usual, I led off with my list of questions or comments, and Ruth agreed that Bret's level of argumentation and language were at a new height for the court. I had reduced to two the number of texts where I was uncertain what he meant. One was a misinterpretation, as "usurpation" had been written as "user patient"!

She agreed that Bret had given a brilliant performance, but he had all the facts with him. Even the best of lawyers would have struggled with the prosecution case, as they had no corroborating evidence and in none of their scenarios did the evidence fit. All that said, the director of public prosecutions gave an inglorious performance, completely faithful to the precedent of the majority verdict delivered by Victoria's two senior judges. When you add the recent failings of police commissioners Ashton and Overland in the Lawyer X saga, you have an ugly picture of the Victorian legal system.

Like me, Ruth would be very surprised if we lost the appeal. Bret spoke on when the judgement might be released, that the judges are good people and will do their work quickly; but he was unable to be more precise on what that meant. All in all, I was encouraged by the meeting.

Earlier in the day, I had a boost from receiving by mail the summary of notes from the two-day hearing taken by Terry and Bernadette Tobin. Some excerpts demonstrate their flavor:

Day 2
Thorough thrashing of the prosecution's case from the Bench.
As I see it, the prosecutors have no respect for the primacy of evidence.

[Bernadette's notes include]
Crown changes its evidence as trial and appeal proceed.
Various bits of evidence unchallenged.... They just don't deal with
   some evidence.
Crown misdescribes key bits of evidence.

And so on.

In my mind, all the comments were accurate, and once again it was good hearing them from experts.

No new cases of coronavirus in China, but 415 deaths in Italy. New restrictions and financial helps announced in Australia, and foreigners banned from entry here. Catholic churches will remain open, but no Sunday Masses, and only family allowed at funerals and weddings, etc.

I need to offer a few more prayers for the end of the pandemic, being too concerned with my own situation. So I invoke the help of St Joseph on both issues:

> *Joseph, wise ruler of God's earthly household,*
> *Nearest of all men to the heart of Jesus,*
> *Be still a father, lovingly providing*
> *For us, His brethren. . . .*
>
> *Saint of the dying, blessed with Mary's presence,*
> *In death you rested in the arms of Jesus;*
> *So at our ending, Jesus, Mary, Joseph,*
> *Come to assist us!*

P.S.—Richmond won the opening match of the AFL[3] season against Carlton in an empty Melbourne Cricket Ground stadium.

---

[3] The Australian Football League (AFL) organizes competitions for professional men's Australian Rules football, which is a game more like Irish football than American football.

Friday, 20 March 2020

The big news of the day arrived around 4:00 pm, when a warder gave me a printed two-page announcement that personal visits to prisoners in Victorian jails are being banned from tomorrow.[4] This is yet another (secondary and lesser) reason for a verdict next week! I was able to phone Tim O'Leary, who was due to visit tomorrow, but only managed to leave a message. So I phoned Kartya, who said she would spread the word and make sure Tim knew.

The letters continue to arrive at about the rate of fifteen per day, and, if anything, the mix is more exotic. Karen in Alaska sent me some beautiful coloured photos of images of the mystical visions of Hildegard of Bingen: the kingdom of God, Christ Pantocrator, and another of the fall of the devil and the origin of hell.

Another regular correspondent from Plano outside Dallas in Texas sent me an article, "Safety Last", by Robert Royal, telling how another conservative speaker at a university had been banned to protect the safety of the students.

Royal quotes from Dante's *Divine Comedy* where Dante and Virgil meet a large band of the condemned, stung by wasps and flies and running after a blank flag. These are the uncommitted souls and neutral angels, who followed neither God nor the devil.

> The world allows no rumour of them now.
> Mercy and justice hold them in contempt.
> Let's say no more about them. Look, and pass.
> (*Inferno*, III, 49–51)

Today our distracted and restless lives make it easier to be superficial and sentimental much of the time, blotting out death and sickness, downplaying evil and sin. I don't think Dante would be allowed to speak at many of our universities, as he would disturb too many personal spaces with his strict moralism. I also find it too much, but probably need to hear it.

Jonathan from near Fiesole in Italy sent me a kind letter and five medals of Jesus' Holy Face for prisoners or guards. All were confiscated and the letter was marked "not to be distributed".

---

[4] Because of the coronavirus restrictions.

A pro-life and pro-family senator from Italy wrote a beautiful five-page letter affirming my innocence and telling me of his own problems, being accused of the defamation of homosexuals and fined a substantial amount. He is appealing the decision and hopes to meet me soon in Rome.

The majority of the letters and cards come from Australia: one from a retired Aussie Rules follower in Western Australia, saying that I shouldn't have the wind blowing against me in all four quarters!

I received a couple of copies of the prayers of the 2–10 March novena, the Memorare, and prayers to St John Fisher and St Thomas More.

One of the altar servers from my time in Mentone wrote to express his support, saying that we last met in Rio de Janiero in 2013, when he was a young leader for the Melbourne CEO at WYD. He was kind to acknowledge: "you have had a very positive influence on myself and others, and we are hurting for you at this time."

The coronavirus is now known as Covid-19, and while the situation is stabilising in China, the pandemic spreads elsewhere at different rates. Unfortunately, four hundred people died in Italy in twenty-four hours, most of them elderly and with a preexisting health condition such as tuberculosis. For small gatherings in Australia, each person must have four square metres [thirteen square feet] of space. Hands are to be washed regularly and not used to touch your face.

Katrina Lee was delayed forty minutes before we met, but we had a good hour together, discussing my prospects for release and canvassing how we might reply if the ABC regurgitated any of the St Joseph's Home allegations which had been dropped. My instinct, like Katrina's, was for swift and decisive action, if it could be financed.

As it is a Friday, we might pray an Irish prayer.

O King of the Friday
Whose limbs were stretched on the Cross,
O Lord who did suffer
The bruises, the wounds, the loss,
We stretch ourselves
Beneath the shield of thy might,
Some fruit from the tree of thy passion
Fall on us this night!

Saturday, 21 March 2020

As I was walking around the lawn soon after 8:00 am, Paolo, one of our gang of four who are confined in Unit 3, called me to the glass partition. "They've stopped visitors", he exclaimed, shrugging his shoulder. "We'll go mad." I don't think there is any chance of this for him, or three out of the four of us, but it made me wonder about the reactions of some of the prisoners.

An hour or so later, I was called over again, and their attitude was more upbeat, as they had heard that 370 lawyers, with more to come hopefully, had signed a petition asking for prisoners with only six months (or was it two years? They were unsure) of their sentence remaining to be released.[5] So, too, for the old and infirm prisoners. Paolo thought I would meet the age category but looked too healthy. I was tempted to appear weaker and failing but have no intention of doing so. I am grateful to the Lord for my good health.

At lunchtime, while I was on the treadmill, we were all returned to our cells because of an "Aqua Alert", which means a disturbance is occurring somewhere in the jail. On a couple of occasions in the next hour or so, I heard voices shouting and, probably "putting two and two together to make twenty-two", wondered whether they were part of a protest. If something had taken place, we would be the last to be told.

The *Australian* this weekend had an eight-page supplement on Covid-19, the coronavirus pandemic, full of excellent and informative articles. That gave me a wake-up call because I had been hoping the number of deaths and seriously ill would be kept low, that the lockdown, limited or severe, would last weeks, not months, that the economic decline might be 2 to 5 percent, not 25 percent as Goldman Sachs is now predicting for the US, and that unemployment might rise to 5 or 10 percent, not 20 percent plus, as is quite possible. The personal consequence is that if I am released after more than twelve months in solitary confinement, I face the prospect of another six months in comparative seclusion.

Paul Kelly wrote a magisterial piece outlining the prime minister's major task as maintaining morale, which will be built on the success

---

[5] To reduce numbers in confined spaces, because of the coronavirus contagion.

of slowing the disease's spread and limiting financial damage. It will be interesting to see the level and spread of altruism and the willingness to sacrifice. Kelly has been among the first in the Australian commentariat to ponder the consequences of Christian decline in Australia for secular Australia, especially the secular establishment.

So he concluded his piece with these words: "But it is impossible to overlook the obvious: at some point, the idea of God-created morality was swept away in favour of another principle: that man, not God, is the centre of the universe and has the ability to control the fate of humanity. This crisis will test that belief with the outcome unpredictable."[6]

Geoffrey Blainey had a typically erudite and sympathetic piece drawing on previous epidemics such as the Spanish flu after the First World War and the SARS epidemic in 2003. He pointed out that in World War II, Australians were forbidden to hoard as the government did the rationing.

Angela Shanahan spoke of her home village of Introdacqua in Abruzzo, Italy, pointing out that the death rate in Italy is so high because of the disproportionately large percentage of the elderly, a consequence of the low birthrate.

The most interesting article of them all was an excerpt of a speech Tony Abbott gave in Tokyo on Thursday, where his basic point was logically unassailable and at this time politically unrealisable. He maintained that "the real China virus" is not the contagion but "our overdependence on just one country for vast swathes of our supply chain"—one of the consequences of free trade with a country that does not believe in it, but sees trade as a strategic weapon. Any serious country must have a capacity for manufacturing what is essential in a crisis and stockpiles of essential commodities. Bob Santamaria was making this point when I was a boy. Abbott went on to restate the obvious: that we need to be building baseload power stations and new dams. Please God, after this crisis, these rudimentary truths will be recognized and acted upon.

One of my surprises in jail is the absence of cursing, and I didn't even hear the Holy Name used much when I was at MAP, and most

---

[6] Paul Kelly, "Coronavirus: 'Whatever It Takes' Must Be Our Motto", *Weekend Australian*, 20 March 2020.

of the other prisoners would not have known I was there and cared less. I therefore wrote to my most regular correspondent, who has been in jail for more than two decades, asking about this. While he is now deeply religious, he replied that "most prisoners have a strong to ardent belief in God, in having a reverence and a fear of transgressing against God further." Men can lie to each other, but not to themselves or God. He added, "Those who do not believe in God keep their views to themselves for fear of offending those who would take offence." Some pray when they are in trouble, but "after these people are out of prison or hospital, they simply forget the promises made to God." I suspect that the significant presence of Muslim prisoners has helped produce this godly silence.

Yesterday, 627 people died in Italy, and Fr Robbie is stranded in the United States, trying to return to Italy.

We will close with some lines from John Donne's Holy Sonnet 5.

> *Batter my heart, three-person'd God, for you*
> *As yet but knock, breathe, shine, and seek to mend;*
> *That I may rise and stand, o'erthrow me and bend*
> *Your force to break, blow, burn and make me new.*

WEEK 57

Silence So Far

22 March–28 March 2020

Sunday, 22 March 2020

John's Gospel today for the fourth Sunday of Lent about Jesus' cure of the blind man at the pool of Siloam is one of the finest narratives in the New Testament. It is a great story, well told, of increasing tension and, indeed, confrontation between the blind man, who came to see physically and spiritually, and his religious opponents, poisoned by antagonism, who went farther and farther from the truth. The blind man had lived on the streets and survived by begging. He knew how to look after himself with his tongue, was not looking for trouble, but was determined to defend his benefactor, the man who had cured him.

He knew a man called Jesus had performed the miracle, and he defended him as a prophet, not someone who broke the sabbath. He knew Jesus was no sinner and rebuked his opponents for not listening, asking them sarcastically if they, too, wanted to become his disciples. If this man, his benefactor, was not from God, he couldn't do a thing. They drove him away, where Jesus met him and explained he was the "Son of Man". "Lord, I believe" was the response of the man who could now see. His truthfulness and courage had brought him to faith.

Fr Shabin again celebrated the Mass and preached a good sermon, linking the Gospel with St John Henry Newman's hymn "Lead Kindly Light".

After John's Gospel, Joseph Prince's sermon on "Live the Faith" fell a bit flat as he explained the differences between a blessing and a curse; Jesus has redeemed us from the curse of the Law. As always, the sermon was well prepared. As the world gets darker, the Church gets brighter. Look how the mustard seed grew.

Once again, Joseph had a darker jacket and trousers, with a slightly different ensemble, e.g., a dark tie and white shirt. As he does once in a while, he shouted a bit.

Joel Osteen was on theme, urging us to ask God for something big, as it is the devil who tempts us to ask for small things. God is omnipotent. We are to ask God for an overflow of gifts so we, in turn, can help others. Asking God for our dreams is one occasion when it is not bad to have a big mouth! Joel commended Elisha for asking for double the spirit of Elijah, and, in fact, according to Joel, he performed twice as many miracles as Elijah. I have always regarded Elisha's request as bad form!

He concluded with the homely wisdom that you cannot speak negative words and live positive.

The jail was locked down until 10:00 am so that I was a couple of hours late for my exercise around the lawn. No reasons were given, but it had nothing to do with health requirements.

When I returned to my cell for *Songs of Praise*, the press conference on the virus from the prime minister and treasurer was being broadcast. They announced a huge financial package, equivalent to 10 percent of Australia's GDP, and further restrictions on, e.g., interstate travel. I thought they both did well in their speeches and in their answers to questions.

At halftime in a good match, where Hawthorn defeated Brisbane, the AFL's chief executive, Gillon McLachlan, announced that after today's games, the season, including team training, would be suspended until May 21. While not unexpected, this is an earthquake, as even during two world wars the football continued in Australia. I felt it, as I particularly welcome the games each week on TV as a distraction from my life in jail and was hoping for a similar bonus during my quiet times, enforced because of my age, when I return to Sydney (provided I am acquitted).

My self-centred reaction was set in perspective when I switched over to the second program on the Hitler Youth, who were brainwashed for years, conscripted in the last months of the war, and shot if they deserted. Most fought bravely, some heroically. A twelve-year-old and a sixteen-year-old were given the Iron Cross by Hitler. Thousands were killed. The corrupting of these youths was also a war crime.

These are early days for Covid-19, and the future is unknown. The infection rate of 0.7 percent of those tested is the lowest in the countries affected, and the symptoms here in Australia are generally mild. Not so in Italy, where 793 died in the last twenty-four hours, while the situation has worsened in Spain; China, South Korea, and Singapore have done well in their crisis situations.

I am proud of the pilgrim path I had installed at St Patrick's Cathedral in Melbourne, and a Melbourne correspondent sent me a photo I had not seen of the length of the fountain of living water from the Apocalypse, featuring the Paschal Lamb outside the south transept. It is inscribed:

The angel showed me a river whose waters give life,
it flows as clear as crystal from the throne of God and of the
  Lamb.

Monday, 23 March 2020

It was cold and overcast when I was outside this morning, so I told the warder I was keen to come in lest I die of frostbite. He replied that "we wouldn't want that."

One small mystery was revealed in today's *Herald Sun* with the news report that gangland murderer Steve Asling and a companion had climbed onto the roof of their unit here at Barwon as a protest against the cancellation of visits. This was the reason for the lockdown, and the voices I had heard were probably part of the excitement. The report did not speak of violence or of anyone being hurt. When I mentioned to the warders that I wasn't thinking of climbing onto the roof, they didn't seem to be either impressed or relieved.

No news of any result from the High Court. In speaking to both Chris Meney in Sydney and Tim O'Leary, I recommended that churches should not be closed for individual prayer (Masses have been cancelled) because of Covid-19, but the distance rulings should be enforced, and the maximum number of people in the church should be specified. Apparently, a Polish cardinal in Rome refused to close his church, saying they had not done so for the Nazis and were not doing it now. I well remember Kenneth Clark in his splendid series *Civilisation* in the 1960s remarking that St Paul's Cathedral in London had been closed soon after World War II was declared, and he commented that this would never have happened in a Catholic country. Late in life, he became a Catholic. The news tonight suggested that in Victoria, at least, the churches had been closed.

Australia now has 1,711 cases of the virus, but only seven deaths, which is a very low rate. Tragically, my dearly loved Italy, where I have lived for eight years, now has a higher number of cases than China, if China's statistics can be believed. Yesterday, 650 people died in Italy, but there is a glimmer of hope in the fact that this was a decline on the previous day's total of 793. In Spain, the situation continues to be bad, while the US now has 33,000 cases located primarily in New York, California, and Washington State. South Korea continues to improve.

The Australian Parliament held its last sitting, possibly until October, legislating twenty-four measures to help and injecting $83 billion into the economy.

Graeme Putt, a retired physicist from New Zealand who had written to me previously, sent me a week or so ago a very interesting 2005 article by Elizabeth Loftus, from California, summarising thirty years of investigation, in which she herself has been heavily engaged since the time of President Nixon, on the topic of planting misinformation in the human mind. This research explored the processes by which people came to believe falsely that they experienced rich complex events that never, in fact, occurred.

The first experimental work using neuro imagery on the mechanisms of the "misinformation effect" was done in 2005, and we now know from hundreds of studies much about the degree of memory distortion.

Many factors are at work. Misinformation is more likely to be accepted as true when the original memory has started to fade due to the passage of time. Age matters. Both young children and the elderly are more susceptible to misinformation, to accepting it as true, as are those with the personality variables of empathy, absorption, and self-monitoring.

The "source misattribution effect" concludes from the evidence that "misled subjects definitely do come to remember seeing things that were merely suggested to them", although the size of the effect varies, and it is quite a different thing to plant an entire memory for an event that never happened from mistakenly believing some element or aspect. But it occurs.

Experiments have shown that many subjects "have come to believe or even remember in detail events that did not happen, that were completely manufactured with the help of family members, and that would have been traumatic had they actually happened".

Some have called this "the familial informant false narrative procedure", and many studies using a procedure called "lost in the mall" have shown that an average of "30 percent of subjects have gone on to produce either partial or complete false memory." Some have even come to believe in alien abduction memories!

At a minimum, all this demonstrates that credible witnesses have to be judged from the evidence for their reliability. Even genuine sincerity is not enough.

We shall all have to answer before our great, just, and compassionate Judge, who will separate the sheep from the goats, so that we hope and pray that many, or most of us, will enter:

> *O holy city, seen of John*
> *Where Christ, the Lamb, does reign,*
> *Within whose four-square walls shall come*
> *No night, nor need, nor pain,*
> *And where the tears are wiped from eyes*
> *That shall not weep again!*

Tuesday, 24 March 2020

Unlike my usual practice, I started to prepare for this entry during my lunchtime outside my cell in the indoor common area, as my lunch had not arrived around 11:15 am, the usual time. Abdullah told me that the government's distancing regulations had delayed the work, so that the food arrived an hour late. 12:15 pm is actually a better time for lunch than earlier, and I regularly wait until then to eat. One reason I order so many salads for the evening meal is so that I can keep the food for the three hours after it is delivered and eat around 6:30 pm. If I have a hot meal, as I did today, I eat it while it is warm and appetising. The afternoon meal did not arrive late, because the staff knock-off time around 4:00 pm would have put the distance regulations into a new context.

Silence continues to reign from the High Court, although police and prison officials were to contact Kartya in the afternoon after indicating that a press conference by me would not be possible because of government regulations. Obviously, I will be able to issue the words I have prepared—if the decision goes in the correct direction.

We now have 300,000 cases of Covid-19 throughout the world, with the last 100,000 cases coming in only three days. My information is incomplete, as the SBS newsroom has an infected staff member and the nerve centre has been shut down. Boris Johnson in the UK has imposed a total lockdown for three weeks. Four thousand health workers are ill in Spain, and one more person died in Australia. New York is the epicentre in the United States, although the curve might be flattening in Germany. I am hoping that "no news" from Italy "means good news", so that at least the daily number of deaths and infections is not rising.

To my mind, President Trump made a sensible point saying that in three weeks' time the situation will need to be evaluated to ensure the cure is not causing more damage than the disease. I presume they are hoping to flatten the curve in three or four weeks, because the economy cannot grind to a halt, and I'm not sure how long non-stoical Western world citizens will stay at home for a disease where most of the victims have the equivalent of a bad cold.

I have received an interesting letter from Fr Andreas Hornig, a parish priest and prison chaplain in Austria. He described the Church situation there as "deplorable", saying that very little is to be gained by preaching and protesting as "the only method to heal our Church is praying and suffering." I suppose if I lived in Austria, I too would be a bit "down".

Fr Andreas also mailed a deeply Christian talk by an official who had worked in jails for forty years and finished as deputy governor of a jail with 450 prisoners. His topic was "How to Bring the Good News to Offenders". He explained the closed world of the jail, the tensions, the diversity of nationality, religion, and irreligion among the prisoners, their low level of education, and the fact that 90 percent come from broken families. These Austrian characteristics would run in parallel with the Australian scene.

He was very clear about the importance of the prison ministry, the presence of pastoral volunteers, and especially the presence of the priest. The fruits of this work are invisible, receiving no acknowledgement or thanks. But Christ commended visiting those in prison.

He explained how Christ's parable of the talents helped his work with difficult prisoners. If a man came from a dysfunctional family and a bad environment, his starting point might be minus 50. If he struggles consistently, he might succeed in reaching minus 10. Another person might come from a good family and live in an excellent environment, starting life at plus 30. But he is lazy and selfish and only finishes at plus 35. So the deputy governor concluded: "In the eyes of God, the apparent bad man had won 40 points. The apparent good, only 5 points. And according to that, they will be judged and rewarded."

I often used to explain in my sermons that, in God's eyes, life was like a handicap horse race, not a championship weight-for-age race for thoroughbreds.

Already in Old Testament times, this teaching on the importance of compassion for prisoners was present in Psalm 101.

> *Let this be written for ages to come*
> *that a people yet unborn may praise the Lord;*
> *for the Lord leaned down from his sanctuary on high.*
> *He looked down from heaven to the earth*
> *that he might hear the groans of the prisoners*
> *and free those condemned to die.*

Wednesday, 25 March 2020

Today is the feast of the Annunciation of the Lord, a principal Marian feast, when the young Virgin Mary, betrothed to Joseph, agrees to cooperate in God's great plan of salvation to be effected by his Son, Mary's Son, Jesus. "I am the handmaid of the Lord; let what you have said be done to me" (Lk 1:38), she replied to Gabriel, the messenger of the Divine.

In our era of partnerships, much later marriages, and childbearing when mothers are often in their thirties, we regularly forget how young Our Lady was, probably no more than fifteen. The *Golden Legend*, a collection of lives of the saints, also using non-biblical stories popular in the Middle Ages, drew heavily on the apocryphal second-century *Proto-Evangelium of James*, and we read there that Mary had been raised in the Temple in Jerusalem from a young age, devoting herself to prayer and desiring to offer her virginity to God. The high priest Zechariah thought she should be married and was therefore uncertain how to proceed, when he heard a voice while he was praying telling him to choose one of the young local men for her. And so we have St Joseph.

This beautiful embroidered legend is not in the Gospels, but it embellishes a vital truth. The one true God needed Mary's free cooperation so that the whole Incarnation project could proceed. Mary's *fiat*, "let it be done", is a crucial turning point, not just in salvation history, but for all history. As Pope St Leo the Great wrote, "Lowliness was taken by majesty, weakness by strength, mortality by eternity." This is our faith. We are proud to profess it.

The Covid-19 pandemic continues to spread, but at different rates, so everywhere countries are facing two crises: in health and finance. Australia now has 2,400 cases. In Italy, deaths and new infections had declined for two days, but the number of deaths bounced up to 743 yesterday, still below the peak. Prime Minister Modi has locked down the whole of India in an attempt to prevent the country "going back twenty-one years" economically. Spain now has a higher infection rate than Italy, and Trump hopes the worst will be over by Easter. It would be good if we could all then go to church, he said. Leaders have to tread a narrow path to avoid panic and pessimism, enforce obedience to the restrictions, and encourage some hope without stimulating false expectations. The US share market rose 11 percent at the prospect of a $6 trillion stimulus package, and the Australian market rose 5 percent.

For no adequate reason, I was somewhat agitated this morning by the fact that we still had no news from the High Court, so at lunchtime I phoned Paul Galbally to suggest that he phone the High Court to make sure they were still delivering judgements. Paul was sure that this was continuing, and the ever-practical Kartya confirmed it on their website. Earlier in the week, Ruth had suggested to Bret that we might apply for bail for me in the interim, but they decided against doing that. I was steadied by the fact that the work was definitely continuing, while Bret and Ruth believe we might hear something in the next couple of days—or, of course, next week.

From the transcripts, I cannot see how the decision could again go wrong, and I surmise that the delay could be because the judges want to be careful, knowing the public examination the verdict will receive. And I still have hope that they might break new ground in the judgements, making it more difficult to convict, or even charge, people in situations like mine.

Derek received the good news that his appeal against his conviction for murder will be heard, nineteen years after being sentenced. If it is proved that he was framed, it would be, as Paolo said, a game-changer. The injustice against me pales into insignificance in comparison with this outrage. I pray that the truth will out.

The governor of the jail on his weekly visit said I will be able to watch the replay of the two-day hearing in Canberra on a computer.

Another complication is that nonessential travel across the New South Wales and Victoria border is prohibited. One response would be for someone to drive me to Bendigo to see the family, for David to drive me to the border, and for Chris Meney, or someone, to drive me to Sydney. But we can cross that bridge when and if we come to it.

We conclude with a couple of intercessions from the feast. Today, we celebrate the beginning of our salvation in the Annunciation of the Lord, and full of joy we pray:

> *Holy Mother of God, intercede for us.*
> *Holy Mary, comfort the miserable and the sick, help the*
> *fainthearted, cheer those who weep in this time of plague*
> *and pestilence:*
> *Holy Mother of God, intercede for us.*

Thursday, 26 March 2020

Yesterday for the feast of the Annunciation, the weather was overcast and the light dull, very dull. Early this morning, the cloud cover was lighter, and I wasn't quite as cold, although it never developed into a lovely autumn day.

One of my prison correspondents threw some light on the men on the roof incident. The leading actor was not Steve Asling, but a Muslim prisoner with a similar name. He and his companion were jeered at and denounced by other prisoners, who resented the lock-down that was being imposed. Apparently, some damage was done to the antenna, and the whole affair ended ignominiously with a climb down when the chief protagonist, brandishing a pipe, offered to surrender it if he was given a drink. Most alternative endings would have been worse.

The United States now has 69,000 persons who have tested positive for the coronavirus, and this despite the fact the US testing rate is low, much lower than in Australia. New York has 20,000 cases, making it the epicentre, although the spread there might be slowing. A seventeen-year-old boy died in California, while numbers continue to surge in Spain. The downward trend continues in Italy although health facilities in the north are under intense pressure. Three people died in Australia, bringing the death toll to thirteen, and the majority of those infected have returned from overseas.

In the UK, Boris Johnson asked for 250,000 volunteers to help the elderly, etc., and they already have 500,000 names. This provides evidence of a social capital which might not be equalled in all or many other Western countries. Prince Charles has tested positive, but Camilla has escaped. The secretary-general of the United Nations was probably heading in the right direction when he expressed the fear that the virus would rage through the Third World, while the First World manages to contain the damage.

In Victoria, the premier finally closed the casino many days after he had closed churches.

The continuing flow of letters reminds me of the many loyal friends I have in Australia and in many other countries.

Fr Brian Kelly, OSB, of Quarr Abbey on the Isle of Wight, whom I had ordained to the priesthood, wrote to assure me of the prayerful support of the community, enclosing an *In Memoriam* card for my good friend Abbot Cuthbert Johnson, who died three years ago and had worked with us on the Vox Clara committee for the English translation of the Roman Missal. Cuthbert was a well-published liturgical expert who was our singing adviser, as you must be able to sing the Mass prayers.

Two good friends from the Australian branch of Opus Dei wrote, both of them medical doctors, one head of a university college and the other a professor at Notre Dame University in Sydney, who commented on how the blessing of hands for the first-year medical students, mostly not Catholics, causes many of them to reflect deeply. Already in Australia, Opus Dei is a major source of spiritual energy, working away from the headlines and strengthening the sinews of the Catholic community.

The Neocatechumenal Way, like Opus Dei, is also a major twentieth-century contribution to the life of the Church, and both are likely to endure for centuries. In my mind, the hand of God is upon them, and both groups have given me wonderful friends and support.

Paolo, a member of the Way, from Perugia in Italy, who was in Sydney for World Youth Day in 2008 (now married with a wife and two young kids), wrote to offer me his "poor support" and to assure me my "righteous deeds have not been forgotten". He wrote that "I feel we are part of the same Body, that we are brothers in Jesus Christ."

Gionata, from a family with whom I have been friendly for about fifteen years, is now a sixth-year seminarian in the Neocatechumenal Redemptoris Mater seminary in Perth. He has just returned from a year on the mission in Papua New Guinea, where the Way now has sixteen communities. They visited four different provinces, Wewak, Mount Hagen, Alotau, and Rabaul to give the First Scrutiny,[1] and he proudly recounted how two hundred of the locals scraped together enough money to make a pilgrimage from their many different regions to Rabaul, to the grave of Blessed Peter To Rot, and the spot where eight missionaries were martyred in 1908. He assured me of constant prayers from the seminary, that "we are following the hearing [of the High Court]. I know it is a heavy cross to carry. I hope God is giving you the strength to bear it." That his sister Micol has just given birth to a 4.2 kg [9 lb] baby boy, called Levi, was his last piece of breaking news.

Patty, a regular correspondent from Dallas, recommended this prayer based on lines from Psalm 31:

---

[1] Part of the preparation for adult baptism.

Lord God,
Let your face shine on your servant.
Save me in your steadfast love.
Amen.

Friday, 27 March 2020

An unknown friend from Lane Cove in Sydney sent me a couple of beautifully written paragraphs by St John Henry Newman.[2] While I have read a lot of Newman's writings, there is more that I haven't read as his output was enormous. I hadn't read these lines.

They are a bleak meditation on the world, history, human achievement, and folly, which concludes with a clear affirmation of faith in God and an equally clear affirmation of original sin, or what Newman calls "some terrible aboriginal calamity".

It would be interesting to know the saint's circumstances and state of mind when he wrote this piece, one I would not have written and could not have written so well. While I was born during the Second World War, I was too young to know that war, did not struggle through the Depression, and have lived a charmed life, albeit with some challenging personal trials, through more than seventy years of increasing prosperity—until Covid-19. I and many of my generation of Australians have had it easy.

But back to Newman. He writes of "the world in its length and breadth", of "the many races of man" and their "forms of worship"; "their random achievements" and "aimless courses"; of "the tokens so faint and broken of a superintending design".

He captures "the greatness and the littleness of man, his far-reaching aims, his short duration" and "the dreary hopeless irreligion", which is much stronger today. "All this is a vision to dizzy and appal; and inflicts upon the mind the sense of a profound mystery, which is absolutely beyond human solution."

He concludes, "*If* there be a God, *since* there is a God, the human race is implicated in some terrible aboriginal calamity."

Charles Dickens has described the squalor and the degradation in earlier Victorian times, miserable living conditions of twelve- to

---

[2] *Apologia Pro Vita Sua* (1864), chapter 5.

fourteen-hour working days for men and sometimes women and children in dangerous factories and mines, of the Great Stink and the cholera epidemic; life was harsh for most of the population as it is still for many people around the world.

Newman was not a sentimentalist, not someone to be tricked or reassured by attractive superficialities. He was led gradually by God's "kindly light" in good times and climes and in bad. He assented really and truly to God's love in the world and in his heart. So must we, even as we pray, quite legitimately, that we be not put to too much of a test.

The coronavirus is flowing around the world following the travel routes. The US now has 85,000 cases with 1,000 deaths and has overtaken China for the top spot; a dubious distinction.

Australia has 3,167 cases, two-thirds of them among travellers returning home from overseas, with a very high rate of testing and a low infection rate. From tomorrow, returnees from overseas will spend fourteen days in quarantine in a hotel. Worldwide, the numbers have topped half a million, while Italy could be returning from the worst. The Australian government is preparing a third tranche of economic measures to put Australian businesses into "hibernation", so they can start up again when the worst is over.

We all should be praying in this crisis, especially for the weak and the vulnerable, and that means many millions in the Third World. And we should be praying that we learn from our hard times and be consoled by the fact that our suffering, joined to Christ's, can be turned to good account. It is a teaching moment for bishops and priests.

The weather was better today, so that I sat outside in the sunlight for much of the morning. A little disappointed that we still have no news from the High Court, but I reread the transcript of the hearing again, and this always gives me heart.

During my thirteen months in jail, I have discovered many beautiful prayers, generally sent to me by correspondents, especially some by St Thomas More and even more by St John Henry Newman.

This excerpt from Newman finds him in a more positive state of mind.

God has created me to do Him some definite service; He has committed some work to me which He has not committed to another. I have my mission—I never may know it in this life, but I shall be told it in the

next.... I am a link in a chain, a bond of connection between persons.
He has not created me for naught. I shall do good, I shall do His work;
I shall be an angel of peace, a preacher of truth in my own place, while
not intending it, if I do but keep His commandments and serve Him
in my calling.[3]

Saturday, 28 March 2020

I now subscribe to the *Weekend Australian*, and it is a lifeline, a gateway to understanding, not available through TV and the few magazines and articles sent to me. Because of Covid-19, Kartya was unable to pass in my *Spectators* to me; but even when they are available, it is somewhat frustrating when they are four or six weeks out of date.

The Inquirer section of the paper has some of the finest journalists in Australia, many of them regularly outstanding, as are the editorials.

So I was able to read Greg Sheridan's evaluation of the efficacy of the different national approaches to the virus, of the US and China blaming one another, of the efficiency of the South Korean policies, of the relationship of the health and financial challenges and the need to avoid disaster in either area.

J.P. Morgan estimates the Chinese economy will shrink by 40 percent in the first quarter of this year, while Goldman Sachs predicts a slump of 24 percent for the US in the second quarter, and Morgan Stanley put it higher at 30 percent. One writer compares the crisis to the First World War rather than the Great Depression.

The pandemic has only started in many Asian countries. Fears are held for Indonesia, which already has 1,000 cases and only one-tenth pro rata of the number of doctors in Italy, where they are already close to breaking point in the north.

With my monthly allowance of $140, plus $50 extra for the phone, I cannot afford *The Australian* every day, as this would exhaust around two-thirds of the entire sum. The number of mobile phone numbers allowed on my list is limited, and this is sensible because mobile calls are horrendously expensive.

The prospects for the plague are grim, much worse than I had hoped for originally, and they certainly dwarf my personal concerns

---

[3] *Meditations and Devotions*: "Hope in God the Creator".

about my verdict and set them in a proper perspective. After three disasters, I find it difficult to feel confident, although I know the signs are good, if not excellent: first of all, because I was given leave to appeal and, secondly, because the two days in the High Court went so well. I don't doubt that God is with me, caring for me, but I don't know what he will allow. Just as surely as I do know what would be just and good for me, and good also for the Church in Australia and more widely.

Michael Casey passed on to me a couple of phone messages from a dear friend in the United States, a good bishop, who has taken leave because of anxiety and depression. He wrote that "not a day goes by that I don't think and pray for Cardinal Pell." He is offering Mass for me and promises "unfailing support and prayers". I asked Michael to phone my best wishes and the promise of my prayers. I confessed I am an inveterate meddler, and I am sure he has expert help, but I urged him to pray (which he would be doing) and to walk, walk, walk. I reminded him of the victim of Auschwitz who, when he was badly down, would often walk and walk, almost to the limits of his strength. Then he was much better able to sleep a healthy sleep. And I reminded him we are preaching Christ, not our poor Church, or her leaders, or ourselves. Please God he will be able to battle through this bad time.

I have long realised that no matter what our mood might be, even when we don't feel very Christian, we can often find a verse or two in the Psalms which enable us to speak to the good God. The morning prayer in the *Magnificat* today uses Psalm 7, and a couple of verses might overstate my goodness but, otherwise, capture my prayers exactly.

> *Lord, my God, I take refuge in you.*
> *From my pursuer save me and rescue me,*
> *lest he tear me to pieces like a lion*
> *and drag me off with no one to rescue me....*
>
> *Give judgement for me, Lord; I am just*
> *and innocent of heart.*
> *Put an end to the evil of the wicked!*
> *Make the just stand firm,*
> *you who test mind and heart,*
> *O just God!*

WEEK 58

Old Accusations Resurface

29 March–4 April 2020

Sunday, 29 March 2020

The weather showed promise when I went outside at 8:00 am, but that promise did not materialise for most of the day; the afternoon saw some heavy rain, but it was confined to showers.

I felt lethargic this morning and decided to take my pulse, which was as regular as clockwork at around 70 bpm. No problems here, although I decided to eat my three Weetabix and a splendid banana before I commenced my half-hour walk. I dozed again after that and prayed my Office of Readings and morning prayer when I returned to Cell 17.

The coronavirus has hit the *Mass for You at Home*, as we did not have today's Mass for the Fifth Sunday of Lent, but a previous Mass for the Australia Day weekend, the First Sunday of Ordinary Time, celebrated by Fr Andrew Jekot. The background music was "Come as You Are", and the Gospel told of the brothers Peter and Andrew answering Jesus' call to follow him and become "fishers of people".

Fr Andrew preached a good, well-prepared sermon, listing and praising the best Australian qualities, which are expressions or extensions of following Jesus. True Blue Catholics first change their own hearts to follow Jesus and then help others to Advance Australia Fair. A welcome change from the run-of-the-mill sermons.

For the second Sunday in a row, I was not much taken by Joseph Prince's sermon on "Prosper through Prophetic Teaching", although he was informative on the pure gold menorah, the seven-branched candelabra, which he linked with the seven lamps around the good God.

He then went to the seven lampstands and two olive trees of Zechariah's vision. A mountain can be levelled by grace. It is God who calls the end result, who does not see us as we see ourselves. We have to pray to become children of God, and Joseph promised that he would make sure we are always full of Christ.

Joel Osteen preaches a prosperity gospel more regularly and explicitly than Joseph, but I prefer his sermons, perhaps because I am tempted by the prosperity gospel, but more exactly because Joel's topics are taken often from the New Testament and are good as far as they go. Often it is not so much a love of the cross or a recognition of the importance of suffering, but a weakness of faith which impedes our asking for God's help. Jesus himself commended those who asked in faith for miracles, sometimes far beyond any human expectation.

We should start to expect God's favour, he insists, and search it out with all our heart. In so many places, there are embers waiting to catch fire. God doesn't bring us so far and then leave us. This is completely true, and Joel has encouraged me to continue to ask the good God that I will be exonerated from the remaining charges.

Phoned around my regular circle of friends as well as David and managed to have a good chat with Margaret. She has a cough, so is in isolation in her retirement home. All seemed well and relaxed, although Margaret mentioned that David had seen advance publicity about my being in the ABC program on Tuesday. Margaret herself mentioned that she had seen nothing more recently. Obviously, it is a cause for controlled concern, as Katrina Lee foreshadowed nine days ago, but I don't know what they might say or show, and I don't know whether we have responded or acted in any way. Kartya didn't mention anything on Friday, but I will phone her tomorrow to see if she knows more. When we know what is happening, we can then decide what should be done and judge how damaging it might or might not be.

Since early afternoon, very strangely, I have not been able to obtain the ABC on television or radio, although my TV is otherwise working well. A couple of informal enquiries have elicited no useful response. This is another issue I will try to clarify tomorrow. Naturally, I wonder whether it is somehow connected with the ABC's Tuesday program.

The prime minister has brought in tighter regulations, so that only two people can get together rather than the ten previously allowed, and those over seventy should stay at home. The number of deaths around the world from Covid-19 has topped 30,000 with more than 10,000 in Italy, although the infection rate there is flattening. When Rhode Island closed its borders and President Trump suggested New York and surrounds should be isolated, the mayor of New York claimed it was a declaration of war! Trump quickly softened his prohibition into a suggestion. In Australia, we have 3,981 cases and two new deaths, bringing the total to sixteen, probably reasons for a cautious initial optimism, because of the low infection rate and the increase of cases at 9 percent yesterday, rather than the rate of 25 percent plus some days ago.

Given the uncertainties in my situation, it seems appropriate to conclude with the final section of St John Henry Newman's reflection.

Therefore I will trust God. Whatever, wherever I am, I can never be thrown away. If I am in sickness, my sickness may serve Him; in perplexity, my perplexity may serve Him; if I am in sorrow, my sorrow may serve Him. My sickness, or perplexity, or sorrow may be necessary causes of some great end, which is quite beyond us. He does nothing in vain; He may prolong my life, He may shorten it; He knows what He is about. He may take away my friends, He may throw me among strangers, He may make me feel desolate, make my spirit sink, hide the future from me—still He knows what He is about.[1]

Monday, 30 March 2020

Let me start with the least important piece of news. My television and remote-control have both been replaced, and all is working perfectly. The malfunction was simply that and unrelated to any other factor, and they decided on replacement, because they couldn't correct the older equipment.

In his *Confessions*, the first autobiography in Western literature, St Augustine recounts how he heard a child chanting in a garden *tolle, lege*, Latin for "take and read", when he was pondering his return to the Catholic faith. He opened the Bible at random, finding chapter 8

---

[1] *Meditations and Devotions*: "Hope in God the Creator".

of St Paul's Letter to the Romans, outlining the alternatives of a spiritual or unspiritual life, a choice of life or death. And a promise followed: "Everyone moved by the Spirit is a son of God" (Rom 8:14).

Some people when they are in doubt or distress still open the Bible at random to find a text for prayer and meditation. This is not one of my practices, but the readings and prayers today are immensely consoling.

The Scripture reading in the *Magnificat* for the morning prayer is taken from chapter 54 of the prophet Isaiah. There we read: "My love for you will never leave you and my covenant of peace with you will never be shaken, says the Lord who takes pity on you." And in the next paragraph, God is still speaking: "Should anyone attack you, that will not be my doing, and whoever attacks you, for your sake will fall."

These words were balm for my soul, as I was feeling aggrieved by the prospect of a new set of accusations on Tuesday night. I knew and know God has not left me, and during the night I repeated my love for the Lord; but it was still good to hear these basic truths once again and realise that God is to be dissociated from the attacks.

The first reading at Mass is from the prophet Daniel and recounts the story of the beautiful Susanna, who resists the advances of two lecherous judges and is framed by those who make false allegations about her and a young man. She is tried and condemned; then Daniel objects and proves the accusers are lying.

I, too, have been falsely accused by a number of men who are either fantasising, telling lies, or victims of altered memories; and I am not yet vindicated.

When an atmosphere becomes poisonous, many start to believe the worst or want so to believe. It is not hard to envisage a scenario where it is difficult to prove innocence, although technically that is not necessary in our legal system. I thank God regularly that I have not been in that situation, and I thank God for my Daniels; first of all, my legal team, but also writers like Andrew Bolt and Keith Windschuttle in Australia, George Weigel and Fr Raymond de Souza in the US and Canada, and Christopher Friel in Wales. Many others have contributed, also.

The Gospel reading is from chapter 8 of St John's Gospel, telling of the woman accused of adultery, threatened with death by stoning, and saved by Our Lord. It is another of my favourite passages, only reluctantly accepted as canonical by many, who felt Our Lord could not have acted so "softly". Today, most of us don't have any problem on that score, but we do need to point out that Jesus did not tell the unfortunate woman (whose male partner in crime is not mentioned) to keep up her good work, but to go and sin no more.

At lunchtime, I phoned Kartya to learn what the situation was about tomorrow's ABC television show. It appears that a former resident at St Joseph's Home in Ballarat has repeated accusations that were put to me by police four years ago, were answered, taken to court, and dropped by the prosecution. If this proves to be the case, the man involved is a most unfortunate, unwell individual. And I never had any role at St Joseph's in any official or unofficial capacity, not knowing either nuns or residents at that time, forty to fifty years ago.

Katrina Lee has sent a message to this effect, which the program should mention. It will still be ugly, and it appears as a disgraceful exploitation by the ABC of an unfortunate, deluded man. This information has provided me with a degree of reassurance, and I have prayed for the accuser.

The prime minister and treasurer continued to perform well, announcing a $130 billion package to pay $1,500 a fortnight to six million workers over the next six months. This represents 17 percent of GDP. Our infection rate remains low for Covid-19.

Trump no longer hopes for salvation in the US by Easter. Chinese equipment to Spain has been returned, as 30 percent of one item was found to be ineffective, while the death rate in France is five times higher than in Germany. Frydenberg[2] the treasurer says the weeks ahead will be tougher than the present situation for us in Australia.

The intercessions are from the *Magnificat* morning prayer:

> *You are our help and defender, O Lord, in time of trial.*
> *To you we flee for protection, praying:*
> *Save us, O Lord.*
> *When Faith wavers in the face of suffering:*
> *Save us, O Lord.*
> *When evil tempts us to doubts and darkness:*
> *Save us, O Lord.*

[2] Joshua Anthony Frydenberg (b. 1971) is Australia's federal treasurer and has been the deputy leader of the Liberal Party since August 2018.

Tuesday, 31 March 2020

The entrance antiphon for today's Mass strikes the right note: "Wait for the Lord; be strong, be stouthearted, and wait for the Lord."

I am doing my best to act as instructed. Eugenio Pacelli sent in a copy of *Magnificat* for April, which was confiscated, as no books are being allowed in. This morning I asked for an exceptional approval to be given, but have heard no reply, as I am writing this in the early afternoon.

The day dawned fine and clear, the best for some time, but things have slipped somewhat and the clouds have made a bit of a comeback.

Some days ago Bernadette Tobin sent me a copy of Fr Frank Brennan's Barry O'Keefe Lecture, sponsored by the Law School of Australian Catholic University on "Do We Need New Laws to Protect Religious Freedom in Australia?"

Barry O'Keefe was one of New South Wales' leading Catholic laymen, who was a Supreme Court judge with many other interests, such as local government and the National Trust, which he once chaired. He became the first chairman of the Truth, Justice and Healing Council, which the Catholic Church set up to guide us through the Royal Commission on sexual abuse. He kept himself alive, battling cancer, to see me through the first round of these troubles.

Brennan's paper sets out elegantly and concisely the present situation legally, politically, and with public opinion. He recognizes that times have changed with an increase in anti-Catholicism as well as the spread of secularism. The sex abuse crisis was a disaster for the victims and for the standing of the Catholic Church, but it has provided an unusual opportunity for anti-Christians, which they are exploiting methodically.

Australia, unlike the UK and New Zealand, does not have a Bill of Rights, which I publicly opposed,[3] but Victoria, Queensland, and the Australian Capital Territory have a Charter of Human Rights, which is a weaker form of protection. By and large, the freedom of religious bodies is protected by exemptions, and religious behaviour

---

[3] In 2008 Cardinal Pell argued against a proposed bill of rights for Australia by saying that human rights are protected better by a democratically elected parliament than by the courts, where disputes over rights end up in countries with a Bill of Rights, such as the United States.

by exceptions. These are always liable to further restriction and are in no sense ideal.

As with all freedoms, the right to religious freedom is limited and has to be weighed in the balance with conflicting rights. As a member of the Ruddock review,[4] Brennan does not believe religious freedom is in imminent peril, but it does require "constant vigilance". Religious schools, for example, should be able to constitute their own faith environment, just as a political party creates its own political environment. He wrote, "Religious schools should remain free to teach their doctrine respectfully and reasonably, in season and out of season." Some or many Christian teachings are countercultural, e.g., on forgiveness and sexual behaviour, and Brennan quotes two of these: Christ's teaching on riches and on marriage and divorce.

Brennan does not favour a Religious Freedom Act, but proposes a carefully worded Religious Discrimination Act, particularly because of shortfalls in legislation in NSW and South Australia.

Potential areas of tension are religious schools and hospitals which receive government funding and insist they should be able to maintain their distinctive practices and teachings and select staff to maintain an ethos which enables this.

I am not among those religious leaders who have changed their minds and now prefer judges in the courts, through an act, to defend religious freedom. Values in Australia are changing, and this will have religious consequences, but a populace can change their politicians, while they cannot change judges who give unwelcome decisions.

A lot will depend on the political capacity of the different religious bodies, working cooperatively as much as possible, to defend their freedoms through public debate and the ballot box. We should be espousing reasoned discussion extolling the virtues of a free society, including freedom of speech, which respects the separation of church and state and so limits the powers of governments and bureaucrats to interfere in church life (and in the life of synagogue, mosque, and temple). As always, religious people in a democracy will have to use their opportunities to preserve their freedoms. Legislation can help,

[4] During a 2017 parliamentary debate over whether religious institutions may uphold their sexual morality in employment practices, Prime Minister Malcolm Turnbull's government created a panel to review the question. Headed by former attorney general Philip Ruddock, the panel also included Fr Frank Brennan.

but is always the product of a changing society, so that religious citizens will need to continue to be seen and heard in public.

I watched the ABC show giving a harrowing description of the sex abuse crisis in the Newcastle Diocese and among the St John of God Brothers, and at the end they announced there would be new revelations about me next Thursday night. The complainant's voice was briefly featured, and I believe I recognized it from the committal hearing. All in all, an unpleasant couple of hours and more to come on Thursday. It is a consoling Christian belief that we can offer up our suffering and join it to Christ's for some good purpose.

In Australia, we had a 9 percent increase in Covid-19 cases yesterday and one more death, while 812 people died in each of Spain and Italy, although the infection rate is slowing in both countries. The number of deaths in the United States has reached 5,000, and the peak is expected in the UK in a couple of weeks.

I conclude as I began this entry with the antiphon:

> *Wait for the Lord; be strong, be stouthearted, and wait for the Lord!*

Wednesday, 1 April 2020

As winter approaches, the sun is arriving later, so that today, while the weather was clear, it was greyer than previously as I went outside for my half-hour walk around the lawn. It became sunny and pleasant as I had my breakfast of Weetabix and a banana and then went through my prayer routine. I recite a couple of rosaries during my walk; one extra for Lent.

My *Magnificat* booklet still hasn't been passed through, although senior officer Murphy (with three pips on his shoulder) promised he would go personally to collect it after an initial knockback.

My night's sleep had not gone too badly, as I had slept until just before 4:00 am and then prayed a rosary, which nearly always puts me back to sleep. Surprisingly, my sleep apnea machine showed that it hadn't been needed much at all during the night, registering the lowest reading for months.

At 10:00 am, I was called to the phone by my lawyers, with the suggestion they wish to initiate a video link. They informed me that

was not possible, so we chatted on the phone for ten or twelve minutes. Their call was very welcome, as they had already concluded a
half-hour phone hook-up with Katrina Lee, Danny Casey, Michael
Casey, and Terry Tobin, my good friends and brains trust.

Katrina and the whole team, with Paul and Kartya, insisted strongly
that there was no point in our commenting on Friday morning, as it
would give oxygen to the public reaction. My concerns were allayed
by the news that many were outraged and a good number ready to go
in to bat in the media and social media on my behalf. Neither will it
be useful to call out the abuse of process, because that would remain
there to be used in each set of eventualities.

Paul explained that this example of persecution will demonstrate
why the trial by jury went off the rails. In response to my question,
he insisted that this turmoil would have zero impact on the timing or
substance of the ruling from the High Court.

Paul also believes that the complainant was the same as in the
committal, and he was interested in my "recognition" of the voice.
According to him, the allegations referred to an "incident" of forty-
seven years ago, nominating 1972 or 1973. I was not in Ballarat in
1972—although, in fairness to Paul, he was not making too high a
claim on his recollection of the dates. My subsequent thought is that
even if it is another person, the duplication of the story of the earlier
complainant also provides grounds for suspicion.

All in all, I was buoyed by both the support and the developments, asking Kartya to bring my brother up to date. She promised
she would do so immediately after our call. We continued to have
no news on the timing of the High Court verdict, with Paul again
pointing out that with a successful outcome we will be much better
placed to plot our course. I repeated my conviction that some decisive measure will be needed to stop the flow of false allegations.

I then spent over three hours watching a recording on iPad of the
first day of the appeal. Anne McFarlane's claim was validated that it is
easier to follow the argument by watching them than by reading the
text, although the language and level of argumentation were high (as
appropriate with High Court judges), higher in my estimate than in the
Victorian Court of Appeal. Certainly no judge made any elementary
error in law as Maxwell did in referring to the non-calling of Fr Egan.

Bret systematically demolished the arguments of the Victorian
majority, showing the circularity in their arguments, how they

reversed the onus of proof, and demonstrating against them that showing X is possible is not the same as proving X is true beyond reasonable doubt.

The judges were younger than I expected and looked "reassuring" to me. Time will tell. All except Keane spoke on the first day, and their comments were worthy of their high office. I thought Bret answered their concerns well, and I presume their silence as he spoke meant at least that he was not making legal errors. This was in marked contrast to their treatment of the director of prosecutions.

The Covid-19 virus curve continues to flatten in Australia; more than 800 died once again in Spain and in Italy, which now has more than 12,000 dead, and the US is preparing for a shocking death toll. António Guterres, the secretary-general of the United Nations, was warning of looming disasters in the Third World and of the need for help from the First World. Similar fears were expressed for the health of the homeless in Los Angeles, and it was conceded that social distancing in India is almost impossible, especially for those still travelling home to their villages. May the good God help us if the virus starts to rampage through India or Africa or Indonesia.

So tonight I pray Psalm 17 from the Office of Readings, not so much for my personal concerns, but for the hundreds of thousands caught up in this pandemic.

> *I love you, Lord, my strength,*
> *my rock, my fortress, my saviour.*
> *My God is the rock where I take refuge;*
> *my shield, my mighty help, my stronghold. . . .*

> *In my anguish I called to the Lord;*
> *I cried to my God for help.*
> *From his temple he heard my voice;*
> *my cry came to his ears.*

Thursday, 2 April 2020

It was a tumultuous day, but a good day. The rain was falling as I showered, and it continued lightly as I went outside at 8:00 am. My half hour's exercise was done under cover in the open gymnasium, where I followed my usual routine of breakfast and then prayer. As I was expecting to continue watching the High Court appeal on the iPad, I consumed my toast and jam after the Weetabix, rather than when I came back to the cell.

At 10:00 am, I was called to my viewing, and I moved immediately to the second day to watch Kerri Judd, the Victorian director of prosecutions, strut her poor stuff. It was more encouraging than the written text, because you could see the long pauses, the shuffling and searches for documents, the infrequent appeals for help to Gibson, her supporting barrister, and her persistent evasions.

Unexpectedly, around 10:00 am, a senior officer, whom I had not met, perhaps the deputy governor, informed me my lawyers had phoned to say that the High Court decision would be handed down at 9:30 am next Tuesday, April 7th. This was good news and a big relief, so I returned to my viewing with an increased enthusiasm.

On the first day of the appeal, Bret Walker had worked hard to establish that a witness judged to be credible might still be judged to be unreliable in the light of contrary evidence. In bringing a verdict of guilty, the jury accepted the complainant was credible. This is their function, and it is not the proper role of the appellate court to repeat that exercise on credibility.

So something like the first hour of the prosecutor's time was spent on the propriety of the Victorian judges viewing a video of the complainant's evidence, twice in fact, and once before they (the majority) had read the text. Did they have to establish a forensic reason for watching the video, and was there an error in law in their so doing? The prosecution emphasised that they had not requested such an activity, although they had acquiesced against our objections.

Another theme investigated was whether the majority judges reversed the onus of proof by equating the possibility that X happened to the claim X actually happened, a factual claim beyond reasonable doubt.

I am finishing today's journal after breaking to watch the ABC TV program *Revelation*. Two of the fellows who had accused me, and whose cases had been dropped, featured in a long program which covered much of my life, generally, but not always, presenting me in the most unflattering light. Bernie's accusations are so fantastic, ranging from accusations at St Joseph's Home, where I had no role, officially or informally, and only visited one or two times (possibly) in my twelve years in Ballarat, to accusations at St Patrick's Cathedral, Ballarat, where I never lived and had no role.

The program could scarcely have been worse, although no new ground was broken, and the bizarre allegations against me in places where I neither lived nor worked will help in the short and especially in the long run, because they are so false and counterproductive. The ABC's exploitation of Bernie, that poor man, is disgraceful.

There seems to be no alternative to suing, although we have to receive a good verdict from the High Court to enable this. Some years of struggle lie ahead, and financing the struggles might be beyond me, as there are limits to the burdens friends can be asked to bear.

There are now 938,000 Covid-19 infections reported around the world, with 5,133 cases in Australia and 20 deaths. The trajectory of the disease in the US is judged to be similar to Italy's, while the first death has been reported in a Mumbai slum. Spain had 864 deaths in the last twenty-four hours, but the contagion rate is stabilising there, and in some places in Italy parents have been allowed to take their children out for a walk. The Australian government announced child-care subsidies, suspending fees for working parents.

A couple of verses from Psalm 26 are *ad rem*.

> *Instruct me, Lord, in your way;*
> *on an even path lead me.*
> *When they lie in ambush, protect me*
> *from my enemy's greed.*
> *False witnesses rise against me,*
> *breathing out fury.*

> *I am sure I shall see the Lord's goodness*
> *in the land of the living.*
> *Hope in him, hold firm and take heart.*
> *Hope in the Lord!*

Friday, 3 April 2020

It is raining heavily as I write this in the evening at 8:50 pm, although the weather was so good this morning that I sat out in the sun, doing nothing, after I had finished my breakfast and prayers. A quiet day after the tumult of yesterday evening's show. A thoroughly nasty program, which Terry described as the most anti-Catholic he had seen in sixty years of viewing. I would have to agree.

It is provoked by, and a product of, the awful crimes committed in the Church and the spectacular failures of leadership, not universal. The suffering, sickness, and anguish produced cannot be denied or written down. But that is not the whole of the story, as I feel certain the Spirit of Evil, the devil, is also at work, fomenting the hatred, trying to damage the Church further and reduce us to silent impotence. Pope Francis was heavily criticized in the program for saying the devil was at work in the crisis.

The Church is much weakened, but she is like a patient who has had a terrible cancer removed, an absolute necessity, but is only slowly returning to health.

My paranoid fears that the press would run riot with the revelations was not at all justified. The media hardly touched on the issue, with even *The Age* having a short straightforward article on page 17. The coronavirus, of course, at the moment does not tolerate rivals for top billing, and this was the major factor. Three other factors were also important. These allegations had been raised by the police and answered in 2016; they had been brought to court unsuccessfully, while their main actor, Bernie, came through, not only as troubled and suffering, but also as highly disturbed as he listed his bizarre accusations.

Perhaps I should take a small, wry consolation from the fact that my enemies, the Church's enemies and the Evil One, still see me as worth destroying.

Sr Mary, the senior Catholic chaplain, drove down from Melbourne to see me, a gesture I deeply appreciated as we had a good yarn for about one-and-a-half hours. Naturally, she had watched the program and was, I think, a bit concerned about how I might have reacted. As a general rule, I am better at coping with reality, less anxious or pained than when I am waiting for the unknown. My time with Mary was great therapy as I was able to run through why Bernie's story was so wrong, implausible, and impossible. We then ranged more widely on how the Church had allowed herself to be reduced to such ignominy and pondered the roles of a couple of the leaders.

She is a woman of authentic faith, humanity, and wide experience. I have found her to be a huge help. She reminded me I had four more sleeps here (at least!). I hadn't counted, and I have not started packing or throwing out most of the articles, etc., I have received. At her suggestion, however, I did commence enquiries on whether my suit is hanging or packed. Someone had claimed that it had been hung up, which would be preferable.

This afternoon, I completed my viewing of the High Court appeal with the final section of the prosecutor's shambolic presentation, which was punctuated by regular interventions from the bench, and then Bret's contribution for one hour. He was rarely interrupted at all until a final section of dialogue on a couple of legal points.

He lived up to his promise to be in "hunt and kill" mode; something he accomplished with logic and precision, denouncing the "improvised and rickety construction of a Crown case to make something fit that will not fit". He spoke of improvisation, misreading of the evidence, and a reversal of the onus of proof. I think I identified Justice Bell giving an occasional nod of approval.

Even a couple of weeks ago, I was badly underestimating the likely extent and virulence of the Covid-19 pandemic. Today we have around the world more than one million acknowledged cases, while the Australian chief medical officer, Prof Brendan Murphy, believes that the real numbers are in fact five or ten times higher, because testing is so restricted in most countries. In the US, which has 245,000 thousand cases and 1,000 deaths, 100,000 body bags are being made available. The infection rate is slowing in Australia, and the prime minister has announced that those of our 580,000 foreign students who are not self-sufficient should return home. And so it goes on.

St Francis of Paola was a fifteenth-century hermit from Calabria who provided some good advice.

Remembering grievances works great damage. It is accompanied by anger, fosters sin, and brings a hatred for justice. It is a rusty arrow spreading poison in the soul. It destroys her virtue and is a cancer in the mind. It thwarts prayer and mangles the petitions we make to God. It drives out love and is a nail driven into the soul, evil that never sleeps, a sin that never fades away, a kind of daily death.

Be lovers of peace, the most precious treasure that anyone can desire.

Saturday, 4 April 2020

For me this was another quiet day, but the prison was locked down just after 1:30 pm with an aqua alert; which means violence. This was confirmed in the evening news with headlines on violence at Barwon. At this stage, I have no further information.

The weather this morning was cold and overcast while I walked for thirty minutes and then had my breakfast. Heavy rain started to fall, so I went inside when some warders passed by. By coincidence, I had to take my first urine test at Barwon, preceded by a perfunctory strip search by a friendly and decent guard. Let us hope this is the last time.

Made a round of phone calls at lunchtime, although I was not able to reach Margaret. David feels, as I do, that some action is needed after the ABC show, because he felt that Bernie came across as "credible", as people would not have realised the matter had already been to court.

Terry gave me the welcome news that Fr Frank Brennan, SJ, had drafted a strong statement denouncing the disgraceful behaviour of the ABC, e.g., by claiming "revelations" and "two new complaints", when in truth there was no such thing. We also discussed the difficulties in financing any action for libel as well as paying what remains of legal costs already incurred.

Finally managed to contact Tim O'Leary, who has been busy working with Archbishop Comensoli. Young Joe, his youngest son, is delighted because four of his five brothers and sisters are home with him. I had been keen for a few days to inform Tim that a mutual friend, whom I had coached in a successful rowing crew, had written to express his support and thank me: "I think of you often and reflect on the good you did in my life." He mentioned that his father, who was at school ahead of me, was studying theology part time. I will write in reply and suggest that he might take a unit or two himself, because when he was at university, he liked to talk theology with me. Perhaps a better word for some of this would be "argue", and I am not sure I made much ground theologically. He concluded with the words, "I trust your faith and spiritual foundation are helping you negotiate this difficult time."

No letters arrived yesterday, which is unusual, and none arrived today, which was to be expected, as letters usually are not delivered on weekends, but I had recently received a number from Italy. A maths teacher from Rome, who teaches handicapped children, wrote "to encourage you in this difficult moment".

A retired university professor in Italy wrote to tell me he fully shared my views which challenged "the theory of the anthropogenic origin of global warming". He very kindly applied to me the beatitude of Matthew 5:10–12 and added, "Unfortunately, in the de-Christianized West, the Church is going to face a persecution.... They want to silence it by every means possible, because no other voice has remained to defend the little ones and the poor of God." I am an incorrigible optimist, and we are a long distance from persecution in Australia, but I have been struck by the number of writers from a variety of countries who have these fears.

A group of cloistered Carmelite nuns of the ancient observance from the Monastero Sant'Elia in Campobasso-Bojano wrote to bring me "all our affection" and "the certainty of our constant prayers for you". They hope it is true, rejoice, and thank the Lord "that you are fine and that you are quite serene". Well, I am serene most of the time.

A parish priest from San Vincenzo in Liguria wrote that he remembered me often as he celebrated Mass and placed me under the protection of the Blessed Virgin and St Joseph; while, finally, a family man from Foligno, near Assisi, who felt close to me in this time of humiliation, wrote and asked for my prayers for a couple of his difficult teenage children.

I believe deeply in the spiritual efficacy of these prayers, but they are also a psychological boost, evidence of the universality of the Catholic Church and reminders of my beloved Italy, which is suffering so grievously from the coronavirus.

In the Redemptorist Church in Via Merulana in front of the Basilica of St Mary Major, Rome, we have the ancient image of Our Lady of Perpetual Help, which tradition ascribes to St Luke, although Our Lady is in Byzantine dress. It is my favourite image of Mary, a devotion which was very strong in the Australia of my youth, fostered by the Redemptorists and the Christian Brothers.

All powerful and merciful Lord,
you gave us the image of the Mother
of your Son to venerate under the title
of Our Mother of Perpetual Help.
Graciously grant that in all the
difficulties of our lives (and especially in this time of plague),
we may be assisted by the continuous protection
of the Virgin Mary and obtain the
reward of eternal redemption.
  You live and reign forever and ever.
   Amen.

WEEK 59

Convictions Quashed

5 April–8 April 2020

Palm Sunday, 5 April 2020

It would not be true to say that Palm Sunday began in Cell 17 with a comedy of errors, but it did begin with a series of misunderstandings due to the fact that I had forgotten Summertime (Daylight Saving Time) had ended.

I awoke at 6:23 am and realised to my annoyance that I had missed the televised Mass. There was a brief temptation to go back to sleep and skip Joseph and Joel, but I quickly concluded that was not appropriate. And it is the start of Holy Week.

My shaving and shower were duly completed, and at about 7:02, I turned on the TV once again for Joseph Prince, only to discover Bishop Terry Curtin just commencing Palm Sunday Mass. It was a previous year's celebration, because the sign of peace was exchanged with a handshake and Holy Communion was distributed under both kinds. The music initially was haunting, the plaintive ancient chant with its refrain of Jesus' words, "My God, My God, why have you forsaken me?"

Even with an abridged reading of Matthew's Passion, the bishop had no time to preach, but asked us to pause and put to ourselves the question Jesus asked Peter, "Do you love me?"

Initially, I thought that good sense had prevailed and that the Mass had been promoted to a better time because of the importance of the feast; neither was I surprised that breakfast did not arrive around 7:15, because the jail was in lockdown from yesterday. Later I learnt from the other prisoners that violence had broken out between seven inmates and three had been hospitalised a violence that was probably hastened by the cessation of visitors for prisoners.

Brian Houston from *Hillsong* appeared, and it was only after I decided to watch him for a small Lenten penance that I remembered the change of time. Part of the prison life is that such events are not announced, that each has to cope for himself, which is a small penalty.

The reverend's sermon was also a rerun, which had nothing to do with Lent or Easter but explained the theme "Understanding the Realm of Dreams and Visions", starting with Daniel and Joseph from the Old Testament. Once again we heard almost no New Testament teaching, as he explained that God had an uncanny way of bringing dreams alive and that he doesn't know anyone who has dreams of failure who has the Spirit of God in him. What was unusual was the amount of time at the end devoted to exhorting his listeners to make a personal choice for Jesus Christ. His preaching is not secular, not merely horizontal or "this worldly"; it is certainly God-centred, but strangely silent on the life of Christ and silent about most New Testament preaching.

Joseph Prince, soberly dressed and with only a couple of rings, preached that we inherit God's promise by faith, not works. Quoting Romans 4:4–5, he urged faith, not work, recommending that we rest and believe. If we are Christians, we are Abraham's seed, which enables us to push all our sins onto God's account. As always, his teaching was based on a series of Bible passages, usually from the New Testament.

Without any doubt, Joel Osteen is a charmer, and his initial silly story usually has a point. Today the young boy was asked, "Where is God?" three times by the pastor, prompting him to bolt home to his brother and blurt out that "someone has stolen God, and they are blaming us."

Joel pointed out that our time on earth is limited. More to the point, the only thing you owe people is to love them: we don't have to keep everyone happy. We must not let others control us, and one of our greatest freedoms is to get free from other people—especially those in the social media.

You cannot be a people pleaser and reach your destiny, while he explained that he hasn't forgotten where he came from; he just didn't want to stay there.

Every good person in the congregation would have been emboldened and every upwardly mobile Christian consoled.

The Songs of Praise was one of the best, coming from Scotland, with a rousing selection of hymns sung by a choir and full congregation with "Christ Is Made the Sure Foundation" and Susan Boyle singing "Amazing Grace" as two highlights. I was intrigued by the sequence on the Dutch painter Vincent van Gogh, who came from a religious family and underwent a further religious conversion when in London, where he was a lay preacher at Wesley Church. He abandoned in his mid-twenties the idea of becoming a pastor before he fell into his cycles of depression and then tragic suicide.

The weather in the morning was cold and windy, so that I was let out late when the lockdown was ended. I walked for an hour and then returned to my cell.

I phoned the friends I had not reached yesterday and learnt I will probably stay with the Carmelite Sisters in Kew if released.

The critical points in the battle against the coronavirus are changing. In comparative terms, Australia is doing "well" with 5,689 cases and 35 deaths, while the death rate and new infections are still high in Spain and Italy, but stabilising or declining. Crisis point is approaching in the United States with 312,000 cases and 8,500 deaths, with a maverick governor in New York, where the city has received 1,000 ventilators from China. With 96,000 infections, Germany has more than France, but the death rate in France is six times higher than Germany's. The trouble is only beginning in the Third World, and it is here that we could see chaos beyond anything yet experienced in the West.

Christ's entry into Jerusalem was a false start to Holy Week, a small triumph which points in the wrong direction, the prelude to a tragedy, but a life-giving tragedy.

They brought the ass and the colt, and put their garments on them, and he sat thereon. Most of the crowd spread their garments on the road, and others cut branches from the trees and spread them on the road. And the crowds that went before him and that followed him shouted:

Hosanna to the Son of David!
Blessed is he who comes in the name of the Lord!
Hosanna in the highest!

Monday of Holy Week, 6 April, 2020

The day started well as the front page of the *Herald Sun* announced only eleven new cases of Covid-19 in Victoria yesterday, continuing a dip for four or five days. Across Australia, the increase was only 3 percent. We are entitled to rejoice in good fortune close at home, even when it isn't universal.

As I don't know whether excitement or disappointment will come tomorrow morning, I should remind myself of the Holy Week we are entering by quoting one of the prefaces.

ICEL commissioned the translators of the third Latin edition of the Roman rite, who remain anonymous. Some of the translations of the prefaces are beautiful, particularly well done, such as these lines of the second Passion Preface.

> For the days of (Jesus') saving Passion
> and glorious Resurrection are approaching,
> by which the pride of the ancient foe is vanquished
> and the mystery of our redemption in
> Christ is celebrated.

Holy Week reminds us of the perpetual struggle between good and evil, light and darkness, which simmers or rages in our hearts and families, in societies and within and between nations. Each of us has to commit to faith, love, and hope.

I spent the afternoon packing up and sorting my documents, hundreds of pages, finding again texts and articles.

One of these is from the Curé of Ars in France, the nineteenth-century St John Vianney, spelling out two truths, each contentious: "When people wish to destroy religion," he wrote, "they begin by attacking the priest because where there is no priest, there is no sacrifice."

The conflict between God's Kingdom and the world is not a hyperbole or a figment of the imagination of the religious right or religious left, but the defining issue in salvation history. The Son of God was murdered, put to death, and the fruits of his Resurrection have not yet prevailed.

And the priest, preacher of the word, celebrant of the Eucharist, forgiver of sins, is one important warrior in this strife. He is a servant leader, the crucial figure in our parish communities, and when he (and the bishops) are corrupted by the Evil One, the damage is profound. St John Vianney is correct.

I also found again an interview with Sir James MacMillan, a Catholic from Scotland and our foremost composer, talking on suffering and silence; in 2016, he lost his young multi-handicapped granddaughter, who was blind, partially deaf, and immobile.

His grandfather was a coal miner, who loved his music, performed in choirs and bands, and knew classical music well. Music scores were here and there through the home, and his mother played Beethoven and Chopin. In Scotland then many such working class families flourished.

As a young man, James joined the Young Communist League but didn't stop practising his faith. He now concedes that it is counter-cultural to be a Catholic, "because you just seem to be against the grain all the time". He sees Catholicism as a comprehensive, unsentimental, "habit of being", following Flannery O'Connor, and sees composers in the Catholic Church as "midwives to faith, because they have inspired the prayers of the faithful". All composers are "searching for the sacred in different ways".

The death of his five-year-old granddaughter, Sara, did not dent his faith: "Actually, it's the exact opposite". "First of all, your Catholicism kicks in, the liturgy gives shape to the suffering, which is transformed into something beautiful." For him, that wee girl brought tremendous joy, a deeper religious understanding to all of them, especially the mother, "whose life changed forever when she said yes to new life", against the advice of some helpers. MacMillan explains grimly that the concept of *lebensunwertes Leben* (life unworthy of life) did not disappear in Nazi Germany, but is "here now in our modern, oh-so-caring-and-sharing nice democracies". Not surprisingly, he accepts that this kind of massive convulsion has had an impact on his music.

No one escapes suffering. The challenge for a Christian is to use suffering properly, so that it strengthens faith, hope, and love in the patient, family, and friends. And some find this harder than others.

Around the world, 70,000 have died in the coronavirus pandemic, and 1,200,000 have been infected. The Queen has spoken to her people, reminding them of her first speech with Princess Margaret in 1940 during the Second World War and hoped that those strengths, that self-reliance, still remained. In the US, they have 337,600 cases, and the director of health spoke of an approaching Pearl Harbor moment. The death rate is falling in Italy, and Japan is heading for worse trouble.

In the midst of such an international tragedy, where we do pray to God that it will end soon, I feel a little guilty praying for myself. But tomorrow is also important for me—and the Church.

Today's entrance antiphon is from Psalm 34.

> *Contend, O Lord, with my contenders;*
> *fight those who fight me.*
> *Take up your buckler and shield;*
> *arise in my defence, Lord, my mighty help.*

Tuesday of Holy Week, 7 April 2020

Last night, although I worked until around midnight tidying and packing documents, I did not finish the work so that I would have something to do this morning.

My sleeping was not too bad, although I was awake before the 7:15 am breakfast call with my milk, three Weetabix, two rounds of toast, butter, and jam.

As always, the shower water was hot, and I shaved. No paper this morning, as I have ordered for Monday, Wednesday (for the weekly television programs), and Saturday, when I receive the *Weekend Australian*.

By a happy coincidence, the work of packing, sorting, and discarding was completed by 9:30 am, so I was able to commence my Prayer of the Day, my breviary. Matins and Lauds were completed by 9:50 am, when Paolo, who was in the kitchen area, told me Channel 7 has a reporter at the court in Brisbane and that the result would be announced quickly.

One or two minutes passed as I watched, until a surprised and disconcerted young reporter announced that the appeal had been accepted and the convictions quashed. He was in shock.

Some little time later, he received another, worse shock. The judgement is "seven-zip" or "seven-nil". I cannot remember what he said, but my more learned friends took considerable delight in using the word "zip", a term which was new to me.

A loud cheer went up from somewhere nearby outside Unit 3, probably from my most regular correspondent, who strongly believed in my innocence. As a religious man, he also had a premonition that I would be freed.

Paolo and Derek both then came to my cell and through the small window on my door expressed their congratulations and best wishes. Abdullah was locked in his cell, but I farewelled him before I left.

I had no surge of elation, but I punched the air a couple of times in relief and then prayed the Te Deum, the traditional prayer of thanks. Unfortunately, I had only an English translation, and I couldn't remember too much of the Latin original, which is a masterpiece. Then a rosary in gratitude, as once again I did not want to be like the nine lepers.

All remained quiet for about half an hour when my cell door was opened, and three prison officers stood there saying nothing. I broke the silence by asking, "Any news?" "No", came the reply. "Actually, there is a bit," I volunteered, "as I have just been acquitted."

We then started to walk toward the central office, and the taciturn leader remarked, "Miracles will never cease!" I issued a short correction. "This was no miracle. It was justice."

I moved slowly to the change room, where I was relieved to see that my suit had been on a hangar, as I had been told, and was not badly creased. My belt had arrived without my braces, which I had to call for as my trousers would not stay up without them. I had lost fifteen kilos [33 lbs].

Ruth, Paul, and Kartya had come down to be with me after the result, good or bad, and were excited and delighted, giving a small round of applause. The team have given me marvellous support, personally and professionally, beyond the call of duty, and I am grateful.

The prison officers were friendly and cooperative as Kartya negotiated my exit, and I went to the property office to collect a surprisingly large amount of material: letters, gifts, books, and journals.

I was travelling in the backseat of Kartya's car, which was a good one, but provided a better look than Paul's Mercedes, which preceded us.

The gates swung open to reveal about twenty cameras and photographers spread along the far side of the road, the requisite distance apart because of the Covid-19 pandemic.

It was wonderful to see the countryside, the flat plains which were green and friendly although no one would mistake them for the Swiss Alps.

The police cars were accompanying us, as press cars followed at a distance and two helicopters flew overhead. I was providing a much-needed break from the dominance of coronavirus news.

We attempted to direct Paul to continue along the Eastern Freeway as we came off at the Burnley Exit, and this was achieved after we stopped for an explanatory chat. To no avail, as the press followed us closely at a safe distance until we entered the Carmelite Convent in Kew, where other photographers were already stationed.

The convent is surrounded by high walls around extensive buildings and a beautiful garden. The gates swung open, the car entered, and I was greeted by Reverend Mother. In the next day's paper was a photograph, taken from the helicopter, of me walking the ten metres [11 yds] from the car to the main entrance.

The nuns could not have been more welcoming as I moved into the chaplain's apartment, considerably larger and nicer than what I had been used to.

I then celebrated Mass in their beautiful chapel, where the relics of St Thérèse, the Little Flower, and her parents, Monsieur and Madame Martin, were waiting out the shutdown. Chris Meney served me, and I thanked God for my liberation.

A steak and three vegetables were the main course for the evening meal. Katrina Lee, who had done such great work preparing the ground for the media reports, was keen for me to give the interview to Andrew Bolt as soon as possible, but I did not feel up to doing so tomorrow.

Chris had brought in a bottle of red wine, so I had a glass as we chatted together. Although it was a good wine, I didn't enjoy it much. Please God, this distaste is not permanent. That would be a blow!

Fr Vincent Twomey, a leading Irish intellectual, champion of orthodoxy, larger than life, had again emailed me to offer his congratulations. His few lines from Shakespeare's *Othello* provide a fitting conclusion for my day of liberation, in Holy Week, just before Easter.

Who steals my purse steals trash; 'tis
something, nothing.
'Twas mine, 'tis his, and has been slave to thousands,
But he that filches from me my
good name
Robs me of that which not enriches him,
And makes me poor indeed.

Wednesday, 8 April 2020

Originally, I had planned to stay in Melbourne for up to a week after my release to see my close friends and family and visit my oldest surviving cousin, Bob Burke, who is in Nazareth House. Press interest made this impossible, and I decided to leave immediately for home in Sydney with Chris Meney as my driver.

I celebrated Mass once again in the Carmelites' beautiful and empty chapel with the relics of the three Martin saints. It was good to return to the routine of daily Mass.

We breakfasted, packed up the few belongings we had brought into the convent, and headed to the gate which was opened for us. Perhaps a half-dozen photographers were waiting for our exit and had been there during the night. Apparently, they had attached a bicycle to the main gate, which would have made a giant racket if we had attempted to escape during the night.

We were followed immediately, and at a couple of crossings in the northern suburbs, when we had to stop and wait at the traffic lights, a couple of photographers, one of whom was particularly grim-faced, raced up to bang on the car windows and take photographs.

I had originally hoped that they would stay with us only until we left greater Melbourne, but they followed us all the way to Good Shepherd Seminary in Homebush, Sydney.

My brother had wanted to drive from Bendigo and meet briefly at Seymour, keeping the requisite social distance, but I told him not to do this as I did not want them dragged into the publicity. He reluctantly consented, but we both agreed in retrospect that it was the correct decision.

As I had taken my usual diuretic tablet in the morning, it became necessary to make a comfort stop, which occurred by chance at the BP service station in Glenrowan. The solicitors had recommended that I remain seated and mute in the car, while Chris bought petrol. However, this was not possible, and I judged it was not desirable, either. So, I had a little fun, asking the photographers to keep the requisite social distance as I emerged from the car. Friends of many years were pleased to see and hear that I had not completely lost a rudimentary sense of humour as I responded to the question about how I was, explaining that I was well until I saw them.

I was able to buy *The Australian* and *Herald Sun*, and when I crossed paths with a middle-aged blond lady, she hissed, "Bloody Catholics". The shop assistants were kind as I purchased the wrong connection to charge my phone.

Chris had to do all the driving, a mighty job as he had driven down from Sydney on the previous day.

Approaching Goulburn, we decided to go to the police station to enquire whether they could prevent the press from following us.

Within the city, we performed a number of convoluted manoeuvres, which the press might have thought were designed to confuse them and throw them off our trail. The truth was that we were lost and could not find the police station. The police were generally sympathetic but could do nothing to stop the pursuit.

The New South Wales police seemed to be more cooperative than those in the southern People's Republic, but that might simply have been our bias.

In any event, they accompanied us to the rear entrance (in Broughton Road) for the seminary, where another group of intrusive photographers jammed their cameras into the glass of the car windows for a photo. The rector, Fr Danny Meagher, and Michael Digges, financial administrator of the Sydney Archdiocese, were there to greet us, although we missed the entry on the first drive past.

We drove in and parked out of sight from the road. I was home, back where I had lived happily in the seminary for a couple of years and in Sydney. I was pleased and relieved.

The house was spotlessly clean, and all was prepared for my arrival. Only the seven first-year students with the four-priest staff were in residence because of the coronavirus.

I asked Chris to stay for a while after our meal but insisted he should not think of staying the night as he needed to be home with Mary Clare and one of his children who was sick.

I had adapted well, perhaps too well, to solitary confinement and now had to find a new equilibrium in a locked-down world. In some ways, my four hundred days in jail were a good preparation for the degree of isolation required by the health authorities.

Naturally, I had phoned my brother and sister yesterday after my release and spoke as well with Archbishop Fisher.

My sister, Margaret, is now living in a beautiful retirement home in Bendigo, the home city of my brother, David, and his family, who are very attentive to her.

She believes that I called in to see her briefly yesterday, gave her a kiss, and apologised for not being able to stay long. She was delighted I had been freed, and when David, in response to her question, told her that I had not called to see him, she received another boost. Whether it was a dream or imagination or a small gift from God, it is a lovely story and a small recompense for her suffering and prayers.

For seventy years, I have been writing and often found it hard work, a bit like prayer. But I didn't find it difficult to write this long journal; words flowed regularly, and on some occasions I suspected this might be providential for some, perhaps many, so I hope that these pages will be helpful religiously and socially to more than a few adults, be they Catholic or non-Catholic, believer or agnostic. After all, Christ rode into Jerusalem on his donkey.

In a few days on Holy Saturday night during the Easter Vigil, the Paschal Candle will again be blessed and dedicated to the man-God, whom I love and serve, whom I have followed for all my life, just as saints and sinners, firebrands and the lukewarm have done for nearly two thousand years.

> *Christ yesterday and today.*
> *The beginning and the end.*
> *The Alpha and the Omega.*
> *All time belongs to Him,*
> *And all the ages.*

AFTERWORD

by George Weigel

A grave injustice was reversed when the High Court of Australia vindicated George Cardinal Pell and restored him to liberty on April 7, 2020. What the world could not have known then, and what readers of all three volumes of Cardinal Pell's *Prison Journal* have now discovered, is that the cardinal put his 404 days of imprisonment, most of them in solitary confinement, to good use. He prayed, not least for victims of clerical sexual abuse. He read, studied, and deepened his thinking about the contemporary situation of the Catholic Church, about his native Australia, about reform in the Vatican, and about a troubled world. He participated in the work of his defense team. And he produced a prison memoir that is a shining testament to the power of faith, hope, and charity to see a man through the most difficult of circumstances.

Thanks to these journals, and thanks to the dignity and equanimity with which he has borne himself since his release from prison (not least in an hour-long interview with Australian broadcaster Andrew Bolt), George Cardinal Pell has become a spiritual hero to many. That this is to the consternation and fury of the cardinal's many enemies is a source of considerable satisfaction to his friends. But not, I think, to George Pell himself. For as these journals have revealed, he is a much bigger man than his persecutors and his rabid critics. He holds no grudges. That they do is to their further shame.

Cardinal Pell is moving on with his life. As he marked his eightieth birthday on June 8, 2021, he could look back on eight decades of adventure, accomplishment, and sorrow overcome. He is not a man to spend large amounts of time looking in the rear-view mirror, however. His days of service to the Church are by no means ended, and his status as one of Catholicism's most influential elders has been enhanced, not least by these journals. The cardinal is not looking back. Others should, however.

For friends of Australia who are not caught up in the maelstrom of politics Down Under, it is difficult to understand why there has not been a public reckoning with the travesties of policing and prosecution, and the failures of the justice system in the State of Victoria, that were laid bare in the Pell affair.

Why has there been no state or federal investigation into the Victoria police department's "Operation Tethering", in which, as commentator Michael Cook put it, the police went "trawling for complaints against a public figure"? Surely the public interest would be served by knowing whether personal animosities, political grudges, corruption, or all of the above were involved in an otherwise inexplicable fishing expedition.

Why has there been no state or federal investigation into why the Victoria Office of Public Prosecutions took to trial a case that was implausible to the point of impossibility? What role, if any, did the crowds baying for George Pell's blood have on that decision? In the State of Victoria, is it now the case that unhinged mob rage is sufficient to bring to trial a case in which the prosecution has no case? (And speaking of mobs, who was paying for those professionally printed placards visible outside the court during the Pell trials?)

Within the Victoria justice system, has there been any consideration of whether the trial judge's decision to put a media blackout on the cardinal's trials was prudent? I am not alone in believing that the trial judge ordered the blackout in the hope of keeping the trials from becoming a media circus. Nonetheless, the blackout ensured that the most lurid anti-Pell stories continued to circulate in the Australian press; that the cardinal's defenders were largely if not totally muzzled; and that the public did not know that the prosecution's case had been shredded by the defense in the cardinal's first trial. That trial ended in a hung jury that seems to have been overwhelmingly in favor of acquittal. But no one knew any of that, which could not help but have an effect on the retrial.

Within the Victoria bar, has there been any reckoning with the fact that the two appellate judges who upheld the cardinal's conviction at his second trial were eviscerated, legally speaking, by the High Court, when it unanimously decided to quash the guilty verdict Judges Anne Ferguson and Chris Maxwell had upheld and enter a judgement of innocence in the case of *Pell v. The Queen*? Judge

Mark Weinberg's dissenting judgement in favor of Cardinal Pell's appeal seems to have decisively influenced the High Court. One can only hope that others on the Victoria bench have learned something about legal reasoning from their colleague Mark Weinberg— and about the importance of standing up to the mob and the media when justice demands it.

Then there is the matter of Louise Milligan, an employee of the publicly funded Australian Broadcasting Corporation, whose lurid and fanciful 2013 book, *The Cardinal*, helped set the persecution of George Pell into motion. Why is a tax-supported employee of a state broadcasting entity permitted to publish rubbish and then promote it at the public expense? Why has there been no parliamentary inquiry into ABC's professional standards and practices in general and about Louise Milligan's jihad against George Pell in particular?

No one knowledgeable about Australian public life over the past several decades will deny that Cardinal Pell was a lightning-rod for all sorts of culture-war issues, especially those involving the sexual revolution and climate change. But is the state broadcasting company in Australia to be permitted to persecute a public figure because his views do not comport with the woke shibboleths of the Australian media? And if ABC can commit calumny after calumny against a public personality it dislikes because of his politics, how does that distinguish ABC from state-funded media in the People's Republic of China or Vladimir Putin's Russia?

The Catholic Church, in both Australia and the Vatican, has much to reflect upon in light of the Pell case.

In Australia, George Pell—who as Archbishop of Melbourne was the first bishop in the country to institute a serious program to deal with clerical sexual abuse and provide aid to its victims—became a scapegoat for the failures of other Catholic bishops to deal effectively with these grave sins and crimes. Thus, it was more than a little disconcerting that Cardinal Pell received so little public support from his brother bishops. The statement by Archbishop Mark Coleridge of Brisbane on the cardinal's failed appeal in August 2019 was particularly cringe-inducing, with its waffling call upon Australians to "accept" the judgement of the appellate court while the case played out in its final phase. That dissenting judge, Mark Weinberg, had the courage to say that the appellate judgment made no sense and the president of the Australian bishops' conference could not bring himself to do the same is, at the very least, noteworthy.

George Pell's robust Catholic orthodoxy and his relish in challenging the cultural Left and its political allies made other Australian bishops nervous, even gun-shy, when it came to fighting the Church's battles in the public square—a task admittedly made harder by decades of duplicity and worse in the handling of clerical sexual abuse cases by previous generations of Australian bishops. The answer to that sorry history cannot be cowering before the mob, however; nor can it be to turn Australia into a Church of Catholic Lite on the German model. The only way forward for Catholicism in Australia is to be completely transparent about sexual abuse (commensurate with the obligations of sacramental confidentiality) and to display candor and forthrightness in explaining, defending, and promoting the settled truths of Catholic faith. In all this, his brother bishops of the present and the future can learn lessons from George Cardinal Pell.

Church authorities in Rome also have much to ponder in the aftermath of the Pell case. The pusillanimity of the Vatican Press Office throughout the cardinal's trial and appeals was, in a word, appalling. Did the world really need to hear repeatedly about the Holy See's confidence in the Australian justice system, when it was clear to any fair-minded person that it was the Australian justice system that was on trial—a system that barely escaped with its reputation intact, thanks to the High Court finally giving George Pell the justice he had been denied in his trials and at his appeal?

Then there is the question of a possible relationship between the persecution and prosecution of Cardinal Pell and his work in Vatican financial reform. Much remains to be explored here—and it must be explored, if the Holy See is to rebuild a reputation for financial probity. That reputation has been seriously damaged in recent years. And while the revelations of incompetence and corruption in Vatican finance have been very costly in terms of the Vatican balance sheet, they have been even more costly in terms of the Church's primary work of evangelization. If there are links between financial corruption in Rome and the prosecution of George Pell, they should be identified, not for the sake of retribution, but for the sake of the Church's credibility and its purification.

The publication of this final volume of Cardinal Pell's *Prison Journal* will bring a certain measure of sadness to the cardinal's friends and admirers. Walking this *Via Crucis* with him, day by day, has been for many a kind of ongoing spiritual retreat. Entering prison, Cardinal Pell said to friends that that was how he planned to live the experience of incarceration: as a retreat, an opportunity to grow closer to the Lord. By recording his experience of that remarkable journey of grace and then sharing it with others in these volumes, he has expanded the range of the priestly ministry to which he dedicated himself more than a half-century ago. And through these diaries he has, without a doubt, brought others closer to Christ.

That is how apostles live. Faced with shipwreck, like Paul in Acts 27 and 28, they turn what seems to be disaster into an occasion to expand the Church's evangelical mission. That is what George Cardinal Pell did in prison, and we may all thank him for it.

George Weigel is Distinguished Senior Fellow of Washington's Ethics and Public Policy Center, where he holds the William E. Simon Chair in Catholic Studies. His two most recent books, The Next Pope: The Office of Peter and a Church in Mission *and* Not Forgotten: Elegies for, and Reminiscences of, a Diverse Cast of Characters, Most of Them Admirable, *were published by Ignatius Press. He and Cardinal Pell have been friends since 1967.*